Social Work, Community Work and Psychology

CAROLE SUTTON

Social Work, Community Work and Psychology

CAROLE SUTTON PhD

Senior Lecturer in Psychology
De Montfort University, Leicester

BPS
BOOKS
Published by The British Psychological Society

First published in 1994 by BPS Books (The British Psychological Society),
St Andrews House, 48 Princess Road East, Leicester LE1 7DR.

Reprinted in 1996

A catalogue record for this book is available from the British Library.

ISBN 1 85433 110 8

Typeset by: Arrow Photoset, Leicester
Printed and bound in Great Britain by
Redwood Books, Trowbridge, Wiltshire

Contents

List of figures and tables   viii

Introduction
The contribution of psychology to social and community work   1
    ● the nature of 'theory' ● theories and values
    ● an example of theory: social learning
The contribution of social and community work to psychology
    ● power and empowerment ● values
An all-purpose process of working with people: ASPIRE
    ● ASPIRE: an example

1. Human beings in a 'systems' framework   13
Different perspectives upon human beings
The biological perspective
The psychodynamic/emotional perspective
The behavioural and social learning perspectives
The cognitive perspective
The humanistic perspective

2. Aspects of human development   33
Assessment of development
Infancy and the earliest years of life
    ● bonding and attachment
The pre-school child
    ● socialization ● aggression and anti-social behaviour
The primary school child
Secondary school and adolescence
    ● identity and self-esteem ● employment
The adult
Elderly people

3. Interpersonal skills and communication   56
Research in perception
    ● first impressions and perceived similarity
Elements of social interaction
    ● non-verbal communication ● verbal communication
    ● styles of social behaviour
Interviewing
Communicating with particular groups
    ● children and young people ● communicating across language and
    cultural barriers ● communicating with people with learning disabilities
    ● communicating with older people
Making and sustaining relationships
    ● empathy ● listening ● establishing trust
Social exchange theory
Negotiating and writing agreements

4. Children and their families 78

Partnership with parents

The range of work with families

● separation and divorce ● one-parent families ● reordered families
● Family Adversity Index

The family as a supportive environment

Parenting skills

Communication with and within the family

Family therapy

● social learning theory and family therapy ● the style of the therapist
● evaluation of family therapy ● ASPIRE: work with families

5. Child abuse 97

Estimates of child abuse

Assessment in child abuse

Intervention in child abuse

● primary intervention ● secondary intervention ● tertiary intervention

Neglect

Physical injury

Child sexual abuse

● characteristics of those who abuse ● interviewing young children
● intervention in child sexual abuse

Emotional abuse

● ASPIRE: intervention in emotional abuse

Evaluation of interventions in child abuse

Caring for children in distress

Children as witnesses

6. Crisis intervention and counselling 119

What do we mean by crisis?

Response to crisis

● anxiety ● post traumatic stress ● response to bereavement

Supporting people in crisis

Counselling

The counsellor's repertoire

● dealing with depression ● support in times of crisis or long-term stress
● the problem-solving approach

7. Working for mental health 133

Stress and its management

Women and mental health

Ethnic minority groups and mental health

Classification of mental disorders

● neuroses ● psychoses ● personality disorders ● organic syndromes

Provision of mental health services

Mental health promotion

Approaches in mental health work

● group work ● cognitive-behavioural approaches ● assertiveness training

8. Working with communities and groups 156
Getting to know your community
Forms of community work
● organizing a campaign ● participating in community groups
Group work
● within–group processes ● between–group processes
Group care and residential settings
● children in residential care ● ASPIRE: a residential care context
● young offenders in residential and community settings ● group homes
for people with learning disability ● group homes for elderly people
Group care: a systems perspective
Community care
● the needs–led approach

9. Continuing professional development 185
Becoming research oriented
Research in psychology
● the research process ● some research methods
Professional skills
● negotiation ● advocacy ● educational skills ● decision–making
● record keeping ● writing reports
Administrative skills
Looking after yourself
● recognizing stress ● supervision ● working in a supportive team
Being alert to potential violence

10. Values and ethics 208
The complexity of social work
Dilemmas of social work
● care versus control ● issues of confidentiality ● conflicts of interest
● shortages of resources
Equal opportunity
Accountability
Empowerment
Personal conduct

References 217

Appendix A: Charting several behaviours 227

Appendix BI: An example of an agreement between worker and client 228

Appendix BII: A framework for an agreement between worker and client 229

Appendix C: A framework for an agreement in one–to–one family work 230

Appendix D: Monitoring progress towards goals 232

Appendix E: An example of a questionnaire 233

Index 235

List of tables and figures

Table 1: ASPIRE: A process for practice 8
Table 1.1: Classification of the drives 17
Table 1.2: Piaget's stages of cognitive development 29
Table 1.3: Maslow's model of human needs 31
Table 2.1: The needs of children 34
Table 2.2: Developmental tasks 39
Table 2.3: Childhood temperament 40
Table 2.4: Indicators of secure attachment 42
Table 2.5: Desirable features of daycare settings 44
Table 2.6: Calls received by Childline 48
Table 3.1: Elements of non-verbal behaviour associated with acceptance and rejection at interview 61
Table 4.1: The main concepts and strategies of family therapy 90
Table 5.1: Estimates of child abuse 98
Table 5.2: Child abuse: high risk assessment chart 99
Table 5.3: Nature of sexual abuse sustained 106
Table 5.4: Post-traumatic stress reactions to child sexual abuse 109
Table 6.1: Stages of the grief response 122
Table 6.2: The counselling process 128
Table 7.1: Characteristics of people with positive mental health 134
Table 7.2: Life Events Scale 137
Table 7.3: Children's diagnostic categories 144
Table 7.4: The medical model of mental disorders 146
Table 7.5: Models of care offered by teams in the community 152
Table 8.1: Organizing a campaign 160
Table 8.2: Typical developments when groups polarize 167
Table 9.1: The questionnaire method 192
Table 9.2: Monitoring progress towards goals 194
Table 9.3: Gains from self advocacy 197
Table 9.4: A contract for supervision 205
Table 9.5: Verbal and non-verbal factors in potentially violent situations 206

Figure 1: The ASPIRE process as a cycle 9
Figure 1.1: A system with sub-systems interacting with other systems 14
Figure 1.2: A person as part of many systems 15
Figure 1.3: Elements contributing to the occurrence of a criminal event 20
Figure 1.4: A feedback loop suggested by social learning theory 25
Figure 2.1: Centile charts 35
Figure 2.2: The use of a centile chart for recording growth 37
Figure 3.1: Styles of social behaviour 63
Figure 3.2: An overview of child and worker interactions 67
Figure 4.1: Patterns of parenting and children's responses 86

Figure 4.2: Genogram 89
Figure 5.1: A social psychological model of the causes of child abuse 104
Figure 5.2: A record of particular behaviours 112
Figure 6.1: Model of counsellor methods in relation to client needs 127
Figure 7.1: The stress process 135
Figure 7.2: Levels of arousal and their impact on effective performance 136
Figure 7.3: Genesis of depression: socio-psychological aspects 139
Figure 8.1: 'Core and cluster' principle of residential provision 180
Figure 8.2: The process of care management 183
Figure 9.1: Flowchart of research processes 187
Figure 9.2: Independent and dependent variables in a controlled experiment 190

To Peter, our son, who died in a mountaineering
accident while this book was being prepared.

Proceeds from the sale of this book will be given to the furthering of parent support, education and training through a family trust associated with Peter's name.

Acknowledgements

I should like to express my thanks to many people who have helped directly and indirectly with the preparation of this book. I have been grateful for the help offered by Anita Bishop, Merryl Clarke, Kay Davies, Sue Dewing, Peter Elfer, Beryl Hawke, Barbara Howard, Clive Hollin, Dorota Iwaniec, Janet Kitchen, Lorna Morrison, Rhoda Oppenheimer, Elizabeth O'Neill, Sara Owen, Dorothy Root, Andrew Shepherd, Sylvia Spittle, Rosemary Strange, and Bharat Thakrar.

In addition I have much appreciated the support of my colleagues at De Montfort University: Inderjit Dhalwalia, Cherie D'Silva, Julie Kent, Charlotte Knight, Marcia Stewart, Renu Sudera, George Taylor, Hilary Unwin and Paul Weston.

I am deeply indebted to Rochelle Serwator, of The British Psychological Society, who has spent many hours editing the book and improving upon successive drafts. Thank you, Rochelle.

Finally, to the members of my family, Clive, Cathy, Meriel and Rowan my gratitude for their patience and encouragement during the past months, and to Peter, to whom the book is dedicated.

Copyright acknowledgements
The following figures and tables have been reprinted with permission:
Figure 1.1 and *Table 1.1*: copyright Open University; *Figure 1.2*: copyright C. Sutton and M. Herbert, reprinted by permission of the publishers, NFER-Nelson; *Table 2.1*: copyright British Agencies for Adoption and Fostering; *Table 2.2*: copyright M. Herbert, reprinted by permission of the publishers, NFER-Nelson; *Tables 5.1* and *5.3*: copyright NSPCC; *Table 5.2*: copyright Cyril Greenland, *Preventing C.A.N. Deaths: An international study of deaths due to child abuse and neglect*, London and New York (Tavistock Publications); *Figure 5.2*: copyright *Nursing Times*; *Figure 7.1*: copyright Cary L. Cooper, Rachel D. Cooper and Lynn H. Eaker (Penguin Books); *Table 7.2*: *Journal of Psychosomatic Research, 11*, Holmes and Rahe, Pergamon Press Ltd; *Table 7.3*: copyright Michael Rutter (Penguin Books); Features of a major depressive episode on p.148, Catalan, 1988, in *Essential Psychiatry*, copyright Blackwell Scientific Publications.

INTRODUCTION

What can Psychology offer to Social Workers and Community Workers?

Social workers, probation officers, community workers and psychologists have a common focus of concern: human experience and distress. All these professions, despite different starting points, different traditions and different responsibilities, have a commitment to understanding the causes of distress, to supporting weak and powerless people and to enhancing the well-being of humanity. The fields of practice of all the groups increasingly overlap; they participate more and more in multi-disciplinary teams, and come together with others around the same table in meetings and planning groups.

Since these professions have so many concerns in common, it is likely that we have much to learn from each other's special areas of expertise, research or experience. So, what can psychology offer to the professions of social work and community work, and what can they offer, in return, to the future development of psychology? How can we profitably share our knowledge, values and skills?

Let us first consider the nature of our respective professions. Psychology is first and foremost a *discipline*, a field of study, which examines by scientific methods the nature of human experience: human thought, behaviour and emotion. Those working for a degree in psychology typically devote three years to this study and then continue to study for at least a further two years to apply the principles of psychology to the fields of education, mental health, counselling or industry. Other psychologists are engaged in research.

Social work is primarily a profession in which knowledge is *applied*. Student social workers and probation officers are taught and trained from the outset as practitioners. The responsibilities which they carry, and to which their initial training introduces them, are daunting. A social worker who has specialized in working with children and families, for example, is likely in due course to carry statutory responsibility for investigating cases of suspected child abuse, emotional, physical or sexual; placing children where necessary in foster homes, and supporting both natural and foster parents; receiving applications to adopt children, and undertaking all the associated enquiries and arrangements; as well as carrying out supervision orders made by the courts in respect of young offenders.

Other social workers carry different responsibilities: in particular, the management of care in the community for vulnerable groups: elderly people, people with learning disabilities, people with mental health difficulties and people with physical or sensory impairments. Some of these social workers, with brief additional training, are responsible for supporting, or declining to support, the application made for a person to be compulsorily admitted to a psychiatric hospital.

A further group of social workers are employed in group care settings. Residential social workers care for children and young people and for those with learning or mental health difficulties who cannot live with their families. Daycare social workers support those who attend family and other centres on a day-to-day basis.

Probation officers, a particular group of social workers, have special duties and responsibilities towards offenders (usually aged 17 and over) and other groups of people who come before the courts. They too, however, are employed in day centres and hostels and sometimes undertake community development.

Community work, as distinct from social work, is an emerging profession. The professional community and youth worker is qualified to work both with young people in youth work settings as well as in other ways. These include *community organization*, such as good neighbour schemes and the involving of volunteers in meeting social need; *community development*, in which local opinion is mobilized and people are empowered so that they themselves can address issues such as the lack of services for people with disabilities; and *community action*, in which situations such as unemployment are addressed as political rather than personal issues.

As social deprivation increases, social workers are finding themselves drawing upon the perspectives and skills of community workers. An introduction to community work skills is a part of many social work courses, and the Diploma in Social Work explicitly requires qualifying social workers to be able to demonstrate their ability to 'mobilise the resources of individuals and families within their community, social networks and support systems'. We shall consider community work further in Chapter 8.

There are then major areas of overlap between these professions. It is the aim of this book to examine the particular ways in which the discipline of psychology can inform social work and community work practice, as well as how the discipline of psychology can benefit from the learning, insights and understandings which have been gathered from the practices of social work and community work.

The Contribution of Psychology to Social and Community Work

I wish briefly to consider several concepts from psychology (and other disciplines) and how they can be of relevance to social workers and community workers. First, the nature of 'theory'; second, why social workers and community workers need theory; and third, some specific bodies of theory, based on extensive research, upon which workers can draw in their own practice.

The nature of 'theory'

Some students find this concept rather difficult. They hear a lot about it in college, but there may not seem to be the remotest link between what a lecturer or tutor may have talked about in the classroom and what to do in a situation where a family is so overwhelmed with problems that they have given up trying to cope.

Let's look at this word 'theory'. It derives from the Greek word *theoros*, meaning a 'spectator'. From this original meaning it has come to be linked with what a spectator sees in a field of view. Thus the word has moved from meaning the 'spectator who perceives' to *what is perceived*. Different people, of course, looking at any view, perceive different things in it: predecessors of Galileo 'saw' the sun going round the earth; now we see the earth going round the sun, and there is a lot of evidence that our view is the more accurate one.

Over time, the word 'theory' has developed to mean a *system of ideas explaining something*: a way of attempting to clarify complexity. Researchers in all fields are interested in refining their theories so as to represent as accurately as possible the nature of reality; and in the physical sciences they have enjoyed a good deal of success. Many amazing inventions which we now take for granted – the telephone, air travel, computers, space missions – are based upon a precise understanding of the nature of physical reality. So accurate is this understanding that the ultimate test of 'theory', namely, *its capacity to predict the future*, is taken for granted in many fields of chemistry and physics. Do this, and that will certainly follow – although there may of course be additional outcomes which have not been anticipated!

In the human sciences, psychology and sociology for example, theory has not reached this degree of reliability. Careful research into human development, thought and behaviour began only in the last century and there are, as yet, few theories of human nature which are universally accepted. Research, however, continues upon an international scale, and some very important fragments of theory are emerging.

Few psychologists or sociologists feel confident about making more than very limited predictions about human behaviour and experience on the basis of our present understandings. Yet because members of the public have become used to accurate predictions from other professionals – doctors, chemists and aeronautical engineers, for example – and because large sums of money are spent upon public services and upon training people to administer them, it is naturally expected that those who call themselves professionals shall make accurate predictions. Social workers are expected to be able to forecast whether parents will neglect or injure their children, whether those who have offended in the past will offend again, and whether treating perpetrators of child sexual abuse will have the effect of deterring them from abusing children again. As I have written before (Sutton, 1979):

The irony is that, lulled by the confidence brought by having good intentions and, if they are fortunate, a two-year training behind them, social workers are willing to make or be party to such predictions. They collude with, and thus become victim of, public expectation . . . How can we allow young and inexperienced workers to take decisions and assume responsibility for the lives and well-being of both individuals and whole families while providing them with inadequate resources, inadequate training, or even no training at all?

The succession of scandals within social work which have occurred since I wrote the above passage support my claim. Yet social workers continue to be held accountable for situations which are beyond anyone's ability to anticipate or prevent. Research has not yet provided us with an adequate theoretical base for accurately predicting child abuse, child sexual abuse or offending behaviour – or for dealing with it once it has occurred. Social workers, beware! You take on an impossible job, and are then blamed for doing it inadequately.

Yet if practice should be based upon theory, and if the test of theory is its capacity to predict the future, are there any bodies of reliable theory available? In the sense of there being an integrated, fully understood body of knowledge, on the basis of which one can make confident predictions, there is none. All we have are a few fragments of theory, not integrated one with another, and which may yet be challenged. But some fragments are becoming increasingly capable of bearing prediction. This book is about some of those fragments.

Theories and values

Psychology aims to be an objective science. It seeks, like other sciences, to explore features of human experience, behaviour and thought which are common to all people in all places. But because human beings are so diverse, perceive the world so differently and attach such different meanings to their experiences, it is exceedingly difficult to arrive at the kind of objectivity achieved, say, by physics or engineering. Halsey, Heath and Ridge (1980), writing about sociology, commented of that discipline:

It has never . . . been a 'value-free' academic discipline, if such were in any event possible. Instead it has been an attempt to marry a value-laden choice of issue with objective methods of data collection.

The same is true of psychology: decisions about who or what to study and under what conditions, are never value free and while steps can be taken to seek objectivity, say in gathering data, total objectivity will never be attained.

A good deal of damage has been done by people who believed that they had isolated some truth about human character or behaviour and publicized this conclusion prematurely, only to find that their conclusions were based upon small, unrepresentative samples of participants, or that the same conclusions were not found by other researchers. A similar source of damage has been the tendency to label people in ways which incline professionals to categorize people and to focus on the label (often having negative connotations, such as 'an alcoholic') at the expense of seeing a person first and foremost as a *person* with certain difficulties.

A further cause for concern has been the lack of explicit recognition that psychologists are themselves human and are not always the disinterested purveyors of truth that they might hope to appear. The discipline of psychology is useful, however, when practice can be grounded upon the research findings of psychologists, particularly when repeated studies provide increasing support for a hypothesis, and when evidence is gathered at an international and cross cultural level.

An example of theory: social learning

Social learning theory comprises a large body of concepts which, happily, are recognized by researchers in the disciplines of both psychology and sociology. It concerns how children and adults learn patterns of behaviour, as a result of social interactions, or simply through coping with the environment.

This theory, this system of ideas, contains many concepts which we shall consider further in later chapters; suffice it here to say that social learning theory proposes that we learn much of our behaviour and patterns of thought as a result of several processes. The first process is the imitation of others, especially those with influence upon us, like parents, teachers and respected people in our social circles and communities (sociologists have noted the same process and call those people imitated 'role models'). The second is through the rewards we receive for some of our behaviours and not others; and the third is as a result of cognition – actively thinking through ideas and situations and taking action accordingly.

Consider how a child learns a language. A baby comes into the world innately prepared to speak and to communicate. As soon as the child is born, however, processes of social learning begin to have an effect. Children are born with the potential to learn any language or languages. The language(s) they learn depends upon those that they experience or hear around them during early childhood: English, Gujarati, Icelandic, Greek, British Sign Language or Chinese. The capacity to speak, then, is innate; the form the language takes is socially learned.

As suggested, this learning occurs via three main processes. First, children imitate sounds which they hear about them. Second, they reproduce sounds which people reward them for producing. For example, if a little girl learning Hindi is thirsty and says 'pani', she is likely to be rewarded with the drink of water she is wanting and will probably say 'pani' again when she is thirsty. Third, children make sounds after trying to make meaning of their experience. So a little boy who hears the door bell ring may say, 'Mummy come!' as he interprets the sound in the light of his previous experience. All these examples illustrate concepts of social learning theory.

My reason for choosing social learning theory as an illustrative theory is that this body of ideas has been shown by research to offer a strong framework for much practice within social and community work. It is not so strong so as to exclude all other theory, but an approach based on social learning theory is, as Hudson and Macdonald (1986) claim, especially relevant to social and community work. This is because it suggests how to focus upon the practical rather than the pathological, upon people's strengths and potentials rather than upon their weaknesses or shortcomings, and upon how to empower those with whom we work. Researchers in the field of management have focused on the same body of theory as of key importance in working with people. What's more, I've heard it described as 'refined common sense'.

The Contribution of Social and Community Work to Psychology

So far it may seem that I am suggesting that the flow of ideas should all be in one direction: from psychology to social work and community work. This is not so. The social work and community work professions have developed many concepts which can and should inform and strengthen the discipline of psychology.

Power and empowerment

These are issues of central concern to community workers and social workers. Typically, the people with whom they work belong to low socio-economic groups and lack power and influence. One of the most pressing aims of social and community workers, in whatever arena they work, is to seek to *empower* people. To make influence and power accessible to disadvantaged people is to make them more self-determining, less dependent and more free to develop their own goals. I believe these ideas have been neglected in psychology.

Values

In the requirements for the Diploma in Social Work (CCETSW, 1991) there is an explicit section on 'The Values of Social Work'. These state clearly the positive values which social workers must demonstrate. Qualifying social workers must be able to:

❑ Develop an awareness of the inter-relationship of the processes of structural oppression, race, class and gender.
❑ Understand and counteract the impact of stigma and discrimination on grounds of poverty, age, disability and sectarianism.
❑ Demonstrate an awareness of both individual and institutional racism and ways to combat both through anti-racist practice.

❑ Develop an understanding of gender issues and demonstrate anti-sexism in social work practice.
❑ Recognize the need for and seek to promote policies and practices which are non-discriminatory and anti-oppressive.

This statement of values has been made explicit because social workers and community workers practise in settings where research has shown that prejudice and discrimination are all too common. There is, for example, evidence that minority groups, such as young black people, are dealt with more harshly than their white counterparts in the juvenile criminal justice system (National Council for the Care and Resettlement of Offenders, 1988), and also that members of ethnic minority groups are markedly over-represented in those admitted compulsorily to psychiatric hospitals (see Fernando, 1988, for a review). Social workers and psychologists who hold considerable power need to be constantly alert to such potential for abuse, both to avoid colluding with it and to establish procedures for positive practice.

An All-Purpose Process of Working with People: ASPIRE

The ASPIRE sequence is a process for social work and community work practice which incorporates the aims of working together with people to assess their needs and to negotiate, formulate and implement plans so that people can make decisions and take responsibility for their own lives. It has close parallels with the task-centred approach.

'ASPIRE' is a mnemonic, composed of the first letters of other words (Sutton and Herbert, 1992). It is chosen because these letters represent stages in working with people which offer a useful reminder of the process at times when we may feel overwhelmed by information or events, and need to find our bearings once again.

AS   Assessment
P   Planning
I   Implementation
RE   Review and Evaluation

Table 1 shows that at each of the four stages, specific steps are taken.

AS: Assessment
To assess means to judge or estimate something; the comparable word in a medical context is to diagnose. There are, however, major differences between 'assessment' and 'diagnosis'. In a medical context a doctor typically diagnoses what is amiss with systems internal to the person's body; in a social work or community work context, the worker attempts to gather, organize and make sense of information concerning *people as part of many systems:* family, school, friendship, religious, cultural and many more?'

Table 1 ASPIRE: a process for practice

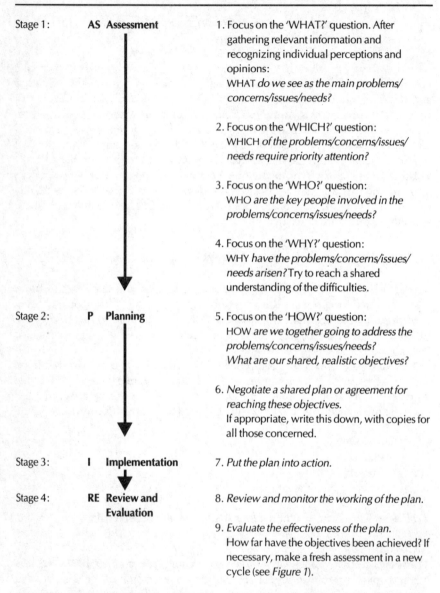

Stage 1:	**AS Assessment**	1. Focus on the 'WHAT?' question. After gathering relevant information and recognizing individual perceptions and opinions: WHAT *do we see as the main problems/ concerns/issues/needs?*
		2. Focus on the 'WHICH?' question: WHICH *of the problems/concerns/issues/ needs require priority attention?*
		3. Focus on the 'WHO?' question: WHO *are the key people involved in the problems/concerns/issues/needs?*
		4. Focus on the 'WHY?' question: WHY *have the problems/concerns/issues/ needs arisen?* Try to reach a shared understanding of the difficulties.
Stage 2:	**P Planning**	5. Focus on the 'HOW?' question: HOW *are we together going to address the problems/concerns/issues/needs?* *What are our shared, realistic objectives?*
		6. *Negotiate a shared plan or agreement for reaching these objectives.* If appropriate, write this down, with copies for all those concerned.
Stage 3:	**I Implementation**	7. *Put the plan into action.*
Stage 4:	**RE Review and Evaluation**	8. *Review and monitor the working of the plan.*
		9. *Evaluate the effectiveness of the plan.* How far have the objectives been achieved? If necessary, make a fresh assessment in a new cycle (see *Figure 1*).

Note: Clauses concerning, for example, statutory requirements, can be integrated into this process, usually at points 1 and 6.

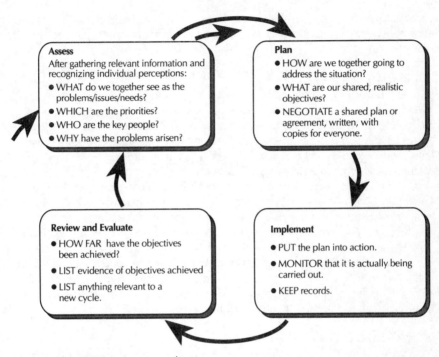

Assess
After gathering relevant information and recognizing individual perceptions:
- WHAT do we together see as the problems/issues/needs?
- WHICH are the priorities?
- WHO are the key people?
- WHY have the problems arisen?

Plan
- HOW are we together going to address the situation?
- WHAT are our shared, realistic objectives?
- NEGOTIATE a shared plan or agreement, written, with copies for everyone.

Review and Evaluate
- HOW FAR have the objectives been achieved?
- LIST evidence of objectives achieved
- LIST anything relevant to a new cycle.

Implement
- PUT the plan into action.
- MONITOR that it is actually being carried out.
- KEEP records.

Figure 1 The ASPIRE process as a cycle

An assessment is based upon information gathered from those involved and, as appropriate, from those closely concerned with them. It may be simple and straightforward, such as the example shown at the end of this chapter, or it may be far more detailed and complex, such as is required when a case conference calls for a full assessment of a child who may be at risk of being abused. Eliciting the necessary detail from sometimes unwilling or hostile clients calls for social work skill of a very high order.

P: Planning action and negotiating objectives
There is a good deal of empirical evidence, quite apart from the democratic principles involved, that involving people in planning action and therefore working towards shared objectives is a far more effective approach than holding them at a distance and deciding on the basis of 'we know what's good for you'. This shared approach facilitates clarity of focus and enlists motivation and commitment.

It is important to work towards *desired outcomes*. These may be long-term, taking perhaps as long as a year. It is difficult, however, for people to maintain such long-term objectives in view. Moreover, we know from social learning theory that achieving goals and the positive feedback we get from this acts to boost motivation. For both these reasons, it is important to break down long-term goals into small scale objectives. These should be attainable within a short period of time, say, days or weeks at most. This serves to boost motivation and enhance commitment.

I: Implementation

Just as the planning of the intervention is, or should be, a shared activity, one which empowers the recipients of a service or one which engages people as far as possible as co-workers towards agreed goals, so the implementation of the plan should, wherever possible, engage the participants as colleagues working towards common objectives. This is the concept implicit in the insistence that social workers shall work *in partnership with parents*.

If the plan has been made carefully, with the worker erring on the side of caution when discussing services and resources which may be available, the implementation of a plan should be a fairly straightforward affair. We should also not forget that we ourselves are part of the 'deal'; for example, people will fulfil a demanding commitment to a probation officer because she has kept her word.

It is also important to monitor developments and to 'troubleshoot' difficulties which arise when, for example, the worker is liaising with other agencies concerning the provision of a service. This should be done early during the stage of implementation, certainly during the first week.

RE: Review and Evaluation

This is the point at which all those concerned come together to review whether they have been successful in achieving what they set out to do. Are arrangements running smoothly and according to plan?

What, though, do we mean by 'evaluation'? To some people it means to discuss informally how they *felt* about such and such an undertaking: 'I felt we did a good piece of work there'. Many psychologists, however, use the term to mean to *measure*, using evidence and verifiable data, the effects or effectiveness of an intervention. If the work has been set up in such a way that the 'desired outcomes' have been negotiated with those concerned, then it is logical and right that those affected by the outcomes shall be central in evaluating whether, or how far, the outcomes have been achieved. While, in the last analysis, no evaluation is wholly objective or value free, many forms of intervention have been statistically evaluated on the basis of evidence as will be seen later in this book.

— ASPIRE: an example —

An elderly person, Mrs Jones, comes into the Area Office with an unpaid bill of £146.88 which has been accumulating for some time. She is very worried. The bill arose when she was taken to hospital in an emergency. Her neighbours kept an eye on the flat while she was away in hospital, but they did not think of adjusting the central heating. The result was that during the months that Mrs Jones was away, the cost of the heating accumulated very fast. Let's look at this situation in terms of the questions a social worker using the ASPIRE process might have in mind when trying to help Mrs Jones.

Assessment
Mr Patel, the social worker, gathers as much information about the situation as he can:

1. WHAT *are the problems?*
- Mrs Jones has a gas bill which she cannot pay.
- She has been warned that her gas is to be cut off.
- She does not think she will ever be able to afford £146.

2. WHICH *are the priority steps to be taken?*
- For Mrs Jones to inform the gas board of the situation and ask that her gas should not be cut off.
- For a letter to be sent asking in the circumstances:
  - a reduction of charges could be made,
  - over how long a period the bill could be paid.

3. WHO *are the key people involved?*
- Mrs Jones
- Mrs Collins, her daughter
- Mr Harris at the gas board
- Mr Patel, the social worker

4. WHY *has the problem arisen?*
- Through circumstances effectively out of Mrs Jones's control.

Planning
5. HOW *is the problem going to be addressed?*
The social worker, Mr Patel, discusses Mrs Jones's situation with her and they agree that their shared goals or objectives are to:
- avoid Mrs Jones's gas being cut off,
- clear the gas bill, either by getting it withdrawn or by finding funds to pay it.

6. Mrs Jones and Mr Patel work out a written plan of action on a carbon sheet, so that each has a copy.
- Mrs Jones will write to the gas board explaining the circumstances and requesting:
  - that she should not be cut off.
  - that the amount of the bill should be reduced.
  - that if it cannot be reduced, she should be sent information about how long-term payment can be made.

- Mr Patel will look through the Charities Register, seeking an organization which might contribute to paying the bill.
- They fix an appointment to meet in two weeks' time to discuss progress.

Implementation
7. The plan is put into effect.

Review and evaluation
8. Mr Patel and Mrs Jones meet two weeks later, as agreed, to review progress.
- Mrs Jones has written to the gas board. A reply has come indicating:
  - she will not be cut off,
  - the bill cannot be reduced,
  - three possible ways of paying the bill.
- Mr Patel has found an organization which may contribute towards the cost of the bill.

The cycle of assessment, planning, implementation of plan and evaluation is complete; the second, and any subsequent ones, continue until there is no need for any more. The example given here is deliberately very simple, but the process which it illustrates can be adapted to the most complex of situations, although many cycles of the process may be necessary.

CHAPTER 1

Human Beings in a 'Systems' Framework

Human beings live within networks of relationships or 'systems'. Let's be clear what is meant by a 'system', since the word is used for both the solar system and for the central heating system which, on the face of it, have little in common! A system has two main features: first, it is an assembly of parts or components connected together in an organized way; and, second, the parts of the system affect each other – a change in one may well precipitate a change in another.

The human body is itself a system, composed of many other systems, for example, the respiratory system, the cardiovascular system, the digestive system, the central nervous system, and many others. All the smaller systems contribute to the smooth functioning of the larger system, the body, and a significant change in one is very likely to affect the functioning of the others.

Human beings also exist *within* systems: family systems and social systems, educational systems and political systems. We are all intimately connected in networks of relationships. Another way of describing this phenomenon is the 'ecological' approach. According to Hicks and Gullett (1981):

The ecological view shows that ultimately every form of life affects every other one. However the inter-relationship may be obscure and insignificant, and may involve many links. These inter-relationships have been called the 'web of life'. Persons and the organizations to which they belong are essential parts of this web.

Figure 1.1 shows a system, limited by a boundary, containing smaller systems in relationship. Other systems feed into and out of it. If this model were used to illustrate an organization such as a hospital, the outer boundary represents the building. It contains smaller systems, the medical, surgical, psychiatric and other departments, linked with the nursing service, the social work department, the pharmacy and the library. Other systems outside the hospital, like government and its funding of the National Health Service, have a strong influence upon the hospital, and the hospital, in turn, affects other organizations – like the district nursing service. *Figure 1.2* represents a family, itself a system and also participating in many systems.

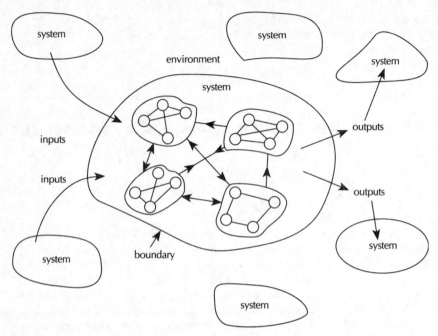

Figure 1.1 A system with sub-systems, interacting with other systems (Open University, 1980)

Human beings then are linked inextricably with other human beings, since our deepest needs can be met only by other people. We are, however, also very different from one another. So we have this tension: human beings are at one and the same time both intimately bound up with each other and yet highly individual.

Different Perspectives upon Human Beings

Figures 1.1 and *1.2* are an attempt to represent the complexity of the human condition. Such simplification is necessary for human beings to be able to deal with ideas of interacting systems in a manageable way. The next idea I want to introduce is also one in which complexity has been simplified in order to make it manageable. This is the notion of having different *perspectives* of human nature. When trying to understand people, the ideal, of course, is a 'holistic' approach, in which each person is perceived in his or her entirety, encompassing the physical body, human experience, learning and development, creativity, individual potential and so on. To represent such complexity, we can use a number of psychological perspectives, sometimes called 'models', of the human being. We shall consider five:

- The biological perspective.
- The psychodynamic/emotional perspective.
- The behavioural and social learning perspective.
- The cognitive perspective.
- The humanistic perspective.

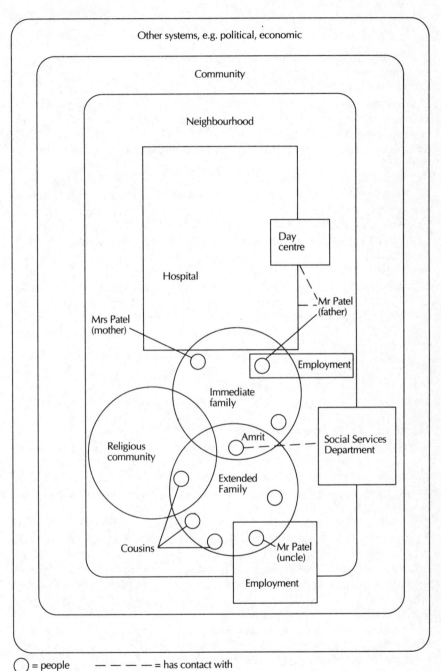

○ = people   — — — — — = has contact with

Figure 1.2 A person as part of many systems

The Biological Perspective

This approach focuses on biology, the study of life. It takes account of genetic influences, genes being those minute packets of biochemical information carried by the egg and the sperm which determine our biological sex and physical characteristics such as our eye, skin and hair colouring. Genes also govern the processes of growth and maturation and *make a contribution* to some of our psychological characteristics. Genes may be implicated in some aspects of our health and mental health, such as sickle-cell anaemia, cystic fibrosis and schizo-phrenia.

This perspective also takes into account the endocrine or hormonal systems of the body which equip it to survive and to function by means of the central nervous system and the autonomic nervous system. The energy arising from these processes is sometimes thought of as 'drives', and *Table 1.1* illustrates both the biological drives which are inborn, and those which are social and learned. Please study this table carefully: it contains a great many ideas about human beings which not everyone agrees upon. Since psychology is a discipline which uses scientific methods to increase understanding, it may be that the table will be amended in the future as new knowledge becomes available. It represents, however, our under-standing of the drives affecting human behaviour at the present time.

How innate factors influence development

This is a complex field of study. One way of going about establishing which characteristics are genetically underpinned (innate) and which are acquired or learned is to study identical twins. These twins are called monozygotic or MZ twins, meaning that they were born from the same egg and are therefore identical, as distinct from dizygotic or DZ twins, born from two separate eggs and therefore non-identical. There has been particular interest in MZ twins who, by chance, were separated at, or soon after, birth. If identical twins who experienced different environments in growing up are found to be significantly similar in certain respects, then this similarity must be attributable to innate rather than environmental influences.

Major studies, such as that of Tellegen and colleagues (1988) who examined 44 pairs of identical twins separated in early infancy and who were subsequently brought together at an average age of 34 years, showed major similarities between the pairs of twins. The highest similarities were found on measures of sociability, intelligence and emotional stability or instability. These findings, which are in line with other studies, suggest that we inherit about 50 per cent of our potential for these characteristics.

These has also been much research into the role of innate factors in infant and child development, for example, in the phenomenon of attachment. This is the term used to describe the tendency of the young of many species to seek closeness to particular individuals from whom they seem to derive a sense of security (see Chapter 2).

Table 1.1 Classification of the drives (Open University, 1970)

BIOLOGICAL DRIVES

To	Breathe
	Drink
	Eat
	Eliminate waste products
	Rest
	Avoid pain

These drives are *inborn*. Upon their satisfaction rests the survival of the *individual*.

To	Mate
	Care for the young

These drives are *partially inborn*. Upon their satisfaction rests the survival of the *species*.

To	Escape
	Attack

These drives have *inborn* and *learned* characteristics. Upon their satisfaction rests the survival of the *individual* and *species*.

To	Explore
	Seek sensory stimulation

These drives may be *inborn* and *learned*. Upon their satisfaction rests the survival of the *individual* and *species*.

SOCIAL DRIVES

To	Praise
	Achieve
	Dominate
	Submit
	Acquire
	Belong
	Help

These drives are *learned* and upon their satisfaction rests the survival of *society*.

Human aggression has attracted much research attention (see, for example, Archer, 1991). Is it innate, related to hormonal factors, or learned? Researchers have concluded that we are all equipped with the *potential* for aggressive behaviour, and are now addressing a more sophisticated set of questions such as: What are the circumstances under which we employ that potential? How do 'nature' (our innate potentials or hormonal factors) and 'nurture' (how we learn to employ those potentials) interact?

Implications for social work practice

It is important that social workers have a good grasp of genetic processes and their contribution to human experience for many reasons. I shall consider three: to underpin their knowledge of child development; to clarify the role of genetic factors in mental and physical health; and to educate people about circumstances which are not attributable to genetic factors.

Genetic processes underpin maturation in child development. For example, children cannot perform tasks such as control of the timing of the passing of faeces or urine until their bodies have matured to the point where they have awareness of and muscular control over these activities. Such awareness and control gradually begin to develop at about two years of age in the case of bowel control and a bit later in the case of bladder control. Parents often do not know that these maturational factors are involved when, for example, a toddler soils or wets a nappy only minutes after being changed. They may believe it has been done deliberately, and may even smack or punish the child. Social workers are in key roles for educating parents about such facts of child development.

They may also point out the role of genetic factors in individual differences between children. Parents may be puzzled why one child is so easy to manage and another is so restless. They may blame themselves with questions such as, 'Where did we go wrong?' if difficulties occur. It is unprofitable for parents to blame themselves or their upbringing of the children for difficult behaviour which may be genetically underpinned.

Research shows that differences in temperament among infants are evident by about three months of age in such characteristics as activity level, attention span, adaptability to changes in the environment and mood. One infant might be difficult to comfort when distressed; another might be easily comforted and so on.

Genetic factors can affect physical and mental health. Research shows genetic variables to be implicated in physical disorders such as cystic fibrosis, sickle-cell anaemia and diabetes, and in psychiatric disorders such as schizophrenia. Members of the public are likely to look to social workers to supplement the information supplied by medical and other professionals. A good grounding in the contribution of genetics seems important if social workers are to be of help to people with these concerns (Rauch, 1988).

Circumstances not attributable to genetic factors. Social workers have an important educational role in conveying accurate information concerning behaviours which are not genetically underpinned. I recall, for example, an occasion when I was visiting a prison, and one of the prisoners began to talk about the circumstances which had led to his being there. He told me that he believed it was because of 'bad blood' and he was very surprised when I not only disagreed with him about the physical cause of his behaviour, but showed him a copy of a diagram presenting other factors which may have contributed to his behaviour (see *Figure 1.3*).

There are many opportunities for social workers, probation officers and community workers to act as educators; for example, there is much ignorance and prejudice concerning differences between people of different races. While genetic factors may account for characteristics such as skin colour or type of hair, there is absolutely no scientific evidence to support the claim of one race to be superior to another.

The Psychodynamic/Emotional Perspective

One of the earliest bodies of knowledge which claimed to be based upon scientific, as distinct from philosophical, ideas about human nature was proposed by Sigmund Freud (1856–1939), and by others such as Jung and Adler, who, at least initially, shared his ideas. Freud, a doctor and neurologist, developed his theories as a response to his search for a treatment for people who came to him with disorders such as inexplicable paralyses of limbs or blindness. Freud found that certain cases were not physiological in origin. In some instances, the opportunity to speak freely, expressing feelings which are often kept hidden – anger, resentment, hatred, jealousy or sexual desire – seemed to relieve the problem. From this and other work, Freud developed his theory of personality.

Freud's theory of personality

The basic components of Freud's theory of personality are:

Id   This is the name given to the energizing force within us. Freud saw it as instinctual, and unconscious, impelled mainly by sexual and aggressive drives.

Ego   This is the name he gave to the conscious self, which he saw as governed by the demands of reality. It arose, he claimed, from the tension between the drives of the id and the inhibitions of the superego.

Superego Freud claimed this develops in response to parental instruction and might be compared with the 'conscience'. Its primary function is to inhibit the impulses of the id.

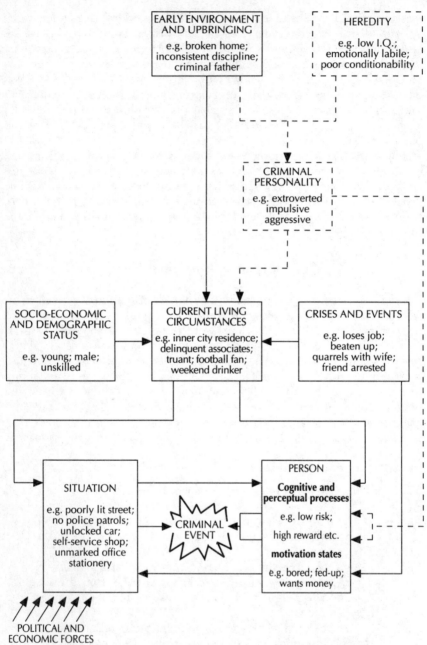

[The examples given within each box will have significance only in respect of particular types of crime]

The dotted lines indicate Clarke's doubts about the influence of hypothetical personality traits.

Figure 1.3 Elements contributing to the occurrence of a criminal event (Clarke, 1977)

Freud also proposed that every child moves through a sequence of *psychosexual stages*, each of which is characterized by a particular unconscious conflict. The successful or unsuccessful resolution of these tensions strongly affects adult personality.

The most significant of these conflicts is the Oedipus complex, which is clearest in the case of a boy. At age five or six, the boy is said to be strongly attracted to the mother, and (unconsciously) perceives his father as a rival for his mother's affection. The boy, however, fears the father who may retaliate against his sexual impulses by castrating him. The resolution of this conflict depends on the boy giving up his attraction to his mother and identifying with the father, so incorporating the values of the father (development of the superego). Little girls, in a similar process, come to identify with the mother. The successful or unsuccessful resolution of the Oedipus complex was thought by Freud to be the major determining factor in later neurosis.

The defence mechanisms

Freud, and his daughter, Anna, also focused upon the nature of anxiety and how human beings cope with it. As we shall see in Chapter 7, all people experience some degree of anxiety, but Freud and Anna Freud drew attention to the 'defence mechanisms' – strategies which people employ against anxiety. These include:

Reaction formation	This occurs when a person sees a characteristic of themselves as unacceptable and reacts against it. An example concerns a young man who, given to incessant talking, entered a Trappist monastery, in which the rule of silence was observed.
Rationalization	This is the process of finding good reasons for behaving in a way which the person consciously thinks is unacceptable. For example, this may occur when people who smoke claim that a little of what you fancy does you good.
Repression	This occurs, for example, when a deeply disturbing event, such as being sexually abused as a child, is 'forgotten' by conscious thought processes, because it is too painful and anxiety-provoking to remember. It is to be distinguished from 'suppression' in which the memory of the event remains conscious, even though a person may temporarily avoid acknowledging it. Freud believed repression of, say, the Oedipus complex is a necessary part of development.
Denial	This may occur when people experience so much anxiety that it may overwhelm them completely. For example, people who have a child or close relative with a life-threatening illness may deny this. Much support is needed in helping them to acknowledge reality, but direct challenge of their denial should be avoided.

A critique of Freudian theory

Atkinson and colleagues (1990) offer an objective appraisal of Freud's theories and work. They point out that rigorously designed studies provide little empirical data in support of Freud's psychosexual stages; moreover, the sample of people upon whom he based his theories was far from representative. However, they consider that Freud, and his daughter Anna, made at least three major contributions towards the understanding of human experience: first, devising the method of free association, that is, speaking whatever comes into one's mind in an uncensored way; second, elucidating the principle that much human behaviour is a compromise between our wishes and our fears or anxieties; and, third, showing that much of our behaviour is influenced by processes which are non-conscious.

Freud regarded the unconscious as the repository of anxiety-laden emotions and wishes of which the person is unaware. While this is, by definition, a difficult area to research empirically, there seems to be much anecdotal evidence that, within a supportive and permissive relationship, people can indeed allow emotions to enter their consciousness of which they were formerly unaware. This may be accompanied by considerable emotional release, for example, when a person recalls, for the first time, times of great distress experienced as a child.

It seems likely that childhood experiences are particularly influential in personality development in that the developing brain is especially sensitive to the impact of early experience and learning.

Implications for social work practice

Social workers play a great many roles in the course of their work. While the majority are likely to be employed within the statutory services, some may find themselves working primarily as counsellors. Whatever their formal role, for all social workers there will be times when they simply need to *listen* – a key feature of helpful therapeutic intervention. Women who have been raped, beaten or emotionally abused; people who have been bereaved in grievous circumstances; people who have had their trust in others shattered, but who have never had the opportunity to talk of, let alone express the feelings associated with these experiences, may find in a trusting and supportive counselling relationship an opportunity for the release of powerful emotions.

Sometimes, because of the horrifying nature of their experiences, people may 'block off' these memories or deny them. This may be so of people who have been sexually abused as children whose only means of coping has been to 'forget' what happened to them. People who were required as children to 'be brave' in distressing situations may experience acute conflict when their experiences provoke grief or despair which they are literally unable to express.

Social workers need to know that defences against anxiety and distress are used by all of us, and that it is damaging to challenge these in a harsh or unthinking way. People who are grappling with conflict, conscious or unconscious, need sensitive and patient responses from us, so that they may cope with the anxiety at their own pace. A broad range of feelings may be expressed – anger, grief, jealousy or bitterness – and they may sometimes seem contradictory. 'I didn't know I felt like that', said one young woman recently when talking and weeping about her relationship with her sister. 'I thought I only disliked her, but now I know I love her as well'. Social workers acting as counsellors need not only specific training for this role, but also skilled supervision – or otherwise they themselves may be disturbed by the expression of powerful emotions.

The Behavioural and Social Learning Perspectives

Behaviourism

In reaction to the claims of Freud and his followers that they had established upon a scientific basis a theory of human development, there arose a number of challengers. The early behaviourists were concerned to place the study of human experience upon as firm an empirical foundation as the physical sciences. J.B. Watson (1930), in an attempt to employ a means of gathering information and evidence about human experience in such a way that it could be tested and verified, proposed *behaviour* as a phenomenon which could be seen, counted and measured by observers. Building upon the work of Pavlov, he was able to demonstrate that a great deal of learning takes place via a process known as 'conditioning'. The term is used because it refers to the learning of a behaviour on condition that it is associated with another event. Two main forms of conditioning have been distinguished: classical conditioning and operant conditioning.

Classical conditioning is the learning of a behaviour because it is associated in time with a specific stimulus with which it was not formerly associated. An example of this in everyday life is a child who has been in hospital showing fear when he or she encounters someone in a white coat, say when going to the baby clinic. The white coat, formerly a neutral object, has become associated with distress, and thus elicits the fear response in the child.

Operant conditioning refers to learned behaviour which takes place because it operates upon or affects the environment. In essence, if a behaviour is followed by an outcome or response which is pleasurable to the animal or person concerned, it is likely to be repeated; if it is followed by an outcome or response which is not pleasurable, or which is actively unpleasant, it is less likely to be repeated. If, for example, a shy student contributes in class and what is said is acknowledged constructively by the tutor, that person is likely to speak again; if what is said is ridiculed, he or she is less likely to contribute again.

Social learning theory

Behavioural theory presents the child as a passive recipient of the conditioning process. While social learning theory also focuses on how an individual learns certain patterns of behaviour in coping with the environment, it places far more emphasis upon the individual and the systems of which he or she is part. Herbert (1981) has emphasized that learning occurs in a social context. Thus a young child learns skills and gains abilities within the larger system of his or her relationships with parents or other caregivers, in a specific setting within the wider social environment.

Mischel (1973) emphasized the multidimensional interactions which are implicit in human affairs, and incorporates this into social learning theory. For example, while people are much influenced by their upbringing and the social-ization experiences they have had, they can also react against these, and actively choose to follow, or not to follow, similar patterns in bringing up their own children. We shall consider three important concepts within social learning theory:

- learning via reinforcement and feedback;
- learning by imitation and modelling;
- learning through cognitive processes.

Learning via reinforcement and feedback

There is no doubt that parents, child minders, playgroup leaders, teachers and all those who take care of children, wittingly or unwittingly, practise the principles of reinforcement. 'You've put all the toys away, Sandra?' You *have* done well!'; 'When you've eaten all your chappatti, Usha, you can have some fruit'. These little scenes capture the processes of feedback which parents offer their children throughout the day. The precise meaning of the terms is set out below.

Positive reinforcement/feedback (reward). This is any event which has the effect of increasing the probability of the behaviour which preceded it occurring again; for example, appreciation, praise, recognition, pay packets or salaries. A child commended for trying hard at her school work is likely to continue to try hard.

Negative reinforcement/feedback. This is, technically, any happening which, because it is unpleasant, such as a pneumatic drill, has a rewarding effect when it stops. In popular usage, however, negative reinforcement or feedback often means a penalty.

Penalty/punishment. This is any event which has the effect of decreasing the probability of the behaviour which preceded it happening again: for example, criticism, blame, being ignored. A child whose efforts to try hard at her school work are criticized or ignored is unlikely to continue to try hard. For some children, however, any attention, even being scolded or smacked, is better than none, so *an apparent punishment may in fact be a reward*.

Desirable behaviour	+ reinforcement (reward)	> more desirable behaviour
Desirable behaviour	+ no reinforcement	> less desirable behaviour
Undesirable behaviour	+ reinforcement (reward)	> more undesirable behaviour
Undesirable behaviour	+ no reinforcement	> less undesirable behaviour

Much learning seems to occur via a series of feedback loops, as shown in *Figure 1.4*. For example, learning the language or languages of one's community, while underpinned by genetically based factors, is obviously learned by the feedback a child receives. Other behaviour, including problem behaviour, may be learned in similar ways. If, for example, a youngster is rude to a teacher, and the teacher not only tolerates this, but the young person's friends admire this behaviour, then being rude to the teacher is likely to happen again. Such sequences can escalate into full confrontations and even violence.

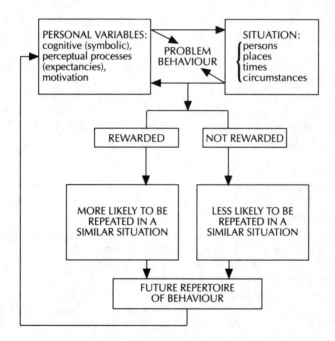

Figure 1.4 A feedback loop suggested by social learning theory (Emmet, 1987)

Learning by imitation and modelling

Social learning theory also takes account of the phenomenon of 'modelling', that is, the way in which people imitate others, particularly those with influence over them. The first models whom children imitate are their parents or caregivers: the way they speak, their mannerisms, their habits, their attitudes and their ways of doing things. This tendency is much exploited by the media and commercial interests who employ people enjoying high status to advertise their products.

Children learn specific roles at least partly through imitation; of particular significance is the learning of gender roles at a very young age. If girls see mostly men in positions of influence and authority, such as doctors, business executives, judges and politicians, they have little opportunity to imitate women in such roles and are more likely to see themselves in subordinate roles.

There is evidence that much behaviour, pro- and anti-social, is learned by imitation. The power of peer group pressure upon young people is well-established, and many young offenders have learned their behaviour from influential members of their peer groups.

Learning through cognitive processes

Mischel (1986) has considered some of the individual differences in thinking, judging and valuing which contribute to the very personal ways in which we perceive and behave in day-to-day life. For example, our different values and aspirations will affect what we find rewarding. Many young children show an amazingly subtle ability to play off one parent against another in such a way as to get their own way. For example, knowing that Mum has already refused a request to stay up late or watch a particular television programme, a child may then gain Dad's permission to do so – Mum and Dad not having been aware of each other's decision. This ability is grounded in sophisticated skills of perceiving parents' likes and dislikes, remembering what happened on previous occasions, choosing the time and place to make requests, selective reporting of the reactions of the other parent and so on. These cognitive processes help us to maximize our personal satisfactions and avoid dissatisfaction.

Implications for social work practice

Social learning theory is far from being an all-inclusive theory, but it can provide people with a framework to enable them to make sense of some of their circumstances. For example, a young man may be able to see that early disadvantage, lack of opportunities and want of active encouragement at school played a significant role in his perception of himself as a failure. This is a *learned* way of thinking, and alternative ways can be learnt. A great deal of research has been devoted to the applications of social learning theory, two of which are behavioural approaches and goal-setting approaches.

Behavioural approaches depend upon precise assessment, intervention and evaluation. If a child is found to be unmanageable in a playgroup or family centre because of attacks upon other children or staff members, and if careful assessment provides no clear explanation of this, a behavioural analysis has been found to be extremely useful (Herbert, 1981).

A   Antecedent: what occurs just before a given behaviour,
                                  or what are the cues to a behaviour.
B   Behaviour: the behaviour itself; what the child does.
C   Consequence: what happens immediately after the behaviour;
                                  that is, is the behaviour rewarded or penalized?

After answering these questions and gathering evidence about the frequency of the specified behaviour (attacking others), research has shown that it is possible to agree with the caregivers how the antecedents and/or consequences of the attacks can be changed. For example, rather than the aggressor being given the (unintended) reward of lengthy reproaches, he or she should be briefly reprimanded, while the victim of the attack should be attended to and comforted. However, staff should be on the lookout for the few occasions when the aggressive child shows kind or considerate behaviour so that this can be warmly commended (see p24). Handled in this way, aggressive behaviour typically reduces in frequency within a few days (Sutton, 1992).

Principles from social learning theory can be applied easily and used by social workers to enhance their clients' well-being. Research has shown that they are relevant to work in a wide range of situations especially child abuse, family work and residential care settings. One principle, for example, is that repeatedly punishing a child may have the opposite effect to that intended; it may increase, rather than reduce, misbehaviour. If a thrashing is the only form of attention a child gets, then that child is likely to misbehave on purpose because that at least guarantees some notice. The research literature repeatedly reports the crucial importance of positive feedback, warmth, encouragement and praise in bringing up children and young people.

Goal-setting approaches derive from many fields of research. Locke *et al.* (1981) have demonstrated that negotiating clear, attainable goals with those concerned is helpful in enabling people to bring about change. Research shows that this approach is effective in a wide range of interventions: helping people to be more assertive (Dickson, 1991), enabling people to gain control over alcohol or drug-related problems (Heather and Robertson, 1981), facilitating self-care among people with learning difficulties (Shearer and Shearer, 1972) and many others. In a community work context, the principles can be used to enable people to set and achieve simple, modest goals before aspiring to more ambitious ones – to raise 100 pounds before aiming to raise 1000, to hold a Women's Day before planning to open a Women's Centre. In this way they receive in frequent small doses the positive feedback of success. There are close parallels here with the task-centred approach (Reid and Epstein, 1972) known to most social workers.

It is, of course, true that these principles can be used unethically, and in a manipulative way. This is true, however, of any body of ideas. One important safeguard is to develop shared goals with the people concerned, and to work towards them together. We should bear in mind, however, that principles of social learning theory are operating whether we are aware of them or not, and whether we like it or not.

The Cognitive Perspective

Cognito is Latin for 'I think', and the cognitive perspective takes account of the evidence that human beings are not simply driven by unconscious anxieties or passively responding to events in their environments. They actively think, judge, assess, gain understanding, plan strategies and initiate activities and are creative in their attempts to make sense of their lives. According to this approach, human beings gather and process information, and then take action on the basis thereof.

Cognitive development

A major contribution to the understanding of the development of children's capacity to deal with incoming information has been the theory of Jean Piaget (1896–1980), a Swiss psychologist. While Piaget's studies have been criticized, they have stood the test of time, and the sequence of cognitive stage in *Table 1.2* is generally recognized.

While there is a good deal of debate about what characterizes the stages proposed by Piaget, there is little debate that a sequence of stages does occur, and in the chronological order shown. Children are likely to progress through them at different rates according to their abilities, opportunities for practice and cultural background.

Implications for social work practice

Social workers should be able to recognize a child's stage of cognitive development and should act accordingly. For example, young children in the preoperational stage, unable yet to understand that there are other points of view as well as their own, may believe that it is the power of their thoughts and wishes which has caused their parents to separate. Such children will also be unable to understand the arrangements made for their care during a separation or divorce. For example, 'to spend every other weekend with Mummy' will have no meaning, as the ability to anticipate the passing of time in this complex way has not developed. Much reassurance and language appropriate to the child's developmental level is necessary.

Practitioners also apply the principles of cognitive theory in order to help people who have distorted pictures of themselves, for example, people who blame themselves for experiences not of their making. There is a good deal of evidence (for example, Beck and Emery, 1985) that both anxiety and depression

Table 1.2 Piaget's stages of cognitive development

Stage	Characteristic
Sensorimotor (Birth to two years)	• The baby comes to understand the boundaries of his or her body, that is, knows that the 'self' is distinguishable from the 'not-self'. • He or she also gradually learns object permanence – the understanding that objects such as cups and toys continue to exist even when the baby can't see them.
Pre-operational (two to seven years)	• The baby comes to understand the idea of representation and learns to represent things by sounds, eventually developing language. • Thinking is 'egocentric', that is, the child has not yet developed the ability to take the viewpoint of another person. • The child gradually learns the principle of 'conservation'; for example, that quantities of water conserve their volume whatever size or shape of container they are poured into.
Concrete operational (seven to 12 years)	• The child can think logically about things and events. • He or she understands the conservation of mass/amount (about age seven) and weight (about age nine). • He or she can classify objects in several different ways, for example in terms of colour and size.
Formal operational (12 plus years)	• The young person can think about abstract ideas such as 'government' or 'justice'. • He or she becomes aware of issues and ideologies and can think abstractly in terms of hypotheses.

can be intensified, if not precipitated, by patterns of thinking which are ill-founded. Helping people to stop blaming themselves for, say, being unemployed, empowers them and enables them to take a fresh perspective upon their lives. Women who blame themselves for being victims of sexual abuse, as many survivors do (Jehu, 1988), can learn to acknowledge that they were powerless in this situation, leading to a marked improvement in self-esteem.

Further areas or cognitive psychology which are receiving research attention are the processes of decision-making and problem-solving (see Chapter 6).

The Humanistic Perspective

This view of human beings concerns itself with more positive and optimistic features of human experience and behaviour. Two psychologists who have made major contributions in this area are Abraham Maslow (1908–1970) and Carl Rogers (1902–1987). Both were interested in human experience in its own right, and have been concerned to examine the circumstances which enable people to live positively, productively and happily.

Maslow and the hierarchy of human needs

Maslow proposed that human beings have fundamental needs, which must be met for optimum development. He thought of these needs in the form of a hierarchy, the most fundamental at the bottom, and more complex ones at the top. The hierarchy is shown in *Table 1.3*.

Rogers' theory of personal growth

There are many similarities between the ideas of Maslow and Rogers, in that both were concerned with the nature of the self and in discovering the conditions and circumstances which enable people to move towards maturity and growth. While Maslow saw the need for personal development as the highest level of aspiration towards which we all aspire but only few achieve, Rogers, a therapist, examined instead the day-to-day conditions which are required for a person to begin the process of personal growth and development – at any age or stage in life. He claimed (1951):

> The organism has one basic tendency and striving – to actualize, maintain, and enhance the experiencing organism.

In order to facilitate this potential for development, Rogers believed that therapists should demonstrate *unconditional positive regard*. This attitude of respect and regard, he claimed, is experienced as healing and restorative by those in distress. Rogers 'client-centred therapy' has been adopted as a foundation to many forms of counselling (see Chapter 6).

Humanistic psychology has been criticized as being over-concerned with personal fulfilment, neglecting social issues and problems. It is no accident that these ideas have emerged in the USA, a country in which individualism and independence are highly valued.

Table 1.3 Maslow's model of human needs

7. Self-actualization needs: to fulfil one's potential.	People can only self-actualize if more basic needs are met.
6. Aesthetic needs: to be creative, to appreciate and enjoy beautiful sights, sounds and experiences.	People's potential to develop and to be creative is always available, even if due to circumstance, it has lain dormant for years.
5. Cognitive needs: to try to find out, to be curious, to try to understand.	Children need to explore and investigate the world as a basis for a lifelong enthusiasm for learning, experimenting and creating.
4. Esteem needs: to feel valued and a person of worth and dignity.	Children need the approval and appreciation of others in order to develop a positive sense of self. As this is a learned characteristic, it can be enhanced or diminished by the way we treat people.
3. Belongingness and love needs: to have close and loving relationships with others.	Babies are born prepared to develop intimate and dependent love relationships with those who care for them. Touch is often a central feature. These early relationships are of great importance.
2. Safety needs: to feel secure and free from threat, physical or emotional.	To maintain our security, we are equipped with two systems: the defence system and the safety system (Gray, 1987; Gilbert, 1989). These underpin our physiological responses to threat.
1. Physiological needs: to have warmth, food, air, water reliably available.	These are the primary requirements for life.

Note: People do not move smoothly up this hierarchy; they move forward and backwards, even within a few minutes, according to circumstances.

Implications for social work practice

Maslow's hierarchy clearly shows the importance of meeting both physical and emotional needs. Certainly, the list of children's needs devised by Cooper (1985) (see p34) is very similar to that of Maslow. Since social workers are all too often involved with children when their needs have not been met, when family care has broken down or when alternative arrangements have to be made, then it is the primary needs, especially the need for security, which call for the most urgent attention. How people express their needs for security may not be understood. The child who clings to the parent who has abused her is probably showing a greater confidence in the known than in the unknown; the prisoner who dreads leaving prison may have experienced the security there as protective and supportive, rather than oppressive. In both instances, it is the need for safety which is predominant.

This fundamental need for safety makes human beings constantly alert to possible threat (Sutton, 1992). When we *feel* threatened, whether this is actually the case or not, we either attack in return, defend ourselves, or remain silent. None of these responses is conducive to effective communication or to learning. People are innately predisposed to be self-concerned when they feel unsafe. For this reason, it is appropriate to treat all those with whom we work with consideration and regard. Even when we have unpleasant tasks to fulfil, like informing parents that we are concerned about their child's well-being, then a firm and respectful manner is absolutely essential.

Whether we appreciate it or not, members of the public often see social workers, community workers and probation officers as threatening. Social workers, in particular, are seen as very powerful people: they can take children into care; they write reports to a court; and some can support an application to admit a person to a psychiatric hospital. Social workers are often strangers, not known people who can be trusted. These perceptions, some accurate, some patently inaccurate, may lead to marked suspiciousness of us. All other roles are obscured by our power and control. We should actively seek to reduce the threat implicit in our role.

CHAPTER 2

Aspects of Human Development

It is possible to devote only limited space to the immense field of child and adult development. We shall start with a consideration of children's needs and then follow the child through particular stages of development, drawing upon the perspectives which we introduced in the last chapter. Only a few topics and studies can be chosen from the vast array of research which has been conducted, but while these seem crucial to include, they may not be representative of the breadth of cultures which social workers and community workers encounter. Readers are asked to supplement the contents of this chapter by their own reading and enquiry. Throughout, an effort will be made to consider the child as part of many systems.

Human needs are particularly acute in childhood, and especially so in early childhood, when children are dependent upon others in every way. Cooper (1985) has summarized the needs of children in the helpful way shown in *Table 2.1*. These needs must be met in order for the child to develop physically and emotionally.

Assessment of Development

Social workers are often in a position to assess whether a child is developing normally. This means taking into account the physical, social and emotional development of the child. In order to do so, it is necessary to be aware of what is considered to signify 'normal' development, that is, estimating whether the child is progressing according to standardized norms, or whether further professional help is needed.

Centile charts are used to monitor physical development in terms of height and weight. As the *Guidelines for Users of Assessment and Action Records* (Department of Health, 1991) emphasize, it is vital to keep records of the growth rates and overall development of vulnerable children. Children usually grow at a regular rate along a recognized curve (centile), so while one cannot judge growth on a single measurement, any unexpected change in growth rate is cause for

Table 2.1 The needs of children (Cooper, 1985)

- **Basic physical care**
  which includes warmth, shelter, adequate food and rest, grooming (hygiene) and protection from danger.

- **Affection**
  which includes physical contact, holding, stroking, cuddling and kissing, comforting, admiration, delight, tenderness, patience, time, making allowances for annoying behaviour, general companionship and approval.

- **Security**
  which involves continuity of care, the expectation of continuing in the stable family unit, a predictable environment, consistent patterns of care and daily routine, simple rules and consistent controls and a harmonious family group.

- **Stimulation of innate potential**
  by praise, by encouraging curiosity and exploratory behaviour, by developing skills through responsiveness to questions and to play, by promoting educational opportunities.

- **Guidance and control**
  to teach adequate social behaviour which includes discipline within the child's understanding and capacity, and which requires patience and a model for the child to copy, for example, in honesty and concern and kindness for others.

- **Responsibility**
  for small things at first such as self care, tidying playthings, or taking dishes to the kitchen, and gradually elaborating the decision-making the child has to learn in order to function adequately, gaining experience through mistakes as well as successes, and receiving praise and encouragement to strive and do better.

- **Independence**
  to make their own decisions, first about small things but increasingly about the various aspects of life within the confines of the family and society's codes. Parents use fine judgement in encouraging independence, and in letting the child see and feel the outcome of his or her own poor judgement and mistakes, but within the compass of the child's capacity. Protection is needed, but over-protection is as bad as too early responsibility and independence.

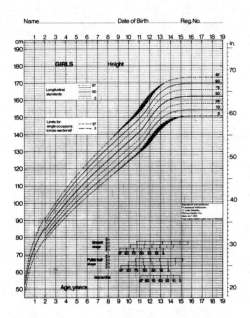

Figure 2.1a Girls' height assessment chart. Girls usually gain height along one of the above curves.

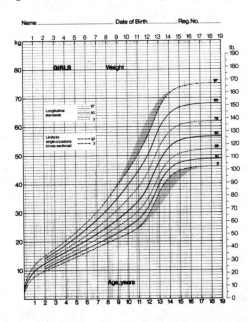

Figure 2.1b Girls' weight assessment chart. Girls usually gain weight along one of the above curves.

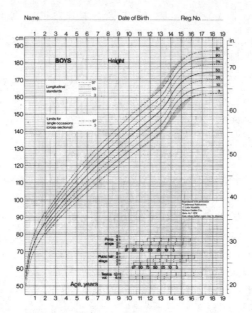

Figure 2.1c Boys' height assessment chart. Boys usually gain height along one of the above curves. The cross-hatched area represents the wide range of measurements characteristically found in adolescence.

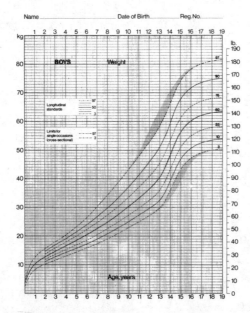

Figure 2.1d Boys' weight assessment chart. Boys usually gain weight along one of the above curves. All charts reproduced with permission.©Castlemead Publications, 12 Little Mundells, Welwyn Garden City, Herts AL7 1EW, from whom further charts may be obtained.

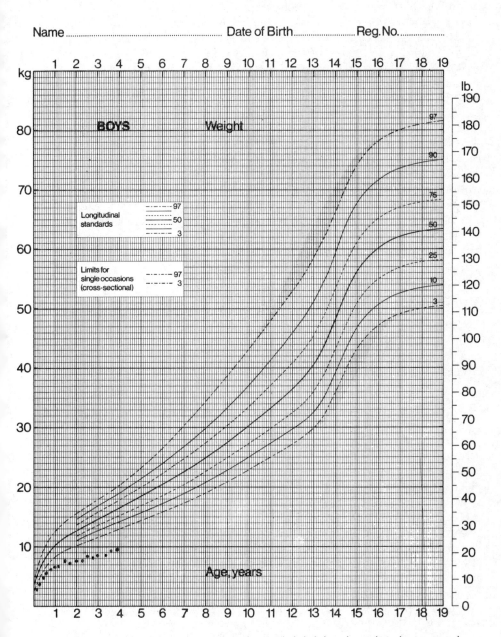

Name... Date of Birth........................... Reg. No. ....

Figure 2.2 This chart shows the actual weight record of a little boy about whom there was much concern.

concern. Children's height and weight should be measured at regular intervals, and children who cross two or more centiles should be referred to a GP or paediatrician for further assessment. Although these charts (see *Figure 2.1*) do not represent data for all communities in Britain, there is cause for concern for any child falling at the extremes of these centiles. *Figure 2.2*, which records the growth of an actual child, shows that there were serious grounds for concern about his development.

Scales such as the Child Development charts devised by Sheridan (1973), the Developmental Scales of the National Foundation of Educational Research (Bellman and Cash, 1988) and the Denver Developmental Screening Test (Frankenburg *et al*, 1992) can all be used to assess and screen aspects of a child's social behaviour, language, play and physical coordination. Such scales should not be regarded as 'tests'; they have not yet been validated across all community groups and are never entirely objective instruments. They can, however, be used when appropriate as an aid to screening. It is also useful, particularly regarding emotional and social development, to refer to Erikson's notion of 'developmental tasks' which children need to negotiate at different stages of development (see *Table 2.2*).

Always bear in mind that:
- Development is a continuous process from conception to maturity.
- Development depends on the maturation and myelinization of the nervous system. Until that has occurred, no amount of practice can make a child learn a skill, for example, to control bowel or bladder.
- The sequence of development is the same for all children; the rate of development varies from child to child.

Infancy and the Earliest Years of Life

The first months after birth are a time of major readjustment for parents. Babies vary enormously: some may be calm and placid, sleeping peacefully much of the time and gazing contentedly at the world during the few hours of wakefulness; others are restless from birth, seldom settling to sleep or feed calmly, and given to prolonged crying. Inexperienced parents need a great deal of reassurance, guidance and support at this time.

Newborn infants are by no means passive recipients of other people's initiatives; they are poised for development, ready to initiate action – albeit at first in the only way available to them, by crying. They are also innately prepared to perceive and react to stimuli in the environment. According to Bee (1992), very young babies can focus both eyes on the same point and follow a moving object with their eyes; they can respond to the mother's or caregiver's voice and smell very early in life; distinguish between sweet and salty tastes and respond to touch.

Very soon, assuming that they are in good health, babies begin to take more initiatives. At about four to five weeks, they begin to produce that delightful

Table 2.2 Developmental tasks (as adapted from Erikson by Herbert, 1991)

Approximate age	Characteristic to be achieved	Major hazard to achievements	Facilitative factors
Birth to 18 months	Sense of trust or security.	Neglect, abuse or deprivation of consistent and appropriate love in infancy; harsh or early weaning.	If parents meet the preponderance of the infant's needs, the child develops strong sense of trust.
18 months to 3 years	Sense of autonomy – child viewing self as an individual in his/her own right, apart from parents although dependent on them.	Conditions which interfere with the child's achieving a feeling of adequacy or the learning of skills such as talking.	If parents reward the child's successful actions and do not shame his or her failures (say in bowel or bladder control) the child's sense of autonomy will outweigh self-doubt/shame/guilt.
3 to 5 years	Sense of initiative – period of vigorous reality testing, imagination, and imitation of adult behaviour.	Overly strict discipline, internalization of rigid ethical attitudes which interfere with the child's spontaneity and reality testing.	If parents accept the child's curiosity and do not put down the need to know and to question, the child's sense of initiative will be enhanced.
5 to 11 years	Sense of duty and accomplishment – laying aside of fantasy and play; undertaking real tasks, developing academic and social competencies.	Excessive competition, personal limitations, or other conditions which lead to experiences of failure, resulting in feeling of inferiority and poor work habits.	If the child encounters more success than failure at home and at school he or she will have a greater sense of industry than inferiority.
11/12 to 15 years	Sense of identity – clarification in adolescence of who one is, and what one's role is.	Failure of society to provide clearly defined roles and standards; formation of cliques which provide clear but not always desirable roles and standards.	If the young person can reconcile diverse roles, abilities and values, and see their continuity with past and future, a sense of personal identity will be developed and consolidated.

response to the human face, the smile. The fact that blind babies smile at exactly the same age as sighted babies indicates that this is one of the social behaviours which is 'programmed' to emerge at this stage of development. Soon they can be seen to follow moving patterns with their eyes in order to explore their environments visually. Activities which bring intriguing results are often repeated, even at this young age, indicating an awareness of cause and effect relationships – 'When I kick, something interesting happens'. This shows that cognitive ability is already developing. According to Piaget, the baby explores the world through movement and through using his or her developing senses. As he or she moves through the sensorimotor period (see p29), the baby learns to distinguish between 'self' (toes at the end of the cot) and 'not self' (a picture at the end of the cot).

In the period from one month to the third birthday, much development occurs. Babies usually take more and more initiative, impelled by the maturational processes within them. They begin to smile spontaneously not just responsively; they reach for toys or objects near them and they begin to roll over and crawl around in preparation for the stages of standing and walking. Already some differences between children are beginning to show: for example, African children are characteristically two to three months ahead of white children in gaining control of the head and beginning to walk (Ainsworth, 1967). Babies also show anxiety about strangers and about separation from the main caregiver.

Many studies have shown marked individual differences between babies in terms of temperament. Thomas and Chess (1977), in a longitudinal study of young babies through into childhood and adolescence, found that 65 per cent of them fell into three main categories, showing characteristics in infancy which tended to persist into childhood and beyond.

Table 2.3 Childhood temperament: patterns among young children which tend to persist beyond infancy (Thomas and Chess, 1977)

The 'easy' child	These young children are adaptable and easy to manage. They move early in life into regular patterns of sleeping and waking, and seem contented and flexible.
The 'difficult' child	These young children are less adaptable. It is more difficult to get them into a routine of sleeping and feeding regularly, and they seem more tense and irritable in their responses to new situations or people.
The 'slow to warm up' child	These children fall between the two patterns shown above, but it takes considerable time to settle them into a routine. Having made that adjustment, however, they are fairly easy to manage.

One particular difference between babies which seems be genetically under-pinned is the response to cuddling. Research has shown that a substantial proportion of babies actively resist cuddling. Since cuddling is often a source of satisfaction to both parents and grandparents, it can be very frustrating to all concerned if, when picked up, the baby arches away, squirms and clearly dislikes this experience. Parents and carers can and do interpret this as a sign of rejection and this can bring disappointment and unhappiness in its train. Parents need to understand that babies are individuals, 'going concerns', in their own right, and that relationships between them and their carers are essentially two-way affairs.

Babies clearly experience feelings – if we take smiling as reflecting a state of contentment and crying as representing distress. Patterns of crying vary greatly between babies and many parents find the early months of life stressful until the baby 'settles down'.

Bonding and attachment

'Bonding' refers to the constellation of feelings of love, protectiveness and closeness which most mothers and fathers come to feel over time for their babies. While some researchers claim that this occurs at a critical period soon after the baby's birth in an almost now-or-never fashion, reviews of the evidence (for example, Sluckin, Herbert and Sluckin, 1983) have shown this to be ill-founded. Typically, parents *gradually* come to love their babies.

The term 'attachment' refers to the constellation of feelings and behaviours demonstrated by babies towards their parents and other caregivers and this, too, is the focus of extensive research. As *Table 2.2* shows, it is during this time that children, ideally, through a network of close relationships, develop a fundament-al sense of trust and security.

According to Bee (1992), infants rarely protest at separation from the main caregiver or show fear of strangers before five or six months, but do so increasing-ly until 12 to 16 months. This behaviour usually declines after this age. By about ten months, however, infants who are securely attached (see *Table 2.4*) are using the mother, or main caregiver, as a safe base and as a reliable source of reference as to whether a new person or situation should be approached or avoided.

While developing close attachments provides children with a sense of security, it would be a mistake to think that they must occur in a once-and-for-all fashion at a fixed point in time. Loving relationships with regular caregivers in the earliest years of life are obviously desirable, but studies have shown that children brought up in nurseries and orphanages, where they received inadequate or inconsistent care, can nevertheless go on to develop close and loving relationships with those who subsequently foster or adopt them (see Schaffer, 1990).

Secure and insecure attachment

This is a field of research which concerns the quality of the relationship between a young child and his or her parent or caregivers during the first twelve months of life. Studies have examined the behaviour of young

Table 2.4 Indicators of secure attachment (Herbert, 1991)

Secure attachments (infant-to-parent) may be indexed by the baby's:

- Interest and attentiveness when with the parent (looking, gazing, listening).

- Relaxation and/or calmness in the company of the parent.

- Dependency behaviours directed at the parent, for example, holding, proximity-seeking (later when more mobile seeking comfort and help).

- Evident preference for the parent to others.

- Curiosity and exploration using the parent as a 'base'.

- Pleasure, enthusiasm, joy (e.g. smiling, vocalizing) in the presence of the parent.

- Protest, displeasure, concern when separated from the parent; comforted when he or she returns.

Note: By four months of age it is possible to observe each of these behaviours in a series of free exchanges between mother and baby. By the middle of their first year, most normal children begin to show attachments to significant people in their environment. From then on young children are much more vulnerable to separation from loved ones (see Schaffer, 1990, for detailed evidence).

---

children in situations in which the mother is present, and then briefly absent, leaving her bag on a seat as an indication that she will return. A person unknown to the child gently attempts to engage the child in play, before the mother returns. Next, the mother again leaves and the stranger returns; and finally the mother returns and stays. Ainsworth and her colleagues (1978) were particularly interested in the behaviour of the babies at the final reunion, and on this basis, classified the children as follows:

Securely attached	With the mother present, the babies play happily and are friendly to the stranger. When she goes out, they are clearly distressed, and may cry and search for her. On her return, they go to her, and only calm down on being hugged. About 65 per cent of children fall into this group.
Insecurely attached: avoidant	These babies are not particularly concerned when the mother leaves and, if distressed, are as readily comforted by the stranger as the mother. On her return, they ignore the mother or look away. About 25 per cent of babies fall into this group.

Insecurely attached: resistant	These babies become very distressed when the mother is not nearby. They seem uncertain about their relationship with the mother, and do not resume playing once she has returned.

Links have been made between the form of attachment demonstrated by the baby, secure or insecure, and the sensitivity of the care which the baby has experienced. It is claimed that mothers of infants who are securely attached are more responsive to their infants' needs, in that they talk to and play with them more and express more affection to them. Babies who are insecurely attached in an avoidant way are said to have experienced hostile or rejecting mothering (see Belsky *et al.* 1984), while the mothers of babies insecurely attached in a resistant way are said to have experienced a general lack of emotional involvement.

In view of the studies by Thomas and Chess (1977) which stress that babies have individual temperaments which tend to persist, and of studies showing the clear effect of cultural patterns upon childhood responses to strange situations, I am not myself persuaded that the causal relationship claimed to have been found between the kind of parenting offered and the child's behaviour in this 'strange situation' test has been adequately demonstrated. Only further empirical research will clarify the matter fully.

Many researchers are continuing to explore this important field with its profound implications for children's development and for social policy concerning, for example, daycare. Crockenberg (1981), for example, has investigated the effects upon the baby of two interacting variables: the infant's temperament and the degree of support available to the mother. She studied a group of 40 mothers and their infants during the first year of the children's lives, from five to ten days old to 12 months. She found that insecure attachment was likely to occur only when the mother had *both* an irritable baby *and* perceived that she had low social support from family and friends.

Attachment and daycare

A series of studies concerning the effects of daycare upon the attachments of very young children has been conducted. Bee (1992) reports that they suggest that there is general agreement that children who first enter daycare at about 18 months or two years show little evidence of loss of security. There is, however, some concern about children who enter daycare earlier than this on a full-time basis. These children were found by Belsky and Rovine (1988) to show higher levels of insecure attachment than those reared entirely at home or by those whose mothers work only part-time. Other researchers, such as Chase-Lansdale and Owen (1987) did not obtain these results, so this is another area where further studies are needed to tease out the impact of daycare on young children in the short and long term. Table 2.6 shows desirable features of daycare settings.

Table 2.5 Desirable features of daycare settings

Aspect of care	Outcome
Caregiver/child ratio	In general, the lower the better; that is, the fewer children per staff member, the better.
Number of children per group	The smaller the number, the better.
Amount of contact with workers	Usually, the more one-to-one time, the better.
Verbal stimulation	The variety and richness of the language used stimulates cognitive development, regardless of, for example, the number of toys.
Space, cleanliness, colourfulness	There is more imaginative play in spacious colourful settings adapted to children.
Carer's knowledge of child development	Children seem to do better in settings where carers have had training in child development.
Continuity of caregivers	In general, the fewer changes among caregivers, the better.

Implications of attachment research

❏ The principle of supporting the relationship between parents and children, enshrined in the Children Act 1989, is a sound one.
❏ Good quality daycare can benefit children who may be receiving little care and stimulation from disadvantaged or severely stressed parents.
❏ Nursery or family centre staff should be encouraged to stay in posts for lengthy periods of time. Young children thrive within familiar relationships.
❏ It is extremely difficult to distinguish insecure attachment from secure attachment. In these circumstances, the list devised by Herbert (1991) can be helpful (see *Table 2.4*). One's assessment should be informed by whether these indicators are present or not.
❏ If 'experts' are still disputing key concepts in child development, it is inevitable that we shall make some mistakes. We have, however, a responsibility to keep abreast of the research in this area.

Areas of general agreement about bonding and attachment:
❏ Babies become emotionally 'attached' to one or more people.
❏ Bonding and attachment develop gradually; not in an all-or-nothing way during the first hours or days of life.

❑ Babies often develop a web of attachments to several people: mother, father, grandparents, siblings, carers, etc.
❑ Sometimes there is a clear hierarchy of attachment, in which one person is selected as the focus of a particularly close relationship.
❑ Close attachment to one figure may be a cultural phenomenon since many babies in extended families develop multiple attachments.
❑ It is in the child's interests to develop trusting attachments with more than just one or two key figures.

Areas where disagreement continues:
❑ The effects of daycare upon young children, especially very young children under the age of two.
❑ The reliability of the 'strange situation' as an index of attachment.
❑ If insecure attachment is diagnosed, the implications of this for the child's future well-being.

The Pre-School Child

This is a time of rapid growth and maturation and one of immense importance for the child's subsequent experience. It has become clear that a great deal of the development of the brain takes place after, rather than before, birth and the importance of early stimulation of, for example, children with learning difficulties has now been recognized.

During the pre-operational period (see p29), the use of symbols develops fast, both in terms of signs and language. Games, such as water and sand play, puzzles, stories and poetry, all enrich children's conceptual understanding as well as providing the means for emotional development. There is increasing consensus among researchers that this is the stage when stimulating activities, in an atmosphere of fun and enjoyment, can markedly increase children's cognitive capacities (see Howe, 1988). Howe points out, however, that 'pressure to succeed' is totally undesirable and stresses that:

Intellectual acceleration cannot guarantee that a person will gain the non-intellectual qualities that real success also depends on, such as self-direction, self-confidence, a sense of commitment and sheer persistence.

Studies in the United States with disadvantaged children who received special programmes of intervention showed that these children made marked gains by comparison with a control group of children who did not participate in such programmes. Early intellectual stimulation has been found to have a significant impact on later school performance, with a stimulating home environment being the most important variable (Darlington, 1986). These and other studies have provided the evidence for establishing programmes of early intervention for children born with learning disabilities, such as the Portage Project (Shearer and Shearer, 1972).

This period is of course of crucial importance to the child's emotional development. According to Erikson (see *Table 2.2*) this is the period when a sense of being an individual in one's own right is, ideally, acquired. It is also a time when the foundations of trust in others continue to be laid down.

Socialization

None of us can escape the experience of socialization – that is, being trained by direct and indirect methods to follow the customs of our family, our community and our culture. At the very least, we learn to speak the language, and because we learn so readily in early life, the influence of this learning often extends throughout life.

As seen in Chapter 1, children learn from the patterns of feedback, positive and negative, which they receive from people close to them and from the models they imitate. This learning will affect their social interactions, their habits and the roles they acquire. It will take effect whether or not caregivers consciously give thought to how a child should be brought up. Children learn specific gender roles, namely what constitutes 'appropriate behaviour' for a girl or boy. A boy may learn not to cry, or to hide his feelings of love and affection for his family. 'I don't like boys being too affectionate; it's a hard world, and they mustn't show their feelings too much', said one father to me. A girl may be denied opportunities to play football or, later, to study science or to learn computing because these are seen as too 'boyish'. In this way, through both subtle and direct methods, gender roles are learned which, in effect, constrain the potential of everyone concerned.

These gender roles are also learned through a broad range of influences such as television, newspapers, magazines, fashion and commerce. These sources have a strong influence upon what is considered desirable by both children and parents.

Aggression and anti-social behaviour

Around the age of two, coercive behaviour tends to increase. The 'terrible-twos' are known for the high rate of shouting and whining which is normal for this time. But tendencies towards aggressive behaviour may become established. By the age of four, coercive behaviour should be considerably reduced. There is good evidence that while all human beings have the potential to behave aggressively, in the sense that we are all equipped with the means of hitting, biting, assaulting or attacking another person, we *learn* whether or not to act upon that potential. This is a matter of major concern, as reports of violence in the home and in public settings increase.

Both American and British studies confirm that many children who display aggressive and anti-social behaviour in early childhood continue to do so in later childhood. Stevenson *et al.* (1985), who followed up a representative sample of 535 children from their third to their eighth birthdays, found that behavioural problems at age three were strongly related to behavioural deviance at age eight. Further studies show that early aggressive and anti-social behaviour tends to continue into later childhood, adolescence and adulthood. Olweus (1979), who carried out extensive longitudinal studies, found that 'marked individual differences in habitual aggression level manifest themselves early in life, certainly by the age of 3'.

Such research points directly to the necessity for *early* intervention to support and train the parents of these pre-schoolers in skills of child management. My own research with 37 families with difficult pre-school children, showed that such training can be effective and inexpensive and that its effects tend to persist (Sutton, 1992).

The Primary School Child

The physiological development of the school child slows down in pace in comparison with that of the pre-school child. Boys and girls seem to enter a plateau in their rate of growth, though towards the end of the junior school period, at age ten or 11, the early developers are already beginning to experience the maturational spurt of puberty. For the majority of children, however, maturational processes occur smoothly during this period, and children gain height and weight more gradually than in the periods preceding and succeeding this stage.

Primary school children acquire a positive sense of self-esteem, and learn to feel competent *if given opportunities to succeed*; they are able to carry substantial

Being left out can be a source of deep distress

Table 2.6 Calls received by Childline between April 1992 and March 1993

Type of problem	Girls	Boys	Total	%
Physical abuse	7884	3356	11240	14
Family problems	8961	2135	11096	14
Sexual abuse	8371	1912	10283	13
Concerns about others	7217	1152	8369	11
Bullying	6038	2090	8128	10
Pregnancy	5712	150	5862	7
Problems with friends	3631	363	3994	5
Sexuality	1649	858	2507	3
Runaways	1505	698	2203	3
Substance abuse	1305	536	1841	2
School problems	1035	351	1386	2
Facts of life	1016	84	1100	1
Parents divorcing	856	165	1021	1
Health	839	166	1005	1
Homelessness	400	330	730	1
Emotional abuse	472	108	580	1
Risk of abuse	464	109	573	1
Bereavement	450	87	537	1
Suicide	458	79	537	1
Other	4726	1409	6135	8
TOTAL	62989	16138	79127	100

responsibilities if their circumstances and/or cultures require it of them. Children of this age need to be able to cope with the demanding environment of school. For some fortunate children, the mixture of cooperation and competition found there can be a stimulating and satisfying experience. For others, perhaps less secure at home or less outgoing, it can be a lonely and frightening world, producing much anxiety. For some, perhaps those from minority cultures or those with disabilities, school can involve experiences of discrimination, rejection and embarrassment. Of the 79,000 children who telephoned Childline between April 1992 and March 1993 over 2,000 boys and nearly three times as many girls complained of being bullied (see Table 2.6).

For children whose lives are made yet more complex by problems at home, this time can be one of intense confusion, anxiety and isolation. To feel unable to talk about being abused or the fear that, because one parent has left, the other may also go, can totally undermine the well-being of children of this age. For yet others, school and understanding teachers may prove a safe haven when home life is too stressful. Children of this age and older desperately want to belong. They need friends and the security that friendship brings. A quarrel or being left out can be a source of distress and depression, especially for sensitive children.

Socialization experiences continue, but now the major influences brought to bear are those of the school and the playground. In this respect, children from ethnic minority groups are likely to be at a disadvantage, since they frequently lack role models from their communities in influential positions. While some children may succeed in the school system, there is much evidence (for example, Tomlinson, 1984), that schools, as white institutions which promote white norms, may be negative experiences for children from minority communities. Similarly, the children of travellers and other groups on the periphery of mainstream society may find school an alien and alienating experience. These factors can inhibit many children from fulfilling their potential.

Cognitive development (see p29) continues and, by the age of six, most children have acquired the abilities characteristic of the pre-operational stage, such as conservation of number and quantity. Their capacity to view the world from the standpoint of others develops, as can be seen from their ability to empathize with the feelings of other children.

At about seven years, children begin to understand and practise concrete operations. As they grow older, they can use words to describe and classify objects in a number of ways, for example, colour, size and shape. If their education is going well, they begin to enjoy using words in stories, poetry, songs and drama. Similarly, they gain confidence in the world of mathematics and science through their explorations of number and the physical world. Ideally, they experience sufficient success in exploration and problem-solving and through the encouragement of their teachers, to see themselves as competent, effective and creative beings.

Secondary School and Adolescence

The hormonal changes which accompany adolescence may contribute to the mood changes which are often associated with this stage of development, but the unpredictability of mood is likely to be as much associated with the young person's preoccupations with the implications of these physical changes. There is much evidence that young people experience concern about the normality of what is happening to them, together with anxiety about their acceptability among their peers, male and female. Research, for example that by Tobin-Richards *et al.* (1983), suggests that young men welcome early maturation and the increases in height and weight which accompany it; late male maturers seem to experience low self-confidence which may persist into manhood. Young women tend not to welcome early maturing, though they also do not want to be noticeably behind their peers in physical development. It is very difficult for young women to remain unconcerned about their weight and appearance when sustained advertising campaigns are aimed directly at them. Such campaigns can lead not only to anxious preoccupation with slimness and dieting, but can contribute to bulimia and anorexia.

On a cognitive level, adolescents become capable of formal operations (see p29). This means that they can conceptualize hypothetical situations, debate abstract ideas, explore notions rationally, and critically examine concepts such as human rights, social justice and individual responsibility. This ability may be associated with the exploration of identity. Many young people become aware that they have been socialized into ways of thinking, believing or behaving which they now question, and search for a set of ideas, patterns of conduct or models of culture which have meaning for them personally. According to Erikson, adolescence is often a time of self-exploration, of discovering who one is and what one's role in life may be.

Emotionally adolescence may be a time of uncertainty, linked not only with increased self-preoccupation, but also with concern about the future. Demands upon young people include learning how to cope with their emerging sexuality, complicated by concerns about possible pregnancy and AIDS; growing wishes for independence from parental control; worries for many about unemployment; and the need for money. While for some, the transition is fairly smooth, others have little to motivate them and few networks of support, and they may experience deep depression and hopelessness.

Sexual experimentation is likely to be high during adolescence, though some communities may prohibit it completely. Evidence from the Brook Advisory Centres (Hadley, 1993) indicates that the age at which the majority of 16 to 24-year-olds (male and female) first have sexual intercourse is 17 compared with 21 for those born 40 years ago. Emotional preoccupation with sexual relationships will vary with parental attitudes, cultural norms and the outcomes of those relationships.

Strong sexual feelings towards members of their own sex may be an added source of conflict for some young people. Researchers estimate that about 10 per cent of the population have a gay or lesbian sexual orientation, although some adolescents may experience a temporary stage of being sexually attracted towards members of their own sex. Rejecting attitudes towards them can cause despair among the young people concerned. A recent publication concerning gay or lesbian young people in care (see Wilkes, 1993) is particularly helpful in clarifying the difficulties they might encounter and in promoting a positive context for training, policy and development.

The peer group is a powerful influence during adolescence, serving both as a reference group and as a source of support. However, it can exact a high price for this support: its power lies in its capacity to reject, to ridicule and to isolate those who do not conform. Since young people at this age are deeply concerned about belonging and acceptance, the possibility of rejection is extremely threatening. It can lead to smoking, to unwanted sexual relationships, to use of alcohol and drugs and to shoplifting and burglary.

There is now clear evidence (see Goodwin, 1989, for a review) that genetic factors make a substantial contribution to the probability of young males developing a pattern of very heavy drinking or use of drugs early in adolescence. This is a relatively new, but very well substantiated, body of evidence. It seems that some people have difficulties in metabolizing alcohol and other substances and that this can be inherited. Youth and community workers, teachers and social workers need to be familiar with this evidence; they may then be able to bring it to the attention of young people with whom they are working, especially if they are beginning to drink heavily at an early age.

A yearning to be accepted may be felt more acutely by young men and women who are disabled. Such people face both practical and social difficulties and may experience a high degree of isolation (see Anderson and Clark, 1982, and Philp and Duckworth, 1982). This is what Kristina Brown, aged 16, has to say (1981):

My feelings are hurt by people who treat me as a freak. I like pop music, books and swimming, and all the things that teenagers like doing. The only thing that is different about me is I don't see as well as other people.

Identity and self-esteem

There is a great deal of evidence that children acquire their view of themselves through internalizing the messages they receive from others. In early childhood the messages, verbal and non-verbal, received from parents are extremely powerful. Messages such as, 'What a bonny girl you are!' are positive and convey to the child acceptance and security. By contrast, to be told 'You are nothing but a nuisance! I wish you'd never been born!' provokes anger, anxiety and self-rejection.

The family is an important influence in the development of identity. Factors such as affectionate relationships and good communication with parents have been shown to be linked with a positive sense of self and high self-esteem. This is enhanced when parents act as positive role models, and establish clear and consistent guidelines for behaviour while still encouraging self-reliance and independence.

But school and the wider society may lead some children to learn largely negative views of themselves. Children who are perceived as being in some way different from the norm are likely to suffer most. According to Brummer (1988):

In a society where negative stereotypes abound, children of Asian and Afro-Caribbean origin are especially vulnerable . . . Negative comments made about their food, language . . . clothes, religious beliefs and traditions can lead to a feeling that the life-styles of their families should be hidden rather than acknowledged. A sense of shame overlies an appropriate sense of pride in, and enjoyment of, their cultural heritage.

There is a good deal of evidence that black children have lower self-esteem than white children of a similar age. Efforts are being made to provide children of minority groups with consistent and positive messages by ensuring that they have role models, such as teachers and youth workers, from their own communities; by actively attempting to value each child's culture in the school setting; by implementing anti-racist strategies of practice in social service, probation and other key departments; by efforts to place children with adoptive or foster parents of the same racial and cultural background; and by attempting to ensure equality of opportunity at all points in the educational and career structures.

It is important to note that self-concept and self-esteem can change over time and adolescence is a time when, ideally, young people can begin to move towards consolidating their sense of identity and developing their potential. Phinney (1990) has described a model of how people may develop a higher awareness of their own ethnic identity.

Stage 1   Lack of interest in ethnicity.
          Views of ethnicity based on opinions of others.
Stage 2   Ethnic identity search: exploration of the meaning of ethnicity for oneself.
Stage 3   Achieved ethnic identity: clear confident sense of own ethnicity.

Maxime (1986) gives a clear example of how a young woman initially rejecting of her own black identity was enabled to move through these three stages. It is possible to learn to feel differently about ourselves – to feel pride where we may have felt uncertainty. Many gay and lesbian people have described the sense of relief and freedom they experienced when they 'came out' and let their sexual orientation be known. One of the aims of the Gay Pride movement is actively to help people experience a positive sense of self in their gay or lesbian orientation.

Other groups who are undervalued in society, such as those who are disabled, may also have to confront particular issues in developing a positive sense of identity. Skilled parents and caregivers, given appropriate and adequate support themselves, can counteract and challenge the thoughtless behaviour of others, at the same time as increasing self-esteem.

Employment

Towards the end of adolescence, employment becomes a crucial concern. The studies of Warr *et al.* (1985) found distress levels significantly higher among both black and white 17-year-olds than among a comparable group of employed young people.

Westland (1986) reported a study in which users of six social services were surveyed: services for people with physical disabilities, learning disabilities and mental health problems; services for children in care and leaving care and for juvenile offenders; and services which dealt with referrals for financial advice and welfare rights. From the sample of 796 cases surveyed, Westland noted:

Only 7 per cent of people were in paid employment . . . Children in care and leaving care were a strikingly under-privileged group. In one area 100 per cent of children of employable age were unemployed . . . Young people from ethnic minorities were seen to be even more at risk than others . . . We found that the generalized effect of economic recession and unemployment is often not perceived by social services staff . . .

This study is in line with many others showing that unemployment has particularly far-reaching and damaging effects. Employment offers not only financial security but a sense of identity: it raises self-esteem, provides opportunities for social contacts, and is a way of structuring time.

The Adult

Despite the huge diversity of people, and of their lives and life styles, and despite the fact that we live within different economic, political and social systems, many adults have common preoccupations in addition to those of identity and self-esteem, already considered briefly. We will consider three here: relationships with other people in marriage or other partnerships; parenting; and the mainten-ance of health and well-being.

People need other people in order to fulfil their deepest needs, indeed in order to be themselves. Developing close personal relationships with other adults is a major concern for all people in all communities. There is much evidence that mental health is associated both with having a number of friends, and with having a confiding relationship with at least one other person. Many people find this support within either heterosexual or gay or lesbian relationships, but all close relationships come under strain and Holmes and Rahe (1967) found divorce and separation to be one of the most demanding stresses of all, second only to the death of a spouse or life partner.

It falls to many adults to be parents, sometimes intentionally, sometimes not. No-one is actively taught or trained how to be a parent. Bringing up children is clearly a very demanding activity, and one of inestimable importance both for individuals and for the whole community.

Bringing up children is a *skill* – that is, a learned ability. In former years, this learning was probably acquired from models within large or extended families. How to bring up children was learned by watching how mothers, fathers, older children and relatives managed the little ones, and by trial and error. Nowadays families are smaller, and many parents are coping entirely alone, with few models and little support. People just don't have the opportunity to learn parenting skills by watching other parents, and many people, like myself, had barely even held a baby before their first child was born.

Social workers, particularly those working in family centres, have the oppor-tunity to support parents and to convey some of the skills of bringing up children. This is not to suggest that there is a limited number of ways of bringing them up – indeed, there is a wide diversity of ways, and each community and many families within those communities will have their own preferred ways. There are how-ever, certain areas of knowledge drawn from research which workers and caregiv-ers can offer to parents to enhance their skills: for example, that children do not learn a language without hearing it spoken to them frequently; that if parents wish children to comply with instructions, they need to give clear and direct messages to them; and that parents are models from whom children learn (see also Chapter 4).

Social workers and community workers are involved in health care at all levels: at 'grassroots' level, alongside people with acute or chronic illness, such as cancer or AIDS; at the level of the issue, such as working out strategies to meet the needs of families with a member with sickle-cell anaemia; and at the level of prevention, such as involvement with anti-smoking campaigns.

The health and mental health of adults is likely to be closely associated with their economic status. Since the publication of *Inequalities in Health* (Townsend and Davidson, 1982), it has been known that poor people are likely to have more health problems and fewer resources available to resolve them, than privileged people. The same is true for mental health: poor people have a higher prevalence of depression, schizophrenia and stress-related conditions than the more well-to-do. We shall consider issues of mental health further in Chapter 7.

Women have their own particular needs. Some experience considerable distress during the premenstrual period, and this may be associated with depression and fluctuations of mood. As men and women age, their bodies cease to be sexually fertile; for men more gradually than for women. The menopause, the cessation of the menstrual cycle, usually occurs during the early fifties, and its meaning for one woman is likely to be different from the next. Studies indicate, however, that only a small proportion of women suffer great distress at this time, though many experience some discomfort.

Elderly People

Few cultures actively promote personal development in older people. While Asian, African, Chinese and Caribbean communities generally offer older people a respected role in which they can enjoy their later years, western white cultures seem often to neglect their needs. Older people are not expected to be active in sport, sexual relationships or competitive situations, and are socialized into passive and caring roles by younger generations, by public expectations and by the media.

There is no evidence of major personality change as people become older. If there are major changes, these are likely to be attributable to the onset of ill-health or the changed social circumstances in which older people find themselves, such as increased isolation. Their cognitive abilities, for example, their capacity to learn, do not normally decrease with age (Schaie and Willis, 1986), although their speed of processing information may be somewhat slower than that of younger people. The brain has the capacity for virtually unlimited new learning, and the number of older people who take up total new areas of interest and acquire new fields of knowledge and skill supports this statement.

People over retirement age now form 18.7 per cent, nearly one-fifth, of the population (Office of Population Censuses and Surveys, 1993). As life expectancy increases, so does people's need for care and support: it is not surprising that those over the age of 75 comprised 20 per cent of referrals to a Southampton Social Services Department (Goldberg *et al.*, 1977). That figure will almost certainly be higher today. McClymont (1991) pointed out that elderly people are three times more likely to live alone than people of non-pensionable age, and many are widowed. There are indications that as people become older more, not fewer, live alone.

There are several major factors to be taken into account when considering the well-being of older people. Major psychological factors are the person's sense of identity and continuity, the availability or not of valued relationships, the losses and bereavements which a person experiences and his or her existing personality. Individual adjustment, however, is not solely dependent on personality or behaviour, but is also affected by the constraints encountered – imposed by health, support networks and personal circumstances, and by the images and stereotypes of ageing held by the wider society.

Coleman (1986) writes that the maintenance of positive attitudes towards oneself seems to be one of the key issues in old age. Enabling elderly people to maximize control over their lives is central in promoting their dignity and self-esteem. The difficulties of isolation, low self-esteem and declining health which many elderly people experience are compounded by the negative view of them and the behaviour shown towards them. This combination of prejudice and discrimination is termed 'ageism'. So pervasive is it that some people, born in the early years of this century, prefer not to seek help rather than to risk being rejected or ridiculed.

In an account of the work of Age Exchange, an organization for older people in South East London, Pam Schweitzer (1991) has recounted the main issues emerging from interviews with elderly people from a wide range of communities who had come to this country from overseas. As they talked of their past lives and their present needs, key concerns which emerged were: loneliness; language barriers; a longing for 'home'; rejection of change in the country of origin; alienation from children and grandchildren; a strong commitment to maintaining cultural identity; the desire for an educational role; a need to be with compatriots.

CHAPTER 3

Interpersonal Skills and Communication

The ability to establish and build effective relationships with other people is an absolute necessity for social workers, probation officers and community workers. Carrying out work of such sensitivity and complexity means that practitioners need to be able to rely on their capacity to get on with people from an enormously diverse range of backgrounds without needlessly irritating, offending or insulting them.

Most clients of social workers come from circumstances of need and disadvantage. The major report by the National Institute of Social Work, *Social Workers: Their Roles and Tasks* (1982), reported of these clients:

The largest group is of elderly people; other groups strongly represented are families in which there are neglected, abused or delinquent children; offenders; physically handicapped people; and emotionally distressed people.

Such people, whom social workers and community workers are employed to serve, are already vulnerable; to ask for help may be difficult, even impossible. A high degree of sensitivity to individual need and circumstance on the part of staff is necessary in order to respond effectively.

Research in Perception

Despite the fact that we are all endowed with the same basic physiological systems with which to perceive the world, we do not all perceive the same things, or attach similar meanings to them. Our perception is individual and selective. We are constantly surrounded by a flood of sensory data – shapes, colours, sizes, sounds – and our brains scan the available data in terms of what is important for us, what has *meaning* for us, at the present time. In some ways, people *learn* how to see; that is, they perceive people, situations and events in the light of their experience. People from differing backgrounds, for example, are likely to perceive a police officer or a teenager quite differently, according to their previous experiences of police officers or teenagers and the meaning they attach to these figures.

For the most part, then, we draw on learned habits of perception and interpretation, while believing that we are seeing things as they really are. Difficulties arise because everyone thinks that his or her view of the world is reality when it isn't; it is only a subjective view of reality.

When we perceive a new person, information about him or her together with new, incoming information interact with our own set ways of perceiving. Sometimes images from the past, for example, from television and the press, are so powerful that we perceive an individual only in terms of a stereotype: a 'young offender' or a 'depressive', so stripping them of all individuality.

Most of us bring prejudice (pre-judgement) to bear upon people whom we meet. Sometimes the prejudice may be of a positive kind and may incline us to see the person in an unduly favourable way; more dangerously, the prejudice may be negative, and if we also possess power, we may behave in a discriminatory way against an individual or his or her group. Many of the groups of people with whom we practise – older people, people with disabilities, those from ethnic minority groups – all experience stigma of some kind. This makes it all the more crucial that we reject stereotypical views of people, as these may incline us to offer a mechanistic or routine service or no service at all, rather than one tailored to each individual's personal need.

First impressions and perceived similarity

Much research has been devoted to what is known as the primacy effect, that is, the importance of our first impressions of a person. An early experiment by Asch (1946) asked participants to report impressions of a person whom he described using a number of adjectives, both favourable and unfavourable. However, the order in which the list of adjectives was presented differed: the favourable adjectives were read first to one group, followed by the unfavourable; the order was reversed for the comparison group. Asch found that each group reported their impressions of the person according to the words which had been read to them *first*; that is, although both groups heard the same words, those which were heard first contributed most to the final impression of the person. This work has been confirmed by later research. Other investigators in this field report that the dimensions 'warm' and 'cold' seem to be primary ones in our assessment of others, whether they pertain to manner, expression or tone of voice.

Another variable which has been found to be of major importance is perceived similarity between ourselves and those with whom we interact. People are generally much more attracted to those who hold similar values and attitudes to themselves. Discovering that someone with whom we work shares our concern about the needs of people with disabilities or likes the same music can provide common ground for work together.

Applying theories of perception

Knowing the powerful effect of first impressions, it is our responsibility to attempt to review and revise any 'snap judgements' that we make. If we find ourselves judging in negative ways whole groups of people, especially those vulnerable to being stereotyped such as 'gypsies', 'mentally ill' people, or 'black youths', then we have fallen into the very trap we need to avoid.

Similarly, we have to guard against forming our impressions from reports written by other workers in case records. All too often such records contain statements representing an opinion as fact, as well as the use of undefined and non-specific words such as 'aggressive', or 'neurotic'. Clearly we must take note of such descriptions, but we should always check how far they are supported by *evidence*. As a wise teacher suggested: 'We should read case records, as they may contain important factual information; but we should distinguish fact from opinion, and then, having set the records aside, judge as we find'. According to William Davies (1990), we need to make a *conscious and deliberate* attempt to set the impressions, but not the facts, aside – so that we may make our own initial contact with as unprejudiced a set of perceptions as possible.

Social workers are sometimes accused of neglecting indications of serious offences or similar previous behaviour. Clearly we have to guard against forming naïve impressions of people who are far from naïve themselves. There is a balance to be struck: again the crucial criterion is evidence. We should be alert to the dangers of forming strong first impressions of a person, favourable or unfavourable, and be ever open to revise them in the light of evidence.

The capacity for 'empathy', the ability to put oneself into the shoes of other people and so begin to understand the world as they do, is desirable in all those who work with people. We shall never be able to see the world exactly as another person does, but the crucial test seems to be whether we can empathize sufficiently for the behaviour in question to make sense to us.

Sometimes, of course, we must actively disconfirm and reject a person's perceptions, such as those of child abusers who tell themselves that the child 'enjoys the game'. Such perceptions have to be challenged and an alternative set of meanings substituted; such as replacing, 'We played the game' with 'I abused the child'. This is an integral part of treatment programmes for child molesters.

Frequently, however, people get into difficulties because they perceive events, in all sincerity, differently from other people – perhaps family members. If a worker can see an event or situation as each separate person does, then it may be possible to take all the different viewpoints into account, for example, by saying to one party, 'From your point of view, it looks as if . . .' and to the other, 'It is natural that you see this situation differently; it probably looks as if . . .' Having had their (differing) perceptions acknowledged, both or all parties are more likely to find common ground.

There needs to be some agreement between participants in an interaction in their understanding of a particular problem or situation if that interaction is to proceed smoothly. It is vital that we try to arrive at a shared understanding of what we are trying to do with people with whom we work. If we cannot communicate in these constructive ways, then people living in multi-cultural, multi-racial society are likely to feel that they want nothing to do with us.

Elements of Social Interaction

There is now a strong body of evidence that there are two parallel but interacting channels of communication: the verbal and the non-verbal. Social workers and community workers should be aware of both these means of communication and their effects upon those with whom they work. People who are already disadvantaged or depressed, or whose first language is not English, may well be afraid of us, or resentful of the power which we hold. They are likely to be more than usually sensitive to cues of superiority or condescension, and alert to subtle signs of which the worker may not even be aware.

Non-verbal communication

According to Argyle (1983), non-verbal communication (NVC) functions in four different ways. These are:

1. *Communicating interpersonal attitudes and emotions.* Evidence shows that emotions and attitudes are largely transmitted by non-verbal means: tones of voice, facial expressions, gestures and so on. The verbal channel is used mainly to convey information.

2. *Self-presentation.* We convey messages about ourselves and how we wish to be seen largely through non-verbal channels. Our choice of clothes, the things we carry, the way we cut our hair, all speak volumes to other people, although, as we have seen, they may not all perceive the same things, or interpret them in the same way.

3. *Rituals.* These, Argyle suggests, are repeated patterns of behaviour having social significance, such as weddings and religious ceremonies. Non-verbal activities often play a particularly important role, such as the joining of hands or the placing of ash on the face.

4. *To support verbal communication.* Spoken messages are supplemented by non-verbal components, such as gestures to convey emphasis or unfinished sentences completed with a shrug of the shoulders.

Argyle (1972) has listed various aspects of non-verbal communication which together convey particular messages:

- Bodily contact: used for greetings and farewells; signals friendship and intimacy.
- Bodily proximity: wide cross-cultural differences.
- Bodily orientation: Co-operating pairs sit side by side; competing or hostile pairs sit facing; those in discussion or conversation prefer an angle of 90 degrees.
- Bodily posture: indicates whether a person is tense or relaxed; the person of highest status sits least formally.

- Gestures: communicate general emotional arousal, as well as specific emotions, for example, fist-clenching for aggression.
- Head nods: act as reinforcers to encourage others to talk more, etc.
- Facial expression: communicates emotions and attitudes to others – though it is heavily controlled and hence hard to interpret. It also provides immediate feedback on what others are saying.
- Eye movements: used to collect feedback on the other's reactions.
- Appearance (of clothes, face, hair etc): used to send messages about the self, for example, about occupation and status.
- Emotional tone of speech: a more reliable indicator of emotions than facial expression, since it is not so well controlled.

A study of particular interest is that of Forbes and Jackson (1980) who examined the contribution of non-verbal components in selection interviews in which candidates were successful or unsuccessful. The patterns of non-verbal behaviour of each candidate were classified during the interview. When, later, the interviews were grouped by outcome – 'Accept', 'Reserve' and 'Reject' – differences were found on several important elements of non-verbal behaviour (see *Table 3.1*). Details are not available about the cultural or racial backgrounds of the applicants and whether different patterns of non-verbal behaviour may have affected the final outcomes.

Table 3.1 Elements of non-verbal behaviour associated with acceptance and rejection at interview (Forbes and Jackson, 1980).

NVC in the accept interview	*NVC in the reject interview*
More eye contact	More avoidance gaze and eye wandering
More smiling	More neutral expression and less smiling
More head shaking and nodding	Head still and less head nodding

Verbal communication

According to Argyle (1983) the main functions of verbal messages are:

- *Social routines*. These include standard sequences like greeting, thanking and saying goodbye.
- *Questions*. These are used to gather information, and can be specific or general. Questions can be 'open' such as, 'How did you feel when you heard the diagnosis?' or 'closed' such as, 'Did you feel relieved when you heard the diagnosis?'.
- *Information*. This may be given in response to an enquiry, or may be volunteered.

- *Instructions*. These can be general or specific: 'Please telephone me if you want me to come again', or 'You should meet me outside the court at 9.00 a.m.'. Important instructions are best written down.
- *Expressing emotion or interpersonal attitudes*. This is likely to be influenced by cultural norms: for example, weeping, laughing or expressing anger.
- *Informal speech*. This consists of messages which 'oil the wheels' of social inter-action: pleasantries, talking about the weather, asking after friends or relatives.

Pitfalls of verbal communication

It is very difficult to communicate accurately. Since different people attend to different cues and different features of a message, it is almost inevitable that even simple messages offered by one person will not be accurately perceived by another. Several barriers to effective communication have been distinguished.

Limitations of the receiver's capacity. This occurs when one gives information which is beyond what the receiver can 'take in', for example, when a community worker is trying to clarify too many details of the local authority 'Structure Plan' or when a social worker attempts to unravel all aspects of welfare rights entitle-ment at once. Here the best course of action may be to try to produce alternative means of communicating such as a diagram or a chart which conveys the same ideas through visual, rather than solely verbal, means.

Distraction. This refers to the factors which compete for our attention when we are trying to talk to someone. I've always found it hard to carry out a difficult interview with the television on. In such situations, we should negotiate with those present to remove the distraction.

The unstated assumption. Countless misunderstandings arise because two parties in an exchange assume that they mean the same thing when they do not. When meetings are planned, people often agree who will attend and the time, day and place of the meeting, but fail to stipulate the precise date. 'Oh, I thought you meant this Friday, the 17th . . .', is countered by, 'No, I meant *next* Friday, the 24th . . .'.

Perceiving things from our own standpoint. Up to a point, this is inevitable. We come from different backgrounds, within different cultures, and our perceptions are moulded by our own experiences. Yet even people within the same family perceive things differently. Sometimes this tendency can lead to a 'blinkered' view of people and situations: white people may not perceive the same realities as black people; a person in employment is likely to see a situation very differently from an unemployed person. Here actually meeting and talking with people can raise our awareness of their realities.

The influence of partly conscious mechanisms. This refers to learned habits of interact-ing with people which we may have been taught, or which we may have acquired from our own experiences. The radio programme 'Does He Take Sugar?', for example, has alerted us to the dangers of avoiding interacting directly, verbally and non-verbally, with people who are disabled. This is a tendency to which we are all vulnerable, and which must be actively resisted.

Confused presentation. In social work and community work we are all too inclined to use jargon. Words and the initials of words become part of our in-group language – to the confusion of those who are not 'one of us'. Consider D.S.S., P.S.R., E.P.O.! We should be aware of the mystifying and alienating effects of using such terms. Most of the things we have to say to people can be said in ordinary, everyday language.

Absence of communication channels. Within most institutions, the channels of communication tend to be from the top down, rather than from the bottom up. *The Client Speaks* (Mayer and Timms, 1970) is one of the earliest sources of information about how recipients perceive the way in which social workers do their jobs. The study of participants in family therapy by Howe (1989) emphasizes the need for feedback from clients. The principle of having agreed objectives, and frequently checking how far we are achieving them *with* those concerned, is a priority as a shared framework for practice.

Styles of social behaviour

Several researchers, on the basis of work with a wide range of groups, have arrived at a model which shows the key dimensions of styles of social behaviour.

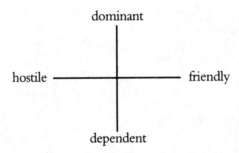

Figure 3.1 Styles of social behaviour (Argyle, 1972)

People have a preferred style of behaving, but Argyle (1972) points out that this style will be affected by the situations people find themselves in. It has also been found that those higher in dominance motivation or extroversion come to dominate in groups and they also talk more.

Whether we describe such people as high in dominance motivation or as seeking high status, the phenomenon is the same. Psychologists tend to use the term 'dominance' and sociologists talk in terms of 'power'. People have a wide range of strategies for attaining power. They may argue more, 'put other people down', use non-verbal strategies such as glares and scowls, or verbal strategies such as personal attacks and deliberate attempts to intimidate others. We should remember that merely being tall, male, or a person seen to be in authority confers power upon us, and this can act to the disadvantage of those with whom we work.

Interviewing

Social workers and community workers conduct many forms of interview including telephone or face-to-face interviews with callers at an area office, interviews to gather information and interviews of investigation (see Chapter 5). The purpose of gathering material in interviews is to inform the assessment, for example, to try to understand the context of a difficulty; the exact nature of a problem; for whom it is a problem; when difficulties first began; what has made things better or worse; and how other people perceive the situation.

There are many sets of guidelines available to inform assessment. *Protecting Children* (Department of Health, 1988) offers a guide for workers undertaking a comprehensive assessment, and Oppenheimer (1983) offers a framework relevant not only to work in a mental health context, but also to family work. The ASPIRE process (see Introduction) offers a structure applicable to practice in general.

Effective communication

Prepare yourself to communicate effectively
❑ What are your objectives for this meeting or interview?
❑ Write down key information required or to be given.
❑ Think ahead about how you are likely to be perceived.
❑ Try to see the situation through your clients' eyes and experience.

Points to promote effective communication
❑ If possible, let people know that you will be visiting them.
❑ Follow social conventions of courtesy; for example, is a morning visit more or less acceptable than an afternoon one?
❑ Take care about how you knock on a door; how you do this matters!
❑ Visit and receive people with sensitivity and courtesy.
❑ If making a home visit, explain clearly who you are, where you are from and why you are visiting. Offer an identity card.
❑ Ask people how they would like to be addressed; many older people do not like to be addressed by their first name.
❑ Always give your full attention; try to avoid being interrupted.

❏ Ask permission to take notes, for example of names of children. Show any notes you have taken before you leave.
❏ Try to convey that you want to be constructively helpful to the people concerned. Establish as positive a relationship as you can in the time available.
❏ Expect hostility and fear: you have considerable power. If people challenge you, try to respond firmly but not angrily.
❏ Know your departmental policy about racism and sexism; act on it.
❏ At the end, invite further questions – to aid clarity.
❏ If you are short of time, give people an indication when you have, say, five minutes left.
❏ Conclude by agreeing who will do what, and by when.

Communicating with Particular Groups

We live in times which make great demands upon our capacity to adjust to change. The major systems of society are in flux as economic and political pressures from central government are brought to bear upon local government and its institutions and services. The legal systems are in flux, and major legislation affects the practice of social workers, community workers and probation officers; and the practice systems are in flux as local authorities attempt to organize and reorganize to meet the ever-changing demands made upon them.

In this melee, vulnerable people become ever more vulnerable: those already at the bottom of hierarchies of power become ever more powerless. I suggest below some principles relevant to those who work amid this flux.

Children and young people

The Children Act 1989 explicitly states that the ascertainable wishes and feelings of the child should always be taken into account. This means that social workers have a responsibility to talk to and interview children. Remember that *any* child is likely to be wary of unknown people, particularly of those like yourself who have great power over them. The children you see may have experienced physical or sexual abuse, rejection, traumatic loss or accident; or sometimes they, themselves, have been responsible for bringing suffering to other people's lives. Whatever the circumstances which have led to a social worker's involvement, the child or young person is likely, at best, to be in a state of confusion, anxiety or anger, and at worse, personal turmoil and misery. Getting through to such children or young people may be a major achievement in itself. It will take time, and cannot be hurried.

Different situations will make different demands upon you and the way in which you work with children. If you are a community and youth worker, you will probably already know that it is inappropriate for you to approach a group of young people whom you do not know and try to chat informally with them. Early learned behaviour about not talking to strangers inhibits the trust needed to make real contact. It is important to work towards gaining acceptance when getting to know children in informal situations, be these residential settings or youth clubs, residential weekends or exchange visits. You may find the following ideas helpful:

❑ Listen a great deal; try to pick up key words and phrases.
❑ Remember that you are the newcomer, the unknown stranger, so take it slowly; several meetings may be necessary before anyone speaks to you first.
❑ Let them know who you are in an informal way: 'I'm Chris – I'm a new worker/volunteer'.
❑ Make a mental note of as many names as you can.
❑ Look relaxed even if you don't feel it.
❑ Another newcomer may be more ready to speak to you than the longstanding members of the group; their status is high, yours is low.
❑ Try talking to one or two people first, rather than a group.
❑ Establish common ground between you and the young people: 'I've got that record' or 'I like that group too'.

It is essential to prepare beforehand when working with children in formal situations. In addition to being absolutely clear about your objectives, you should consider:

❑ What are the implications of a person of your age, gender, race or background working with this particular family/child?
❑ What age is the young person concerned? What are the implications of this?
❑ Do you share a common language? If not, do you need an interpreter (Urdu, Hindi, British Sign Language)?
❑ How much time is needed/available to build up trust?

Some of the things the child may be thinking and feeling about you:

❑ 'What's going on?'
❑ 'Who is this person?'
❑ 'Can this person do me any harm?'
❑ 'She's a white person: I'm black'.
❑ 'She's a posh person: she uses long words'.
❑ 'She says she's a social worker; my mum doesn't like social workers'.
❑ 'I don't want to talk to her; she may make things worse for me. If I do talk to her though, she may be able to help me'.
❑ 'She doesn't talk like I do; she won't understand me'.

Some ways of meeting these (natural) feelings:

❑ Take as much time as you possibly can.
❑ Even if you have to meet the child jointly with the police, try to meet with the child separately as well.

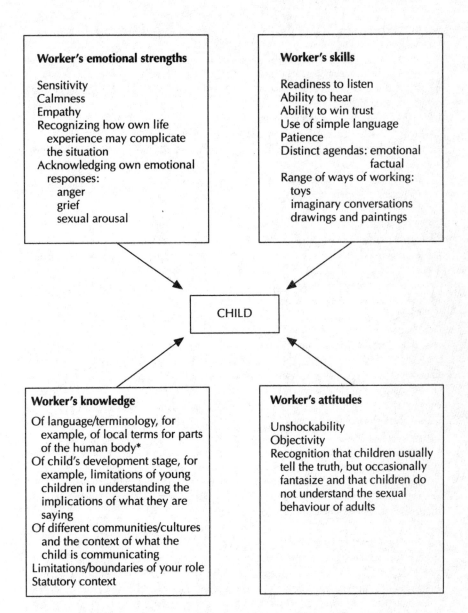

Worker's emotional strengths

Sensitivity
Calmness
Empathy
Recognizing how own life
    experience may complicate
    the situation
Acknowledging own emotional
    responses:
        anger
        grief
        sexual arousal

Worker's skills

Readiness to listen
Ability to hear
Ability to win trust
Use of simple language
Patience
Distinct agendas: emotional
                                    factual
Range of ways of working:
        toys
        imaginary conversations
        drawings and paintings

CHILD

Worker's knowledge

Of language/terminology, for
    example, of local terms for parts
    of the human body*
Of child's development stage, for
    example, limitations of young
    children in understanding the
    implications of what they are
    saying
Of different communities/cultures
    and the context of what the
    child is communicating
Limitations/boundaries of your role
Statutory context

Worker's attitudes

Unshockability
Objectivity
Recognition that children usually
    tell the truth, but occasionally
    fantasize and that children do
    not understand the sexual
    behaviour of adults

* This can be achieved, if appropriate, by drawing outlines of male and female
  bodies and helping the child to say what they call the parts of the body –
  starting with emotionally neutral features. This needs to be done in a low key,
  light-hearted way.

Figure 3.2 An overview of child and worker interactions (with acknowledgements to Bob Trotman,
            Trinity Road Project, Birmingham)

❏ Try and meet on the child's own ground with familiar things around.
❏ Sit down or get on the same level as the child.
❏ Help the child understand who you are and why you're there, but don't give too much information all at once.
❏ Build positive links between yourself and someone you and the child both know and like.
❏ Try to keep the atmosphere calm, relaxed and reassuring.
❏ Don't be too friendly; this can be threatening.
❏ Check that you understand the child's use of words; for example, parts of the body and genitals.
❏ Watch to see if the child is relaxing – observe his/her body language and non-verbal communication.

Play therapy

Play is, among other things, a medium through which children express themselves and their feelings. Through play such as dressing up, copying adults, and imitating voices and behaviours, children explore their own roles. Activities such as painting, making up stories and fantasy give children an opportunity to explore feelings, real and imaginary, and gain control over their fears.

Play therapy is based on the belief that children represent in play form the emotional difficulties they are experiencing, for example, the anger they feel towards a new baby or towards a parent who frustrates their wishes.

Axline (1966) contributed to a growing surge of interest in how children can use play to cope with and recover from major life problems. However, while many children naturally enjoy playing with dolls, paint and the wonderful array of toys usually available, there is very little empirical evidence to support the hypothesis that children play out their difficulties through play. Play can be simple fantasy, and should not always be interpreted as representing reality.

This is not to disparage the importance of allowing children to play, but it is to offer a cautionary note to those who make interpretations of a child's paintings or doll play without seeking additional evidence to support their views. More accurate information is likely to be gained by asking children to tell us about their pictures, rather than by making interpretations ourselves.

Communication with families

It is important to bear in mind that much of the time spent working with children will also involve working with their families (see Chapter 4). The publication, *Patterns and Outcomes in Child Placement* (Department of Health, 1991) emphasizes the notion of working in partnership with parents implicit in the Children Act 1989. Authorities are required to consult and inform parents; ascertain their wishes and feelings about treatment plans; enter into written agreements; and avoid compulsory measures as far as is consistent with meeting children's needs. These four requirements depend on good communication. It is essential always to remain calm and courteous in your work with families even when it is necessary to inform them of unpleasant or undesired events.

Communicating across language and cultural barriers

Mares, Henley and Baxter (1985), working in the field of health care, have suggested five practical ways in which workers can communicate more effectively with people who speak little or no English or who speak English as a second language.

Reduce stress/arousal:
❑ Allow more time than you would for an English-speaking client.
❑ Give plenty of non-verbal reassurance.
❑ Try to communicate something about what's going to happen next.
❑ Get the person's name right.
❑ Pronounce it correctly.
❑ Try to ensure the person meets with the same workers throughout.
❑ Write down any important points clearly and simply for the person to take away.

Simplify your English:
❑ Plan beforehand what you want to communicate to the person.
❑ Be clear which are the essential points to be communicated.
❑ Speak clearly but do not raise your voice.
❑ Speak slowly throughout.
❑ Repeat when you think you have not been understood; don't change the words.
❑ Use words the person is likely to know.
❑ Don't use slang or idioms: for example, 'red tape', 'spend a penny'.
❑ Use the simple forms of verbs – active, not passive: for example, 'I shall send you a letter', not 'You'll be sent a letter'.
❑ Stick to one topic at a time.

Check back properly:
❑ Develop a regular pattern of checking that what you have said so far has been understood.
❑ Try not to ask, 'Do you understand?': you are almost bound to get 'Yes' as an answer.
❑ Ask the person to explain back to you what he or she is going to do.

Points to think about when using an interpreter:
❑ Check that the person and interpreter speak the same language or dialect.
❑ Is there any reason why the person may be embarrassed by the interpreter?
❑ Might the person find it difficult to tell you things because of the interpreter?
❑ Is there any reason why the interpreter might be reluctant to interpret everything the person says?
❑ Are you sitting facing the person rather than the interpreter?
❑ Does the interpreter understand the purpose of your questions and of the whole session?

❑ The interpreter is to be regarded as an interpreter, not as an intermediary.
❑ Give two to three times as much time when using an interpreter.

Learn the client's language:
❑ A few basic phrases in a person's language show courtesy and goodwill.

When communicating with people of a different cultural group:
❑ Acknowledge that the people you are meeting come from a background different from your own, and that they will want their culture and experience to be respected.
❑ Try to use the appropriate terms of address for people of different ages in different communities. The series of books by Alix Henley (for example, *Caring for Hindus and their Families*, 1983) is very helpful and informative.
❑ Acknowledge that you only have limited knowledge of cultures other than your own (as is the case for everyone), but demonstrate your respect for those of others. For example, that you have read some of its literature or know something of its history.
❑ Ask people to tell you, either there and then or later, anything that they would want you to know about themselves or their culture which is relevant to the situation. For example, the dietary factors to be borne in mind for a person entering hospital.

Communicating with people with learning disabilities

The same basic principles for good communication operate here, but because people with learning difficulties need extra consideration and time to handle in-coming ideas, especially from people whom they don't know, preparing to communicate is a particularly important stage (see also advocacy, Chapter 9).

❑ Try to learn something of the person's history from, for example, case records beforehand, so that you can refer to familiar events or people.
❑ Clarify the nature of the person's learning difficulties, for example, autism.
❑ Try to find out how this affects this particular person's ability to deal with speech or to comprehend.
❑ Adapt your communication to the person's special circumstances.
❑ Check that you are facing the person at all times when speaking so that your expressions and body language can supplement your spoken words.

Communicating with older people

As we saw in Chapter 2, there is no evidence that older people lose their abilities to process new information effectively, but they often take a good deal longer to do so than younger people. Coleman (1986), in a sensitive analysis of ageing and its effects upon people, points out that much of the perceived cognitive deterioration of old people should be linked with their increasing isolation, which is known to bring about disorientation. When working with older people, the following factors seem to be important:

❏ Try to spend a few minutes helping people 'locate' you in time and place: for example, 'Good morning, Mr Chan. I am Michael Smith from the social work department. I visited you at home, about a week ago, and we talked about your attending this day centre . . .'.

❏ Spend time making sense of their present circumstances: where they are, and why they are there.

❏ Help them remember or understand where you fit into the overall picture and why you are involved in their life.

❏ Remind them gently of when you last met, and, for example, what you said you would do.

❏ If you have time, help them reminisce a little: for example, about their life as a child in London or in the Caribbean.

❏ If the person is experiencing dementia, avoid going along with their inaccurate perceptions or statements, but correct them gently: for example, 'No, I'm not your daughter. I'm Mrs Boyd, from the social work department. I came to talk to you yesterday . . . Do you remember?'.

Making and Sustaining Relationships

Empathy and appreciation

It is no surprise that empathy, the capacity to *feel with* another person, and so experience something of their distress, pain, fear or anger, has emerged as one of the most valuable components of helpful counselling. This entering into the experience of others is profoundly reassuring to them, because it enables us to cross the barriers of human aloneness and share, however briefly, in the reality of another person's experience. According to Egan (1986):

Empathy in its most fundamental sense . . . involves understanding the experiences, behaviours, and the feelings of others as they experience them . . . It means entering into the experience of clients in order to develop a feeling for their inner world.

Words of appreciation, interest and recognition, where genuinely felt and expressed, reassure, comfort and act as a balm to those who have lost all sense of worth or value in the eyes of the world. Expressing appreciation will open to us doors which are kept closed to others.

Listening

In order to try to make sense of another person's world, we need, first and foremost, to develop our listening skills. We listen to people in order to obtain and clarify information, but Egan (1986) describes listening as being particularly valuable when it is 'listening for understanding'. He emphasizes the need to attend to both the verbal and non-verbal behaviour of those with whom we work and writes:

Listening in its deepest sense means listening to the person of clients as influenced by the contexts in which they live, move, and have their being.

It may be a rare and valued experience for a person who usually has little influence and power to be listened to with respect and concern. Feelings can be expressed, fears shared and anxieties relieved.

I recall several instances when just sitting and listening, saying perhaps only a dozen words within an hour, visibly reduced the level of anxiety and arousal of those I was with. At the end of these times, I was thanked 'for just listening'. Little more was necessary to enable people to go about their lives again. I know that many workers wish to practise in this way, but pressure of work usually prevents it.

When listening, it is important to realize that we cannot do so in a completely unbiased way. Egan draws attention to what he calls 'filtered listening': we are each the product of socialization experiences within a family and a culture and these create a highly selective screen between ourselves and the outside world, determining what we attend to and what we ignore. These personal and cultural filters also introduce bias into our listening – bias of which we are often unaware. According to Egan, we pigeonhole people (consciously or unconsciously) because of gender, race, sexual orientation, nationality, status, religious persuasion, life style and the like. This impedes our ability to listen and understand, particularly when the person has a background and experience very different from our own.

Establishing trust

People whom the world has treated harshly are naturally mistrustful of others. They cannot give us the benefit of the doubt or be forgiving when we break appointments or fail to write the letter we promised. We cannot require people to trust us; we have to earn trust by:

- being absolutely clear about confidentiality: how far this pertains, and its limitations;
- never allowing expectations to be raised when we are not absolutely certain they can be met; it is better to promise to make enquiries than to give assurances which have to be retracted;
- never making an undertaking which cannot be fulfilled;
- being scrupulous about doing what we promised to do.

If you have to give bad news, be open and direct but courteous. There will be many occasions when it is your responsibility to convey to clients that their behaviour is unacceptable, that they have not kept undertakings, that you have been informed that a child has been left alone at night, and so on. On these occasions, it is best to explain simply and directly the facts of the matter and not be gratuitously threatening. Ensure also that the non-verbal components of your message are positive and respectful.

Social Exchange Theory

The word 'theory', as we saw in Chapter 1, means a system of ideas explaining something, and social exchange theory concerns the nature of interactions between people. Social encounters are thought of in terms of exchanges of 'goods' between people in a social context. According to this theory, in all social encounters each person is continually assessing the likely benefits and costs to him or herself, according to individual expectations, values, needs and aspirations. There is an obvious parallel between this idea and that of cost – benefit analysis in the field of economics.

If you are a student, consider your own process of thinking before applying to your course of study. You perhaps thought that, having been interested in social or community work for some time, and having had a good deal of related experience, you would like to apply for a course leading to a formal qualification. You may then have made enquiries about courses of education and training, taking into account their length, their location, their reputation, and your own eligibility for the course.

I suggest that although you probably did not think of it in this way at the time, you were, in fact, carrying out a cost-benefit analysis concerning the advisability of applying to take the course or not. Perhaps your 'balance sheet' might have looked something like this:

Potential benefits
– I can't go further without the qualification.
– I'd like to study full-time.
– I'm really interested in the needs of people with disabilities.
– Lots of new opportunities.
– Plenty of jobs for qualified people.
– Good long holidays.
– The pay's fairly good for qualified workers.

Potential costs
– Do I believe in training?
– Could I cope with the work?
– How could we live on a grant?
– We'd have to move house.
– Would my community approve?
– Lots of stress involved.
– You have to specialize and I don't want to.
– Not a high status job.

Presumably, if you're on a course, your calculation suggested to you that it would be more advantageous for you to go to the trouble of making an application, going through the stresses of the selection process and coping with all the changes in patterns of living which becoming a student necessitated.

Of course, different individuals will have taken a range of very different, perhaps more altruistic, factors into account. Some people may have considered strong personal values, deriving from their political, philosophical, religious or other beliefs. The point that I am making is that ultimately, the cost-benefit analysis is a *calculation* – personal, subjective and highly individual.

Short-term and long-term costs and benefits, values, our own views and those of others are all part of the decision-making process.

Let's consider an imaginary 'balance-sheet' which a woman from an ethnic minority community might draw up when wondering whether to approach a Social Services Department to enquire about the possibility of becoming a foster parent.

Potential benefits
- I should like to help a child in distress.
- My religion and culture say we should help people in difficulties.
- I have room to take another child.
- The child could play with my child.
- There would be help with expenses.
- I should enjoy having another child in the house.

Potential costs
- I might be rejected by the people who make enquiries.
- I shall have to answer a lot of personal questions.
- The child might be difficult.
- The child might hurt my child.
- There may not be enough help with expenses.
- The social worker might not speak my first language.

According to how she assesses the probable outcomes, and according to how she calculates the possible costs and benefits, this mother will either decide to apply to become a foster mother or she won't.

Concepts in social exchange theory have much in common with concepts in economic theory. Some of the fundamental concepts include:

Rewards. These contribute to an individual's sense of well-being, or fulfil needs or wishes. Some common rewards include: increased status; increased power; getting one's own way; friendship or companionship; financial return; reaching a goal or target; gaining support – emotional or practical; improvement in the circumstances of people who matter to us; reduction of anxiety or uncertainty.

Costs. These are the opposite of rewards, namely, anything which detracts from a person's sense of well-being or which causes distress, discomfort or some other penalty. Costs may include: a sense of threat; a feeling of being criticized or looked down upon; lowered self-esteem; financial loss; disappointment; anxiety or stress; the loss of a close relationship; etc.

Outcomes. These are the overall rewards minus the overall costs. They may take some time to calculate, as rewards and costs are seldom clear cut, and the calculation, a cognitive process, is seldom carried out explicitly at a conscious level. A person who is thinking of making a change of employment may be in an interview situation when it suddenly becomes apparent that the post will involve far more travel than was indicated in the job advertisement. Immediately the cost-benefit analysis suggests a far greater cost than was anticipated, the overall outcomes seem less appealing and the person may withdraw from the interview. The only conscious thought may be, 'This job is not for me', but underpinning the decision is a very rapid recalculation of anticipated outcomes.

Comparison level. This is the comparison between the gains to be expected from one interaction in comparison with the gains from others. The implication is that unless an individual achieves at least a slight advantage from an interaction or an experience, he or she may well be reluctant to invest much effort in that interaction on a future occasion. For example, students who have an essay to submit often calculate that it would be more rewarding to stay away from lectures on the day before the submission date. They anticipate that the reward of handing in an assignment on time, particularly if the practice of the tutors is not to accept late work, may well offset the loss of information or instruction which they will experience by missing the lecture.

Applying social exchange theory

It has been shown that people continually assess the costs and benefits of different courses of action on a moment-by-moment basis, and that many variables contribute to each individual assessment. If this is so, then this theoretical idea can help us to understand aspects of people's behaviour which may at first seem incomprehensible.

Why, for example, does a child persist in aggressive and disruptive behaviour despite repeated smacking or thrashing? Why does a wife stay with a husband who beats her? The answers may well lie in the assessment of costs and benefits by those concerned. The aggressive child may get his or her own way by frightening other children. (The same is true of aggressive adults.) This is, of course, rewarding. Alternatively, the child may attract the attention of the parents (a powerful reward) who then punish him or her. There is abundant research evidence that many children see smacking, even thrashing, as a form of attention, and since such children are often deprived of approving attention, even punitive attention is more rewarding than being ignored. The child is then likely to persist in the aggressive behaviour.

Similarly a woman who stays with an abusive husband is likely to have examined the pros and cons of leaving. It may well be that in her personal calculation, the advantages of having a roof over her head and those of the children, together with many small advantages as she perceives them, outweigh the enormous step of leaving. Even if there is a woman's refuge, this is an unknown place where life may have its own difficulties.

You can use social exchange theory to remember that:
- ☐ If someone's actions or behaviour mystify you, it may be that, from their standpoint, the cost-benefit analysis suggests it is rewarding to act in that way.
- ☐ People are motivated not just by hope of personal gain but by their values, their loyalty to a group, their political or religious convictions, their fear of public humiliation, and so on.
- ☐ Involvement with you or your agency may be seen as a cost or a benefit. If association with you constitutes a valued service, then your reward potential will be high; if association with your agency is a stigma, then your cost potential will, at least initially, outweigh all else.

❑ The skilled worker may be able to change perceptions of his or her involve-ment from being a cost to being a reward. For instance, if in investigating child abuse, an empathic worker is able to offer practical help and to ensure that parents receive their welfare rights entitlements and a link with support networks, contact with that worker may become a reward rather than a cost.

Negotiating and Writing Agreements

The ASPIRE process (see Introduction) involves moving, in due course, from a shared assessment of difficulties or needs to one of planning. This too should be a shared process in which the needs of the client, as perceived by him or her, should be a primary focus. The skill of negotiating agreements, whether formal or informal, should be a fundamental competency of any qualified worker. Increasingly, social workers are required, for example, by the Children Act 1989, to devise agreements with parents and other people crucial to a child's well-being.

There are three levels of agreement: primary, secondary and tertiary. *Primary agreements* are typically those made between the courts and a person who has received a sentence, for example, a probation order or a supervision order. *Secondary agreements* are sometimes called 'service' agreements, and typically consist of a negotiation between a worker and a person assisted by that worker. Other secondary agreements are those devised between, for example, parents and a Social Services Department whereby the parents are required to bring their child weekly to a health centre for weight monitoring, and in return the Department offers the family resources, practical help and personal support. *Tertiary agreements*, sometimes called 'contingency' agreements, are those in which three parties are involved: for example, the worker develops an agreement with parents who are experiencing difficulties with a teenage son or daughter. Here the social worker acts first to negotiate a set of undertakings on the part of parents and the young person which will satisfy all concerned (on the principle of give-to-get) and then acts him or herself as a third party to facilitate the implementation of the agreement.

There are a number of important ideas intrinsic to agreements. First, as they are based on the notion of the cost-benefit analysis, *everybody should be able to anticipate gaining something as a result*. This is why writing the agreement may take a long time: it is better to ensure that everybody is satisfied at the outset than try to save time at the risk of being unclear or failing to think of what might go wrong. Second, agreements are expressed in positive terms: that is, what people *should* do, rather than what they should not do. With practice, it becomes possible to express almost anything in a positive form! Third, the agreement should be devised in such a way as to enable people to advance by way of small successes. Agreements do not typically bring about dramatic, overnight changes: they provide a platform and a strategy for people to achieve small gains, which gradually add up to improvement. There are bound to be failures and disappointments, but so long as the general trend is towards improvement, then people's motivation and morale are likely to rise. Finally, it should be emphasized that, like so many other activities in social and community work, writing agreements is a skill, which may be learned. Sample agreement forms are shown in Appendices B and C.

Guidelines for the effective use of written agreements.

When formulating an agreement, it is essential to go through the following stages:

❑ Discuss whether using an agreement is socially acceptable to those involved. It may be familiar for business arrangements, but not for personal ones. If so, invite people to try the idea out.

❑ Focus upon actions or behaviours, rather than attitudes or feelings.

❑ Select one or two behaviours initially. Avoid working with too many problems. Start with an simple goal; early success is vital.

❑ Describe those behaviours in a very clear way. Vagueness may make negotiation seem easier, but all the participants then interpret the agreement differently. This can lead to confusion and anger.

❑ Write the agreement so that everyone understands it. Make the wording clear, brief and simple, and write in each person's first language.

❑ Agreements must give mutual satisfaction. The benefits for each person must be worth the costs.

❑ The agreement should be written in positive language – specifying things which are to be done, rather than those not to be done.

❑ Collect records. It is essential to know whether the situation is getting better or worse. Information can be collected on simple daily charts.

❑ Renegotiate the agreement. A series of short-term agreements is generally more effective than one long-term one.

❑ The artificiality and short-term nature of the agreement should be explained.

❑ The penalty for failure to fulfil the agreement must be clarified.

❑ Everyone concerned must sign the agreement, which should be dated.

❑ As soon as a stable position has been maintained for several months, begin to phase out the agreement.

CHAPTER 4

Children and their Families

Children benefit from growing up in families. By comparison with even the best institutions, the family setting and the opportunities it offers usually seem to provide relationships and experiences profoundly important to the developing child. The Children Act 1989 is an attempt to ensure that local authorities actively support parents in bringing up their children, either by providing services to enable them to care effectively for their children, or by ensuring that if children do enter local authority care, plans are made whenever possible and as soon as possible for children to be restored to their parents. The major report, *Patterns and Outcomes in Child Placement* (Department of Health, 1991) states:

Even when birth families are marginalised by the care process, they remain an important source of continuity . . . Frequent changes of placement and social worker mean that the birth family may in fact be the most stable influence in the child's experience even if actual contact is limited.

A study by Goldberg *et al.* (1977) showed that some 14 per cent of long-term cases allocated to social workers in Southampton related to difficulties concerning children and families. This group consisted mainly of disturbed families among whom desertion, separation, divorce, conflict over who should have care of the children, marital violence, child neglect and adolescent revolt were common occurrences. Recent events, highlighting the prevalence of child physical and sexual abuse, have almost certainly increased this proportion.

Work with families is exceedingly demanding. Working with groups of any kind inevitably makes more demands upon practitioners than working with individuals, because each person brings his or her own perceptions and cost–benefit analysis to bear upon the situation. Work with families is even more complex when we have statutory responsibilities because of the burning importance of the issues involved: children's safety, well-being and sometimes their very survival.

Partnership with Parents

It is noted in *Patterns and Outcomes in Child Placement* that although the word 'partnership' does not actually appear in the Children Act 1989, the concept permeates the sections which deal with services provided by local authorities for children and families, and it is highlighted that authorities will be required to:

- consult and inform parents;
- ascertain their wishes and feelings about placement plans;
- enter into written agreements;
- avoid compulsory measures as far as is consistent with meeting children's needs.

The need to empower parents by developing a working partnership with them arose from extensive research revealing the anger and frustration of many parents whose children were received into care (Fisher *et al.*, 1986). The research points to several practices which can contribute to such empowerment.

- Real partnership must be based on a shared perception of what the difficulties are, why they have arisen and what needs to be done. (The ASPIRE process lends itself to this way of thinking about practice.)
- Written agreements are crucial for partnership work and developing this skill should be a high priority for in-service training.
- Parents should attend reviews, case conferences and planning meetings.
- Relief or respite care schemes offer a useful partnership model.

A key feature of British society is its diversity. Ahmed *et al.*, (1986) in their book, *Social Work with Black Children and their Families*, have drawn attention to the failures of Social Service Departments to offer adequate and culturally sensitive services to many service users. While this has relevance for all aspects of service provision, this has particular implications for the development of a working partnership with black parents and children.

The Range of Work with Families

If we define a family as a network of parents, children or other people in relationship who may be living together, then it becomes clear that in Britain today there is a multitude of diverse family forms. These include:

- stereotypical 'nuclear' families, (father, mother and children) – these now constitute only about 44 per cent of the total of family forms,
- extended families,
- families with step-parents: reordered or blended families,
- families with cohabititing partners,
- one-parent families,
- families with gay or lesbian partners,
- families living in communes.

While the focus of this chapter is upon children, we must not lose sight of the fact that families have other demands upon them. Family members may be caring for sick or disabled relatives, they may be attempting to support elderly parents who live in distant parts of the country or overseas, and they may be coping with pressures of poverty, isolation and unemployment. There is substantial evidence that the practical and emotional needs of those caring for disabled children and other relatives remain unmet (Philip and Duckworth, 1982; Davis, 1993).

The material offered in this chapter constitutes only a summary of some of the main themes of work with families which have been examined by psychologists and other researchers. Readers should supplement their reading with the references provided.

Separation and divorce

Separation of children from parents is clearly undesirable, but social workers often seem to assume in their work with families that separation from parents of itself inevitably gives rise to long-term damage. Studies of children who have had repeated hospital admissions in early life, or who were admitted to care, show that there is no inevitable long-term disturbance following these separations. Long-term problems seem rather to be associated with generalized disruptions of stable and harmonious living arrangements or with marked conflict among parents or caregivers rather than with one or several separations from them. Schaffer (1990) notes in his review of this body of research that:

However traumatic separation from parents may be to young children and however violently they may react at the time, the separation per se *is rarely associated with long-term consequences: the family situation which may have given rise to the need for separation . . . is more likely to be the crucial influence in determining subsequent pathology.*

Rutter (1975) also concludes that it is not so much the separation or divorce which is damaging to children in the long-term as the discord preceding the parting. It is the conflict persisting over time and involving the children, that is, the ongoing disturbance in family relationships which results in stress and insecurity, rather than the break-up itself. In particular, family discord has been associated with anti-social behaviour in children – although again it has been shown that delinquency may be more common in unhappy homes where parents continue to live together than in more harmonious ones where the parents have parted.

It should be remembered that even children with very disturbed histories often retain the capacity to build affectionate and trusting relationships with adoptive parents as late as their teenage years. Overall, the child appears to be far more resilient to even major stresses in early life than was thought to be the case in the 1950s and 1960s.

However, social workers should be aware of the short-term reactions to divorce. According to Wallerstein and Kelly (1980), children under eight characteristically respond with grief, bewilderment, sadness and fear to their parents' divorce, while older children often display a 'fully conscious intense' anger, while still actively attempting to cope with the situation.

One-parent families

Research has shown that children in the growing number of one-parent families can be as emotionally healthy as those in two-parent families. It is not the circumstance of being a one-parent family of itself which may cause difficulties: rather it is the associated social disadvantage. For example, the average disposable income of a one-parent family has been shown to be about half that of two-parent families. One-parent families also typically experience poorer housing and greater social isolation.

A major debate has centred round whether children who grow up in families which do not contain role models of the same biological sex as themselves may be adversely affected. For example, do boys who grow up in households headed by a mother alone, or in lesbian households, develop an uncertain gender or sexual identity? Schaffer (1990) notes that by far the bulk of the research in single parenthood has dealt with the effects of father-absence, and reports that research has consistently failed to show that boys will turn out psychologically 'inferior' in the absence of a father figure, or that the development of their sexual identity will be affected. He also states explicitly that there is no reason to refuse to award custody to a lesbian mother simply on the grounds that she would endanger her child's psychological health.

Reordered families

Many children grow up in families where one parent is a step-parent. Ferri (1984) reported that the development of children with stepmothers did not differ markedly from that of their peers in unbroken families or with lone fathers. However, some children, particularly boys with stepfathers, frequently compared unfavourably with those in unbroken families. Being brought up with a stepfather may therefore not necessarily be more advantageous than being brought up in a single-parent household.

The Family Adversity Index

Rutter (1978) compared the experience of children in two localities, an inner London borough and the Isle of Wight, in terms of child psychiatric disorder and behavioural deviance. Working with sociological, psychological and psychiatric data, he was able to devise a table of 'stress factors' experienced by the children's families, known as the Family Adversity Index:

1. Father: unskilled/semiskilled job
2. Overcrowding or large family size
3. Marital discord and/or broken home
4. Mother: depression/neurosis
5. Child ever 'in care'
6. Father: any offence against the law

This study was conducted at a time of high employment. Unemployment would constitute an additional stress. Rutter reported that if a stress appeared alone, there was no significant associated risk of problems for the child, but if two or more stresses occurred together, there was an interaction effect which markedly inflated the risk of problems for the child. While stresses such as poverty and unemployment are profoundly important, it is still possible to support troubled families in such a way as to avoid further stress (see Webster-Stratton and Herbert, 1994).

The Family as a Supportive Environment

One of the main functions of families is that they provide young children with a security system, a network of dependable relationships in which to grow up. Rutter (1975) has described the essential roles and responsibilities of parents, which are also valid for others who care for children, such as child minders, nursery nurses, teachers and youth workers. These include:

- provision of positive relationships and attitudes;
- provision of security;
- acting as role models;
- provision of life experience within the child's community and culture;
- provision of discipline and a clear communication network.

If children's fundamental needs for security are fulfilled, and if they are offered affection, approval and acceptance by a network of caring adults who act as models and set consistent limits for behaviour, then children are in a position to develop self-esteem and a strong sense of self. Young people also need to be given responsibility in order to foster independence and the ability to make decisions.

Positive relationships
As we saw earlier, it is of great importance that young children develop attachments to others during the earliest years of life. Rutter (1975) writes:

These early bonds probably constitute the basis for later relationships and the child who has failed to make secure relationships in early childhood is likely to be at a social disadvantage when he is older . . . Family relationships continue to be of importance right through childhood and into adult life.

While other caregivers, including foster parents and residential care staff, are unlikely to be as centrally important as parents, they are also responsible for treating children in such a way that they receive positive messages about themselves, are not ridiculed or made the object of prejudice, discrimination or physical or verbal abuse. This is how self-esteem develops, either positively or negatively.

Security

Security is a primary requirement of children. Harlow and Suomi (1979) showed how monkeys are innately prepared to look for safety in their contact with their mother – even when a wire frame covered with terry towelling is substituted. With this artificial mother providing a reliable base, they can move out to explore the wider world. So it is with young children. Rutter points out that going to hospital alone can be a deeply distressing experience for children, yet accompanied by a parent or well-trusted relative, they are relatively calm and untroubled. The same, though to a lesser degree, is true of older children.

Role models

People learn much of their behaviour by copying others. This is particularly true of children, who acquire a significant proportion of their repertoire of behaviour through imitating those around them – particularly their parents and other immediate caregivers. All who have contact with children and young people should be alert to their own behaviour as role models. Personal habits, such as smoking and drinking, the way others are treated or spoken about, are all likely to be copied by children. Gender roles are also learned, either directly through teaching and training, or indirectly through the examples which are provided by people at home, at school and in the media.

Life experience

Parents and caregivers have an essential role in transmitting language and culture. According to Rutter (1975), talking with the young child is important for several reasons:

- it advances the child's development of language;
- important information and knowledge is conveyed;
- it enhances the value of spoken language for the child.

Professional workers have an educational role to play here. One mother, when discussing her child's progress with her social worker, said, 'No, I don't talk to him – he hasn't learned to talk yet'. Happily the worker was able to explain that the toddler would learn to talk by her talking to him, rather than by himself alone. Educational work of this kind can make a crucial contribution to promoting the well-being of children and their families. Parents, teachers, workers of all kinds can offer 'the world in small doses' to young children through stories and conversation, and can introduce them to experiences which will enrich them throughout their lives.

Discipline

In order to feel secure and to know the boundaries of acceptable behaviour, children need clear and firm limits; in other words, they need positive discipline (Herbert, 1989). I found in my own research (Sutton, 1992) that many parents did not know how to set firm limits to children's unruly or aggressive behaviour, but given support and reassurance, they felt more confident in saying 'No, you can't behave like that', and insisting that their children did as they were asked. They learned to set firm boundaries, to stick to them consistently, and to avoid making threats or promises which they did not carry through. Some parents and caregivers seem to fear that children will not like or love them if they refuse to give them what they ask for – even if they cannot afford to do so. The evidence from my study was that, far from disliking their parents when boundaries were set, many children became not only much more pleasant to live with, but actively more loving towards their parents. Older children, above the age of four, need to be given simple reasons together with any instructions.

Good communication, together with the setting of clear limits, seems to provide young people with a set of boundaries which give them security. 'My parents didn't care what I did', said one youngster in care. 'I wish they'd told me I couldn't go to places sometimes. I mean, I'd have made a fuss, but I'd have done what they said because it would have showed they cared what happened to me'.

Communication

Clear communication is important. Homes or residential settings where parents or care staff behave inconsistently are unhelpful to children. If parents and caregivers do not agree between themselves or, for example, tell children that they must not hit other children one day but ignore hitting the next, then those children learn that it is worth trying to get away with bullying. They learn to play off one parent or worker against another with great subtlety.

Parenting Skills

The research available on parenting skills is fairly clear. The following guidelines are derived from the list of principles suggested by Herbert (1989), and confirmed by many studies. Please note that they are principles only, and each culture and family will interpret them in the light of their own values and circumstances.

❑ Foster bonds of respect and affection: the more affection there is, the more notice the child will take of what he or she is being told.
❑ Make firm social and moral demands (set limits).
❑ Prepare children for life by developing family routines, for example, around bedtime.
❑ Choose guidelines carefully: try to make them positive, with not too many 'don'ts'.

❑ Teach children the family guidelines.
❑ Be consistent.
❑ Be persistent.
❑ Give reasons for your instructions, but not too many to the child under four; too much explanation is not appropriate.
❑ Give young people the opportunity to be responsible.
❑ Avoid making threats which you can't or don't carry through.

The impact of different parenting styles

Just as there is increasing agreement among researchers about skills of parenting, so there is increasing agreement about the impact of different styles of parenting. *Figure 4.1* shows two major dimensions of parenting style: warmth (love) – hostility (rejection) and restrictiveness–permissiveness. The words in italics show styles intermediate between the polarities, and indicate characteristic behaviours of parents towards their children. The descriptive words within the four quadrants show the characteristic responses of their children.

The diagram illustrates, for example, how a child who has few clear limits or boundaries for behaviour and who receives little or no affection, is likely to have limited self-control and may use aggression to get his or her own way. Such children, especially if they have aggressive role models at home, tend to become anti-social.

It is known that the strategy of withdrawing approval from a child, that is, telling a child he or she will not be loved for behaving in a certain way, causes children much anxiety. It is likely to lead to compliance, but also to submissiveness and dependency. Indifference and neglect also erode children's sense of security. As *Figure 4.1* shows, and as we have indicated already, children need love and support, confident and pro-social role models, clear guidelines for behaviour, and opportunities for taking responsibility.

Communication With and Within the Family

Social workers and probation officers spend much of their time working with families. A small part of this may be in family therapy, but the greater part is likely to be for less specialized reasons: an application for a child to be 'accommodated' under the 1989 Children Act, negotiating arrangements for a child to be fostered, or in clarifying arrangements for children's welfare when parents are divorcing. Social workers need to be able to communicate effectively with a great diversity of families, but they should also be able to foster good communication within the family itself.

Research has confirmed that people in 'distressed' families have fewer positive verbal and non-verbal interactions than do people in 'non-distressed' families. Falloon and colleagues (1988) carried out important empirical work on how to help families with members with mental illness to interact effectively. They suggest four basic communication skills which are particularly important:

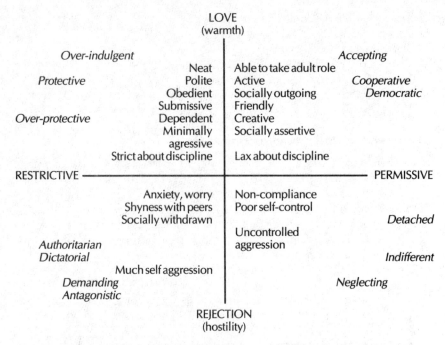

The words in italics in the outer circle denote characteristic styles of parenting. The words inside show the characteristic impact of these styles upon children.

Figure 4.1 Patterns of parenting, and children's behaviour responses (Maccoby and Martin, 1983)

attentive listening; expressing positive feelings; making a positive request; and expressing unpleasant feelings.

Attentive listening

This is essential for good communication. Social workers and community workers should model attentive listening, by turning towards each speaker and demonstrating, through body language, that they are actively listening. When something is not understood, simple clarifying questions can be asked: 'Let me make sure I've got it right . . .'; 'Can I check that I've understood?'. When working with interpreters, things should be repeated until they are clear.

Expressing positive feelings

Falloon and his colleagues found in their research that almost no family with whom they worked demonstrated this skill. Although many members of families *claimed* to express positive feelings towards other members of their families, when the research evidence of their interactions was examined, there was in fact almost no evidence of positive feelings being expressed. Falloon went on to suggest a simple sequence which clients could practise:

- look at the person concerned;
- say exactly what he or she did that pleased you;
- say how it made you feel.

A mother, for example, might say to her daughter, 'Wendy, I was really glad when you came in at the time you said you would. It made me feel that I could really trust you'. Many people find it difficult, and strange, to talk to each other in this way, but as there is a great deal of evidence that members of harmonious families express a lot of positive feelings to each other, this is clearly a valuable communication skill and one to be acquired. Positive feedback also includes giving support and encouragement, doing kind things and generally making life more enjoyable for each other.

Members of harmonious families express positive feelings to each other

Making a positive request

This means making a request in a positive and direct way: for example, 'Please help me with the cooking' or, 'I want you to go to the shop for me'. The *non-verbal* message accompanying the spoken message should be firm but respecting; otherwise the person being asked may perceive a threat and either fight (argue) or flee (walk out or fail to comply).

Expressing negative feelings
Of this skill, Falloon writes:

Blaming, threatening and nagging people will tend to produce bad feelings in them, and will often produce hostile arguments. Making clear, direct statements of how you feel about a specific situation tends to minimize hostility and clears the way for effective problem-solving.

And to clarify the steps to take, Falloon suggests:
1. Look at the person. Speak calmly and firmly.
2. Say exactly what the other person did that triggered off your unpleasant feeling.
3. Tell the other person how that made you feel.
4. Suggest how this might be resolved – either by making a positive request for change, or by arranging a meeting to have a problem-solving discussion.

So, for example, if Michael has upset his mum by shouting at her, she might say calmly but firmly: 'Michael, when you shout at me, it makes me feel upset and angry. If you talk quietly, I will hear better what you say'. This sort of approach might seem altogether too artificial, but the principles are valid, whatever the words chosen to express them. If you are working with a family, and things get heated, unless your agreed goal was to let family members speak their minds, *intervene firmly to stop hostilities between them from disrupting what you are trying to achieve with them.*

To conclude, if you want to help families communicate, remember to practise what you preach: be attentive in your listening, express positive feelings, make constructive requests and express negative feelings (such as disappointment that agreements have not been honoured) in clear, but non-threatening ways.

Family Therapy

The choice of any particular approach flows from the assessment of the difficulties which the family are experiencing. Often the ASPIRE process (see Introduction) will be useful, although the worker will need to supplement this by drawing on a repertoire of skills helpful to families in distress, such as those just discussed.

When working with families as systems (see Herbert, 1993), a skilled therapist can enable many helpful developments to take place by keeping the atmosphere calm and constructive; if this can be achieved, efforts between members to communicate feelings, positive and negative, are much more likely to be successful. Family secrets, long hidden, can be revealed and their implications explored; complex relationships in the past or present can be examined and patterns of alliance within the family clarified. It may also be possible to help a family identify repeated patterns of behaviour in present or past relationships which are counter-productive and to discuss whether they are serving any useful

(a) *Family tree symbols*

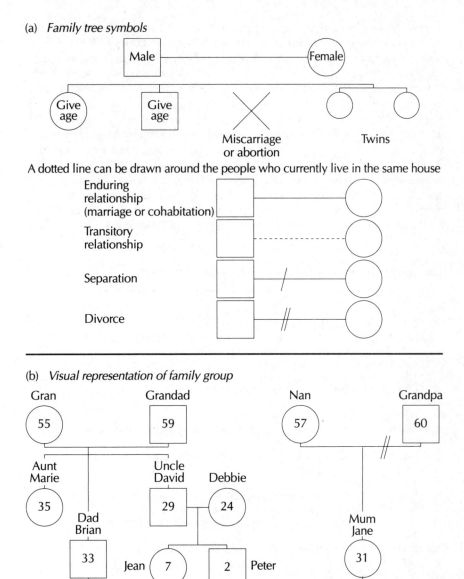

Figure 4.2 (a) How to make a genogram *(b)* An example (Herbert, 1993)

purpose, or whether and how they might be changed. The skilled worker knows when to encourage and when to discourage the release of deep feelings, recognizing that while those of grief, for example, may be acceptable, those of anger, especially when directed against one individual, may cause that person to leave therapy altogether. The worker needs to remain firmly in control in such situations.

If family members can be encouraged to take part, devising a genogram is often a useful method of showing the network of relationships, past and present, within a family (see *Figure 4.2*). Because emphasis is laid upon work with the whole family system, it is important to take account of non-immediate family members, even if they are no longer present. Clarifying events and feelings in the past which are still having effects can help remove misunderstandings, improve communication and open the way to improved relationships in the future. *Table 4.1* shows the main concepts and techniques of family therapy as conceived by Dare (1985).

Table 4.1 The main concepts and strategies of family therapy (Dare, 1985)

The conceptual elements
1. Seeing the family as having an overall structure.
2. Understanding the symptom as having a potential function.
3. Understanding the location of the family on the life cycle.
4. Understanding the intergenerational structure of the family.
5. Making an overall formulation linking the preceding four features.
6. Linking the formulation to appropriate interventions.

The technical elements
1. Making a direct contact with each family member in the meeting or joining process.
2. Engaging children of up to junior school age (0–11 years).
3. Engaging adolescent offspring.
4. Making the parent(s) feel respected and at ease.
5. Eliciting a detailed description of the presenting problem.
6. Facilitating direct interaction between family members.
7. Helping the family develop new strategies to 'solve' their problems.
8. Drawing up a family tree.
9. Devising in-session tasks to facilitate realignment of family structure.
10. Devising between-session tasks.
11. Formulating interpretations.
12. Devising and prescribing paradoxes.

Social learning theory and family therapy

Practitioners are increasingly employing knowledge of social learning theory – formerly called, in its narrowest sense, behavioural theory. This approach uses principles of learning theory, including reinforcement and positive and negative feedback (as described in Chapter 1) to change and improve patterns of family relationships. After careful assessment, a social learning theory approach was chosen in the following example because of the evidence of the usefulness of this approach in the kind of situation described (Herbert, 1988).

Gary was six-and-a-half years old at referral and was described as a very unlovable child. He constantly screamed and shouted abuse at his parents and had violent temper tantrums when he would indulge in physical aggression, hitting and punching people and furniture, and screaming at the top of his voice until he got his own way. He was also persistently defiant and disobedient and seemed to enjoy provoking confrontations with his parents. Observation and assessment confirmed that Gary was indeed showing all these behaviours but also revealed that they were being heavily reinforced by attention from his parents and by the fact that the shouting and temper tantrums usually resulted in Gary's getting his own way and were therefore highly functional for him.

Not surprisingly, against this background, family relationships were very strained and Gary was so unpopular that on the rare occasions when he did behave appropriately it went unnoticed and unattended to, which meant he was only getting attention for anti-social behaviour.

To deal with the shouting and temper tantrums his parents removed Gary from the room as soon as he started to shout. This use of 'time-out from positive reinforcement' was designed to eliminate the possibility of his receiving reinforcing attention for anti-social behaviour and also insisting that he complied with the original request on his return. The parents were able to eliminate these outbursts almost entirely. At the same time great emphasis was placed on rewarding Gary for pro-social behaviour with tokens which he could then exchange for a privilege (such as staying up late) or a treat (such as a favourite play activity with his parents).

This programme was designed to improve their relationship with Gary by providing opportunities for mutually reinforcing activities. By the end of the programme Gary was much happier, showing much more pro-social behaviour and getting on a good deal better with his parents.

The style of the therapist or worker

There is considerable evidence that the therapist, and how he or she behaves, is a major variable in the outcome of family therapy, regardless of the theoretical approach which is employed. Gurman and Kniskern (1981) suggested that there is an association between positive treatment outcome and:

- the therapist's relationship skills, for example, in providing structure and in not being too directive, and
- approaches which enhance a family's abilities to communicate among themselves.

They further reported that the marital-family therapist should provide some structure, but should not confront tenuous family defences very early in the work together. Relationship skills are seen as being as important in behaviourally oriented interventions as in other approaches. The same researchers reported that there was evidence that about five to ten per cent of couples and families became 'worse at least during, if not as a result of' the family treatment they received. They continued:

There is evidence that a particular therapist style is associated with such negative outcomes. These therapists provide little structuring and guiding of early treatment sessions, use frontal confrontations of highly affective [emotionally charged] material . . . rather than stimulating interaction, gathering data or giving support.

Howe's (1989) critique of family therapy carried out by social workers gives further cause for concern. He reported that most families did not like family therapy and 23 of the 32 families failed to complete treatment. The experience of 'Bob' who went for marriage counselling to a private counsellor (Grant, 1992) serves as an illustration of what can go wrong.

Our marriage guidance counselling was the equivalent of putting two people who are not getting along together into a boxing ring and telling them to do their damnedest. It was the worst experience of my life . . . There was no guidance. The counsellor said very little. He was like a silent referee just occasionally asking a question which seemed designed to spur us on to new relevations. I don't know what the counsellor expected the process to achieve. But when we left and went home things were worse than they had been.

This was not counselling or therapy, but inept and unethical practice based on a wholly wrong understanding of how to manage powerful feelings.

Practitioners should be developing ways of working which are appropriate to all communities. In their excellent book, *Transcultural Counselling in Action*, D'Ardennes and Mahtani (1989) write of the appropriateness of client-centred approaches, grounded in humanistic psychology, for working with clients from a range of cultures. This approach, (see Chapter 1) has much to offer to family therapists. Here then are some pointers to good practice with people from all cultures, all races and all communities. It involves:

❑ Using basic principles of good practice: confidentiality, a non-judgemental approach, the expression of empathy.
❑ Always demonstrating respect and regard.
❑ Being clear about your own personal objectives at the outset.
❑ Checking people's expectations, and how realistic they are.
❑ Negotiating the objectives for your shared work together with the family.
❑ Giving support both to the family in general ('This can't be an easy time for you all . . .') and to individuals who seem distressed, ('I wonder if you are feeling a bit isolated, Geraint?').
❑ Trying to help the family members communicate better.

❑ Learning as much as you can of the language and conventions of people from other communities.
❑ Using a repertoire of skills (genograms, agreements, problem-solving) and checking that they are acceptable to families.
❑ Always trying to evaluate your work with those concerned against agreed objectives.

Evaluation of family therapy

In a major examination of the outcomes of family therapy, Gurman and Kniskern (1981) considered 32 reviews of research. They reported:

❑ About 73 per cent of families were seen as 'improved'; however, as few studies used 'control' families, some families might have improved without any formal intervention.
❑ It was impossible to separate out the effects of the person of the therapist from the effects of the theoretical approach used.
❑ The approaches used were never 'pure', that is, based on one body of theory alone.
❑ The studies almost never specified what particular aspects of their interventions brought about the improvement.

Dare (1985), in his later review of the outcome of family therapy in studies which involved children, reported that approaches which employed social learning theory and techniques as well as a systems approach, were effective in reducing intrafamilial behavioural problems (for example, aggressive behaviour) in children and in improving family interactions.

— ASPIRE: work with families —

An ability to assess the urgency of applications to accommodate children and young people as specified by the Children Act 1989 is a fundamental skill required of social workers. Because of the centrality of this skill, a detailed guideline to undertaking a comprehensive assessment, *Protecting Children* (Department of Health, 1988), has been issued. This should be regarded as the context of what follows. Imagine, for example, a young woman, Tracey Harris, comes to the Area Office with a three-year-old and a baby, asking for the older child to be accommodated by the Social Services Department because she cannot control him. How can the ASPIRE process be useful here?

Assessment
Preliminaries to assessment: information gathering
The social worker, Jenny Cooper, who meets with Tracey hears that she is living in a hostel for homeless families, having separated from the children's

father soon after the second baby, Carl, was born. She can stay in the hostel for another three months, and the warden hopes she will soon get a place of her own as her name has been on the housing list for a long time. Tracey is 19 and effectively on her own as her mum lives in Ireland and they have lost touch. When her dad died, her mum moved in with one of his friends sooner than Tracey thought was right.

The three-year-old, Kevin, has always been difficult and Tracey thinks she is losing control of him. He is getting very aggressive, hits her a lot, and she can't leave him alone with the baby. She gives him a slap on the legs now and again, she says, but it doesn't do any good. She wonders if he is missing his dad. So, although she doesn't want to part with him, she thinks that for his own good he ought to go into care. 'I don't love him any more', she says. 'He's knocked all the love I had for him out of me'. However, she doesn't want him adopted.

WHAT *are the problems?*
In discussion, Tracey and the social worker work out a statement of the current problems:

- Tracey feels isolated, depressed and tired.
- She feels she cannot cope with the two children any more.
- She knows she smacks Kevin now and again, but she doesn't know how else to control him.
- She is missing her dad, and understands that Kevin may be missing his dad.
- She wants Kevin to be accommodated by the Social Services Department.

WHICH *are the priority problems?*
From Tracey's point of view:
1. She wants to keep the children, but feels she can't cope with them.
2. She wants the best for Kevin, so wants him to be looked after by the Social Services until she feels better.
3. She would like to feel better about herself.
4. She would like to be in touch with her mum again.

From Jenny's point of view:
1. She knows that her Department is extremely unlikely to take Kevin into care in these circumstances.
2. She is concerned about Kevin, who does seem to be very hard to handle.
3. She is concerned for Tracey, who is young, poor, isolated and depressed and who has not been feeling very well lately.

WHO *are the people involved/affected?*
Tracey, the children's mother, aged 19
Kevin, aged three

Carl, aged ten months
Paul, the children's father – thought to be in Glasgow
Tracey's mother, in Ireland
Trevor, warden of the homeless persons' hostel
Jenny, the social worker

WHY *have the problems arisen?*
Tracey thinks that things began to go wrong when she and Paul had rows over Paul's drinking. He was fine when he was sober, she said, but when he had been drinking he was aggressive and hit her. She is afraid that Kevin has inherited this aggressiveness from Paul. Tracey is very lonely, even at the hostel where there are other young families. She keeps to herself. She feels hopeless about the future, and can only just manage on her Income Support and other welfare money. She doesn't think that Paul is interested in the children. He has another child, a girl, which he always wanted, with the woman he is living with at present, and he never contacts her about Kevin and Carl, or sends birthday gifts or cards.

Planning
It is apparent to Jenny Cooper, after consultation with her team leader, that her Social Services Department will seek to avoid accommodating Kevin. He and the baby are apparently well-cared for: they look healthy and Kevin, a very active and noisy little boy, seems attached to his mother. He is however very disobedient, and Tracey does not seem to be able to manage his naughtiness.

HOW *are we together going to manage the problem?*
Jenny and Tracey have different priorities at present. Tracey claims she wants Kevin to be accommodated by Middleshire Social Services Department, while Jenny knows that this is an unlikely outcome. Jenny listens to Tracey, enables her to say how hopeless she feels, but also detects Tracey's relief when she hears that there is little chance of Kevin's being accommodated by the local authority. 'I thought I ought to give him up', she says. 'I thought I wasn't a fit mother for him'. Once reassured, Tracey enters fairly readily into planning for the future.

Jenny is open with Tracey: she tells her that while she personally notices the close attachment which Kevin has to Tracey, she is required to check that the Health Visitor has no concerns. Tracey agrees to this. They discuss what objectives/goals they want to achieve together and draw up an agreement for their work together (see p.228). A date a week hence is fixed for the next appointment, and both Tracey and Jenny have a copy of the agreement.

Implementation
Jenny Cooper sets about completing her part in the agreement. She contacts Helen Shaw, the Health Visitor. Helen has visited Tracey recently in

connection with baby Carl. She saw him a few weeks ago, and had no real concerns about him. She was aware that Tracey was feeling low, and had encouraged her to visit her doctor. Kevin had been at a playgroup when she called, so she had not seen him. Tracey had told her that 'he was a handful' but had not given her the impression that she felt so upset about his behaviour that she was going to ask for the children to be taken into care. Jenny clarifies the negotiated plan with Helen, and promises to seek Tracey's agreement to a copy of the plan being sent to Helen. Helen says she will visit Tracey again to assure herself that everything she can offer is being done.

Jenny also obtains a list of mother and toddler drop-in centres. She meets weekly with Tracey in order to teach her how to manage Kevin more firmly. Jenny believes that using a social learning approach (see p.23) will be the most helpful way of reducing Kevin's tantrums.

Tracey, in turn, makes an appointment to visit her GP. In between meeting with Jenny she attempts to deal with Kevin's misbehaviour in a more consistent manner. She also visits the welfare rights office.

Review and evaluation

The plan is reviewed briefly each week. Jenny visits Tracey three times at home, for an hour each time. At the time agreed for evaluation, four weeks after their first meeting, Tracey and Jenny meet again and, as agreed, consider what they have achieved – or not.

- Tracey has been to the doctor, and it was found that she was anaemic. She is now on a course of tablets and is already feeling she has more energy.
- She went to the welfare rights office, and although it is likely that she is receiving all her entitlement, this is going to be checked for accuracy.
- After Jenny's teaching her how to manage Kevin more firmly, Tracey feels she can cope with him much better. She has kept a record of his temper tantrums and there have been only two brief tantrums in the course of the last week which she has managed to ignore (see Appendix A for chart). 'He's a much happier child now that he knows how far he can go', she says.
- She has used the information Jenny obtained about the parents' drop-in centre, and has been visiting one with the two children. The people were quite friendly and she might go again.

Things appear to be more optimistic for Tracey, but as Jenny does not feel entirely happy about relying upon her subjective impressions, she asks if Tracey would be willing to complete the Beck Depression Inventory (see p.100). She is willing, and has a score of **6** indicating only very slight depression. Jenny discusses the inventory result with Tracey, and gets further verbal assurance that Tracey is feeling very much less depressed than on their first meeting. Jenny clarifies with Tracey that while she is welcome to return at any time, there seems to be no need at the present for further meetings.

CHAPTER 5

Child Abuse

Child abuse is a topic of enormous importance to social workers. To write so briefly on it can seem irresponsible, but psychologists have carried out important research in this field which can inform the practice of grass roots workers. This chapter will therefore address that research, as well as some other relevant material.

The major document *Working Together Under the Children Act 1989* (Home Office, 1991), which concerns the cooperation of agencies under the Act, contains the following categories of abuse for entry on the child protection register. It is noted that the categories do not tie in precisely with the definition of 'significant harm' in Section 31 of the Act.

Neglect. The persistent or severe neglect of a child, or the failure to protect a child from exposure to any kind of danger, including cold or starvation, or extreme failure to carry out important aspects of care, resulting in the significant impairment of the child's health or development, including non-organic failure to thrive.

Physical Injury. Actual or likely physical injury to a child, or failure to prevent physical injury (or suffering) to a child including deliberate poisoning, suffocation and Munchausen's syndrome by proxy.

Sexual Abuse. Actual or likely sexual exploitation of a child or adolescent. The child may be dependent and/or developmentally immature.

Emotional Abuse. Actual or likely severe adverse effect on the emotional and behavioural development of a child caused by persistent or severe emotional ill-treatment or rejection. All abuse involves some emotional ill-treatment. This category should be used where it is the main or sole form of abuse.

Estimates of Child Abuse

Table 5.1 shows the estimated incidence of abuse to children for the years 1988, 1989 and 1990 based on figures derived from the registers kept by the National

Society for the Prevention of Cruelty to Children (NSPCC) in representative areas of England and Wales. The 'Registered' category includes children entered on the registers for a number of reasons all of which gave grounds for concern, but which were not at that time separated out: neglect, emotional abuse, as well as a category no longer to be used, 'grave concern'. The latter included children who were siblings of abused children, and those thought to be at risk of being abused. The publication *Child Abuse Trends in England and Wales* (NSPCC, 1992) gives further details about the population of children placed upon their registers.

Table 5.1 Estimates of national incidence of child abuse per year* in England and Wales (Creighton, 1992)

AGE AND CATEGORY	ESTIMATED NUMBER OF CHILDREN		
	1988	1989	1990
0–4 Years			
Physically Injured	4,300	4,600	4,200
Sexually Abused	1,500	1,600	900
Registered	12,900	17,000	15,600
0–14 Years			
Physically Injured	8,300	9,700	9,300
Sexually Abused	5,300	5,900	4,500
Registered	25,100	34,100	32,500
0–16 Years			
Physically Injured	9,100	10,500	10,100
Sexually Abused	6,200	6,600	5,300
Registered	27,000	36,300	34,700

* Rounded to nearest 100

Assessment in Child Abuse

An all-purpose framework for assessment, ASPIRE, was given in the Introduction. Assessment in specific situations, such as those in which child abuse is suspected, calls for more information gathering and for informed judgements. A detailed guide, *Protecting Children* (Department of Health, 1988), has been issued for those undertaking a comprehensive assessment (see also Herbert, 1993).

There is always risk in making an assessment, especially those concerning vulnerable children. Whether at the initial investigation or at a subsequent case conference, assessing risk does not simply involve calculating the likelihood that a given event will occur; it also involves considering the outcome *if* the event were to occur. Taking the second factor into account may substantially affect the calculation of the first. The obvious example is the risk involved in leaving a child at home, rather than applying for, say, an Emergency Protection Order, which would temporarily remove the child from his or her family. If the child's life is thought to be in danger, then the calculation is of a different kind from a situation where a child may be neglected, but where there is no danger of physical assault.

The difficulties involved in assessing risk are illuminated by Alaszewski and Manthorpe (1991) who draw attention to two types of error which may be made by social workers. At one extreme, the Maria Colwell situation, social workers did not perceive the evidence of neglect until it was too late; they underestimated the risk involved. At the other extreme, the Cleveland situation, social workers perceived sexual abuse on the basis of inadequate evidence; they overestimated the risk involved.

In an attempt to distinguish families in which children are at risk of being abused, screening techniques of many kinds have been developed. Several instruments are available: that by Greenland (1987) addresses physical abuse and includes variables concerning both parents and children; no weightings are given.

Table 5.2 Child abuse: high risk assessment chart (Greenland, 1987)

Parents	Child
Previously having abused, neglected a child.	Was previously abused or neglected.
Age 20 or less at age of first child.	Under five years of age at the time of abuse or neglect.
	Premature or low birth-weight.
Single parent or separated.	Now under-weight.
Partner not biological parent.	Birth defect, chronic illness,
History of abuse, neglect or deprivation.	developmental lag.
Socially isolated, frequent moves, poor housing.	Prolonged separation from mother.
Poverty, unemployed or unskilled worker.	Cries frequently, difficult to comfort.
Inadequate education.	Difficulties in feeding and elimination.
	Adopted, foster or step-child.
Abuses alcohol and/or drugs.	
History of criminal assaultive behaviour and/or suicide attempts.	
Pregnancy, post-partum or chronic illness.	

Your agency should have copies of two schedules which can be used to assess maternal depression:

- the Beck Depression Inventory, which takes only ten minutes to complete;
- the Edinburgh Post-Natal Depression Inventory, which is also a straight-forward means of assessment, particularly when symptoms have appeared soon after giving birth.

The first of these is American in origin, the second British. Both have been validated for use with European populations, although not with African-Caribbean, Asian or Chinese communities. Steps to do so are being taken at the present time.

It has to be acknowledged, however, that no amount of screening can totally protect vulnerable children from abuse unless it is possible and acceptable to have homes monitored day and night. Furthermore it is vital to avoid misassessments based on misunderstandings due to cultural variables. Okine (1992) has provided important guidelines to bear in mind when assessing black families.

Interviews of investigation

These are extremely demanding occasions, when the anxiety of those involved, together with the associated high levels of arousal, can easily flare into confrontation or aggression. It is vital that social workers enquiring into situations where, for example, there are allegations of child abuse, should prepare themselves fully for this situation. They should not make such visits alone; and they need every possible support, both personal and those offered by clear policies and procedures (see also Chapter 9).

Let's look at the position of the people being investigated. In terms of social exchange theory (see Chapter 3), there is no possible advantage in being involved in an investigation. There are, however, many potential costs in *not* cooperating: a charge might be brought, an appearance in court might follow, a child might be removed. Often then, depending partly on the skills of the investigating worker, people do cooperate in investigations.

Always be open and factual about the reason for your visit, saying who you are and why you are there. If there is concern about a child being bruised, for example, say clearly and in a non-accusing way, words to the effect: 'We've been informed that your little boy has some bruises on his arm, and we've been asked to investigate. We need to talk about this.' This approach may not result in good relationships, but it is likely to prevent the development of the worst hostilities.

Research relevant to the assessment of risk

There are two bodies of research in psychology which are relevant to the case conference situation. The first is the 'move to consensus' phenomenon, that is, when a majority within a group brings pressure to bear upon a minority who disagrees with them. For example, a majority who considers the level of risk to a child does not warrant applying for an order to remove him or her from home may exert pressure upon a minority who takes the opposite view. The effects of the 'move to consensus' can be countered by a good chairperson who can ensure that all views, including those with less formal status within the group, are heard and that premature decisions are not made.

The second phenomenon, the 'shift to risk' (Shaver, 1977), concerns the tendency of groups of people to arrive at decisions which, upon examination, prove to be more risky than those which they would have arrived at independently. This tendency may operate in some case conferences, particularly if responsibility is seen to be diffused, that is, if someone else, rather than oneself, is seen to bear responsibility if anything goes wrong.

Intervention in Child Abuse

Three levels of intervention can be distinguished: primary, secondary and tertiary. The research within each area is extremely patchy – a situation which reflects the nature of the services provided.

Primary intervention

The focus here is on intervening in the overall situations which contribute to child abuse, for example, isolation and lack of support, *before* a crisis occurs. Strategies are developed from a community perspective, that is, services are made available to everybody, not just families identified as being potentially abusive. Community-based responses include the involvement of 'community mothers', experienced parents who offer support and help to isolated young mothers (Early Child Development Unit, 1991), the development of networks of support such as self-help groups as well as visiting schemes staffed by volunteers and guided by professionals. Other schemes include the involvement of 'foster grandparents' who take a particular interest in young families and offer non-judgemental support.

Secondary intervention

Here the focus is upon early intervention to prevent the occurrence of child abuse in specific families. A prerequisite is the detection of families particularly at risk of abusing their children; Roberts (1988) has given an overview of research on this topic. She reports surveys which highlight the relative youth and immaturity of some parents who abuse their children, and how some young deprived parents with unmet dependency needs look to their children for comfort.

Other families at risk include those with children born unwanted and those with babies born sick or disabled. These children are even more vulnerable when these conditions are compounded by other factors such as illness in the parents or bereavement during pregnancy. However, the major study by Browne (1988) concluded that family stress alone is an insufficient explanation for child abuse and that this is compounded by parents' unrealistic expectations of their young children.

Tertiary intervention

The focus here is on intervention in families once abuse has occurred. The main strategies which have been rigorously researched include systemic family therapy and the training of maltreating parents within a social learning theory/behavioural framework, that is, in child management skills. These are examined further in Chapter 4.

The overall picture in this area is complex. What seems to emerge is that intervention at several levels is called for: at the level of community initiatives offering support for young or immature parents, at the level of screening and focused help for vulnerable families, and at the level of direct parent training. Clearly, extremely careful monitoring of all abusive families, whatever the strategies of intervention, is essential.

Neglect

This is a seriously under-researched topic. Because it may be more difficult to detect than child physical abuse or child sexual abuse, and because a child is unlikely to know that he or she is being neglected and so cannot ask for help, there has been very little research attention in this area. Yet the effects of neglect are very serious, both in the short and long-term, in respect of impairment of physical health and low self-esteem, while persistent neglect can result in death.

Non-organic failure to thrive is now included within the definition of neglect. The general term 'failure to thrive' refers to a failure to grow and develop healthily and vigorously. Iwaniec *et al.* (1985) have investigated non-organic failure to thrive, that is, the forms of the disorder not attributable to medical factors. They identify not only key features of the constellation of variables, social and psychological, contributing to non-organic failure to thrive, but also develop an effective strategy of intervention (see p.103). It is highly likely that, as with physical abuse, neglect can only be understood within a multivariate model such as that of Gelles (1979) (see *Figure 5.1*).

Intervention in neglect

Because of the difficulties of distinguishing children at risk of such abuse, it is often only those whose health and development reflect their deprivation who come early to the attention of health and social work agencies. Children who fail to thrive are such a group; many other children almost certainly go undetected. Strategies of intervention are therefore under-developed at all three levels: primary, secondary and tertiary.

Primary and secondary intervention

Careful screening, mainly by health visitors, is the most likely means of detecting the sad, unsmiling and withdrawn victims of neglect. Monitoring of physical development according to centile charts picks up many of those whose feeding difficulties lead to a failure to thrive.

Tertiary intervention

A major research study in the field of non-organic failure to thrive is that of Iwaniec *et al.* (1985b) who describe three stages of intervention using social learning theory (listed below). Evaluation both post-intervention and in the long-term showed very encouraging results.

1. Resolve feeding difficulties and improve feeding style, that is, help mothers to change their behaviour and responses during the act of feeding the child (by means of counselling, modelling and carefully structured feeding situations).
2. In a planned and graduated fashion, create positive interactions and reduce negative interactions between mother, child and other members of the family. It is important to desensitize the child's anxiety about feeding, and to replace a negative and hostile attitude on the part of the mother with a positive one, made increasingly rewarding to her by the child's gradually improved responsiveness.
3. Intensify and increase positive mother–child interactions.

Physical injury

Browne (1988), a psychologist who has done extensive fieldwork in attempting to predict who will abuse their children and in what situations, points out that the ability to predict abuse is a prerequisite for the development of adequate services. He notes that child abuse is one of the most common causes of death to young children in Britain today and that up to four children die at the hands of their parents each week. There is proof, he reports, that at least one per cent of children are badly maltreated in some way, and this is probably just the tip of the iceberg. The National Society for the Prevention of Cruelty to Children holds registers of all children who have been abused in 12 English cities and counties. Of the 2,786 children registered as having sustained physical injury, 1,150 (41 per cent) were bruised on the head or face, 1,206 (43 per cent) were bruised on the body or limbs, 217 (eight per cent) had sustained cuts and 107 (four per cent) had been burned or scalded.

Neglect of children is an offence of *omission*, and once detected, it should be fairly straightforward to monitor that child's progress in cooperation with other professionals. *Child physical injury* , an offence of *commission*, is more difficult to guard against as it can occur suddenly at any time of the day or night.

It has become apparent from extensive research that child physical abuse arises from the interaction of many variables: sociological, psychological, and

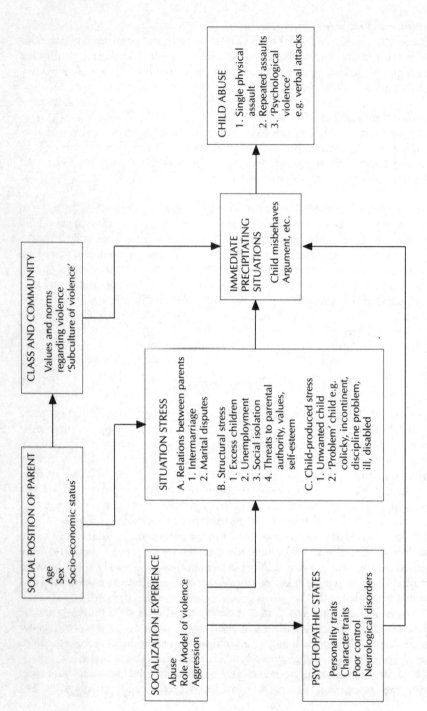

Figure 5.1 A social psychological model of the causes of child abuse (Gelles, 1979)

sometimes psychiatric. Gelles (1979) (see *Figure 5.1*) devised a model indicating the psychological causes of child abuse. In his review of the research literature, he highlights several key variables which are consistently associated with child abuse, wife abuse and family violence.

1. A cycle of violence: the learned transmission of violent behaviour from one generation to the next.
2. Socio-economic status: injury is more likely among, but by no means confined to, those of low socio-economic class.
3. High levels of stress: arising from poverty, unemployment, etc.
4. Social isolation.

Gelles noted, however, the need to exercise caution in accepting these findings uncritically; the above factors are *associations*, not causes, and the research in this field is of great complexity.

Other researchers have emphasized the importance of cognitive factors in child abuse, particularly how the abusers perceive the child's behaviour and the precipitating events which lead to the violent incident. Some parents interpret normal, age-appropriate behaviour as deliberate, and believe that this is part of the child's 'bad' disposition. For example, some parents, having little knowledge of child development, may perceive a baby as crying deliberately to annoy them, or may perceive a baby who soils her nappy just as they were going out, as having done so on purpose. Such incorrect attributions reduce parents' own low self-esteem and may interact with other variables to be the 'last straw'.

With regard to intervention, Nicol (1988) concluded that research indicates that some families where child abuse has occurred can be helped by home-based treatment programmes. It may be appropriate to undertake a trial of treatment in suitable cases, but this should be short-term and form part of the assessment, rather than being seen as a proven and effective method of intervention. Skilled supervision is absolutely essential.

Child Sexual Abuse

Here is an area of such complexity that when the first cases began to come to public attention, there was virtually no research literature to inform practice and certainly no reliable body of experience or procedure to guide the interventions of social workers. The profession was pitched headlong, with neither training nor experience, into managing a flood of referred cases, upon a public stage and under the eyes of increasingly critical media.

There are now, arising from much publicized cases and the ensuing reports, bodies of procedures to follow in all instances of suspected child sexual abuse – as is the case of course for other forms of abuse. There is also the beginnings of a research literature, and this section will attempt to address this. The 1991 edition of *Working Together Under the Children Act 1989* describes sexual abuse as 'actual or likely sexual exploitation of a child or adolescent. The child may be dependent and/or developmentally immature'.

Table 5.3 shows the range of offences included within the term 'sexual abuse' within the registers held by the NSPCC (1992). Readers are referred to the publication itself for details of the ages and circumstances of both the children involved and the perpetrators of abuse in this major report. Despite the huge publicity given to instances of sexual abuse, it is highly likely that only a small fraction of the total number of instances of sexual abuse come to official notice.

Table 5.3 Nature of abuse sustained for 1,732 cases of sexual abuse (1988–1990 combined (Creighton, 1992)

Vaginal intercourse	143	(8%)*
Anal intercourse	89	(5%)
Attempted vaginal/anal intercourse	105	(6%)
Vaginal penetration	194	(11%)
Anal penetration	109	(6%)
Oral penetration	97	(6%)
Masturbation of child by perpetrator	97	(6%)
Lick/suck/spit on child	30	(2%)
Fondle child	370	(21%)
Sexually transmitted disease – child	14	(1%)
Masturbation of perpetrator by child	103	(6%)
Exploitation	15	(1%)
Exposure	32	(2%)
Indecent assault/gross indecency	169	(10%)
Other	117	(7%)

*Bracketed figures show percentage of cases with this abuse.

Concerning incest, Bluglass (1979) reports that sibling relationships are probably the most frequent form, although father–daughter incest is the most commonly reported. Stepfather–stepdaughter relationships (although not legally incest) are also common. Nelson (1982) notes that families involved in incest 'came from every economic, cultural, racial, educational, religious and geographical background. They are doctors, policemen, prostitutes, secretaries, artists and merchants. They are heterosexual, bisexual and homosexual. They are happily married and four times divorced . . . They are emotionally stable and have multiple personalities . . .'

Characteristics of those who abuse

Bluglass (1979) reports that while about 50 per cent of the paternal perpetrators of sexual abuse have one or more of the features of alcoholism, tendencies to violence, or a previous criminal record, the other 50 per cent appear to be a relatively 'normal' group without distinguishing characteristics. The NSPCC report (1992) indicates that 40 per cent of males who abused children either physically or sexually have a previous criminal record. The great majority of child sexual abusers are men. A study by Bentovim *et al.* (1987) involving 274 families, found that 96 per cent of perpetrators were men. However, of the 7,540 children telephoning Childline from November 1989 to October 1990, 12 per cent reported the mother as the perpetrator of the abuse.

Available figures (Home Office, 1989) indicate that of all offenders cautioned or found guilty of sex offences during 1989, 32 per cent were under the age of 21 and 17 per cent were under the age of 16. These 'official' figures do not do more than give an indication of the incidence of sexual offences; wholly accurate figures are virtually impossible to gather.

Sgroi (1982) questions the idea that child sexual abuse is primarily motivated by sexual desires; sexual offenders report feeling powerful and in control when abusing children. She claims that intervention can only be appropriate when child sexual abuse is regarded as a power problem and treated accordingly.

Interviewing young children

Helpful guidelines have been developed by a number of practitioners and researchers; a valuable summary of the stages involved has been suggested by Smith (1991). He emphasizes that the interviewer should proceed from the most general questioning where the child relates the story in his or her own time, using his or her own words, to the more direct, where the child responds to specific questions.

There are five main phases which offer a framework, not a checklist, for the interview.
1. *Rapport building:* children will need to trust the interviewer if they are to share painful information.
2. *Free narrative:* this is the most important phase and should provide every opportunity for the child to give their uninterrupted version of events.
3. *Open questions:* during this phase every effort should be made to avoid suggesting answers to the child.
4. *Specific questions:* this is likely to meet resistance from the child.
5. *Ending the interview:* interviewers will need to deal openly and honestly with the consequences of telling for the child.

Intervention in child sexual abuse

Because the offence is usually so covert, and the perpetrators come from such a wide spectrum of people, it is almost impossible to develop primary, or even secondary, strategies of intervention. At the level of primary prevention, efforts are being directed towards changing the attitudes of adult males towards women, but the effectiveness of such approaches are exceedingly hard to evaluate. Research has therefore tended to focus upon offering help to survivors of sexual abuse, mainly girls and young women, although boys and young men are also victims. A study by Baker and Duncan (1985) found that twelve per cent of young women over 15 years reported having been sexually abused; the corresponding figure for young men was 8 per cent.

The impact of sexual abuse

Sarnacki-Porter *et al.* (1982) report the 'impact and treatment issues' for survivors of child sexual abuse.

- 'Damaged goods' syndrome: a mixture of self doubt, fear and anxiety.
- Guilt: many child survivors feel responsible for the sexual activity even though they are unquestionably not.
- Fear: of being powerless; of being injured; of social responses.
- Depression.
- Low self-esteem and poor social skills.
- Repressed anger and hostility.
- Impaired ability to trust.
- Role confusion.
- Pseudomaturity, but failure to accomplish developmental tasks.
- Failure to achieve feelings of being in control.

These authors claim that the first five characteristics are typical of virtually all sexually abused children, while the later ones typify many others.

Primary and secondary intervention

While acknowledging the contribution of concepts such as power in understanding child sexual abuse, Marshall and Barbaree (1990) have developed an integrated theory of the origins of sexual offending in general, and this includes offending against children. They propose that 'the early developmental experiences of boys who are later to become sex offenders inadequately prepare them for the changes in bodily function at puberty and initiate a strong desire to engage in sex and aggression. Poor socialization, particularly a violent parenting style, facilitates the use of aggression'. Their view is supported by the studies of Rada (1978) who examined the family backgrounds of rapists and the parenting styles which they experienced. The boys were offered little affection or love, and were frequently punished harshly and inconsistently. Finkelhor (1984) has provided similar data for child molesters. It is apparent that preventive methods must begin when the children concerned are very young, yet there is little evidence of substantial sums of money being invested in training people in the skills of consistent parenting.

Tertiary intervention: individualized treatment

Sgroi (1982) suggests that the treatment of a child sexual abuse survivor can be divided into three main stages:

1. *Crisis intervention.* Following disclosure of the abuse by the child or by another person, a great many forms of intervention – medical, legal, social work and other – have to be coordinated. The family is often in a state of acute disturbance and

stress, yet major decisions have to be made against this background. For example, who will be caring for the child? Will the child be remaining in the same house as an alleged perpetrator? and so on. Research relating to crisis intervention is likely to be relevant now. Helpful responses include calmness, providing information, companionship, supportive listening and practical help (Parry, 1990).

2. *Short-term therapy lasting six to 12 months.* Here, the focus of intervention goes beyond the sexual violation. A major part of the work is directed towards strengthening the child's feelings of safety and his or her ability to trust other people again, as well as towards developing self-confidence (Sarnacki-Porter *et al.*, 1982). It follows that the first five of the 'impact and treatment' issues discussed earlier will be a central focus. *Table 5.4* shows other major concerns which may arise. Sgroi suggests that the success of short-term therapy generally depends on the degree of support for the child in her or his family circle or community. The perpetrator's relationship to the victim is also a key factor – whether, for example, the perpetrator resides in the child's home.

3. *Long-term therapy (two years or more).* There may be a need for continued intervention over a longer period. This will be indicated when the symptoms of post-traumatic stress (see *Table 5.4*) persist, or where there are continuing difficulties in terms of expressing anger or feelings of powerlessness or self-blame. These have to be consistently addressed and countered. Making, rehearsing and implementing realistic plans for handling future difficulties, including, if necessary, the relationship with the perpetrator, form part of the intervention. The whole approach rests upon empowering the survivors of abuse, and upon enhancing their self-efficacy.

Table 5.4 Post-traumatic stress reactions to child sexual abuse (Jehu, 1988)

Persistent re-experiencing of abuse
- Recurrent and intrusive recollections of the abuse.
- Recurrent distressing dreams related to the abuse.
- Sense of reliving the abuse.
- Distress at exposure to events resembling the abuse.

Persistent avoidance of features related to abuse
- Avoidance of activities or situations associated with the abuse.
- Avoidance of thoughts or feelings related to the abuse.
- Inability to recall memories of the abuse.
- Dissociative reactions:
  – disengagement,
  – depersonalization,
  – multiple personality.

Persistent increased arousal
- Sleep disturbances.
- Irritability/anger/aggression.
- Hypervigilance.
- Physiological reactions to events resembling abuse.

Emotional Abuse

While physical abuse is relatively easy to detect, and publicity has led to increased awareness of and enquiries into sexual abuse, emotional abuse is still an exceedingly difficult area in which to make an accurate assessment. Since the category should be used only where emotional abuse is the main or sole form of abuse, a limited number of cases have come to light. It follows that there is a small amount of research in this field.

Behaviours contributing to child emotional abuse are:
- the punishing of positive behaviours such as smiling, mobility and the manipulation of objects;
- behaviour that results in discouragement of parent-infant bonding;
- actions leading to the reduction of self-esteem in the child;
- parental actions leading to the punishing of interpersonal skills, such as relating to other people (Iwaniec *et al.*, 1985).

In their work with families of children who fail to thrive, Iwaniec *et al.* reported that the mothers of the children, by comparison with a control group:
- report more often a disturbance in their sense of the child belonging to them;
- express less pleasure in the baby, less sense of the infant being lovable;
- spend less time interacting with the child (outside the time devoted to basic care);
- do not devote as much time to picking up, talking to and smiling at the baby;
- when they do so, they report a lack of pleasure in these activities;
- are less demonstrative in showing affection towards their child;
- play less often with their child for fun as opposed to duty;
- get on better with their other children rather than the index child.

In this study, social learning theory was used as a framework for both understanding and interviewing in situations where children were failing to thrive.

— ASPIRE: intervention in emotional abuse —

A study of a child experiencing emotional abuse (Gilbert, 1976) is adapted here to illustrate the nature and sensitivity of the work required.

When her daughter, Sara, was born, Kathleen resented having to give up her established career. She became very depressed two weeks after the birth and wanted nothing to do with the baby.

A second daughter, Lisa, was born three years later. Kathleen found that she enjoyed this child right from birth, and this made her more aware of the way she was behaving towards Sarah. She started feeling guilty about it, and depressed in consequence. At the time that help was requested, Kathleen could not cuddle or kiss Sarah, the sound of Sarah's voice irritated her, and nothing the child did was right. Kathleen had begun to smack Sarah and was also shouting at her. The relationship between Kathleen and her husband was deteriorating. The problem was not discussed properly and there were no sexual relations between them.

Kathleen realized that she was avoiding any contact with Sarah, and that the child was noticing it. However, she just did not know how to change her behaviour and could not see any way of solving the worsening situation.

Assessment
Key features of the assessment were:
- Kathleen's avoidance of Sarah; her husband cared for the child most of the time.
- Kathleen's fear that she might harm Sarah, but she was also afraid of the harm the lack of emotionally warm contact might produce.
- Kathleen did not know how to bring about any change in her own behaviour.

Planning
- Kathleen needed immediate guidance in order to prevent her from harming Sarah.
- A psychologist would present a 'good' model of how to handle Sarah in an affectionate manner for Kathleen to imitate.
- Once an appropriate way of managing Sarah was established, the psychologist would gradually 'fade-out' from the situation.
- The following objectives were negotiated with Kathleen's cooperation:
  - she would cuddle Sarah at bedtime,
  - smile at Sarah in a natural way,
  - praise Sarah,
  - sit next to Sarah at mealtimes and when watching TV,
  - talk to Sarah in an affectionate way.

Implementation of the plan
- The psychologist played with Sarah, and encouraged her mother to imitate her actions and games with the little girl. This took place twice weekly over three months.
- Kathleen, despite some reluctance, also attempted to interact with Sarah every day according to the negotiated objectives outlined above.
- Kathleen was initially dubious about this, claiming that Sarah would know that she was pretending. In fact, as she tried out the new behaviours, Sarah readily responded to her and Kathleen began to enjoy her child's company.

Review and Evaluation
After three months, Kathleen could achieve all five objectives without feeling anxious. At that point a reassessment was made followed by another

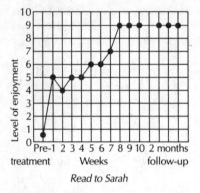

Read to Sarah

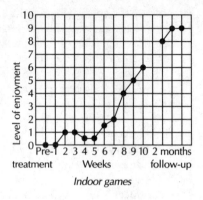

Indoor games

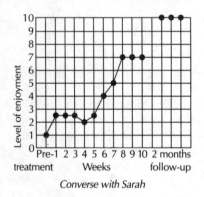

Converse with Sarah

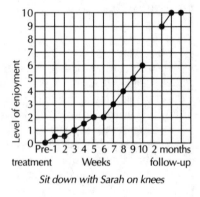

Sit down with Sarah on knees

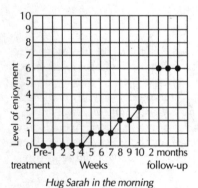

Hug Sarah in the morning

Figure 5.2 A record of particular behaviours (Gilbert, 1976)

intervention to last ten weeks. Further activities involving mother and child were negotiated. These included:

- reading to Sarah,
- joining in indoor games,
- conversing regularly with Sarah,
- sitting down with Sarah on her knees,
- hugging Sarah in the morning.

Kathleen kept a record of her own behaviour (see *Figure 5.2*). This gave her a clear idea of her achievements and a sense of control over the situation. She also rated the enjoyment, not the anxiety, she felt in undertaking these activities. Support from the psychologist was still offered.

At follow-up two months later, the improvement in Kathleen's behaviour was maintained. Sarah did not hesitate to kiss and cuddle her mother. Kathleen had also been helped to discuss her relationship with her husband and this was steadily improving.

Evaluation of Interventions in Child Abuse

The research in this area should make us cautious. There is a shortage in this country of longitudinal studies, although Bentovim *et al.* (1987) followed up 120 of the 274 families referred for treatment of child sexual abuse. They reported that following the therapeutic intervention which the team offered, 'there was an improvement in the victim's circumstances in 61% of cases, and a noticeable reduction in "sexualised" and general emotional difficulties among victims, but there was a reabuse rate of 16%'.

An overview carried out by Cohn and Daro (1987) in the United States gives grounds for concern. They examined a total of 89 treatment programmes for child abuse and neglect, involving 3,253 families. They found that successful intervention, particularly in the case of physical abuse, was associated with a package of services. Those parents who received counselling by lay people, support from Parents Anonymous, as well as group counselling and parent education classes were significantly less likely to abuse their children again than those who did not receive these services. Overall, there were more favourable outcomes associated with the treatment of sexual abuse than with other forms; neglect seemed particularly intractable. However, Cohn and Daro noted that 'one-third' of the parents served by these intensive demonstration efforts maltreated their children while in treatment and over one-half of the families served continued to be judged likely to mistreat their children following termination'.

Cohn and Daro conclude their review by suggesting that services to *prevent* child abuse are called for, rather than attempting to respond after the event. This suggests that an array of strategies to support young isolated families should be made available, through community centres, family centres and health centres.

It is important to highlight that there is no inevitable transmission of learned patterns of abusing children from one generation to the next. Kaufman and Zigler (1987) reviewed the data in this area and concluded that about one-third of parents who were physically or sexually abused, or who were extremely neglected will treat their children abusively, but the remaining two-thirds will care for their children adequately. This is emphasized because it is becoming erroneous common knowledge that children who were abused will in time abuse their own children. I recently heard of a young woman who had been admitted to care after being severely maltreated. She confided to her social worker that she believed she ought not to have children because, having been 'knocked about' herself, she would be likely to do the same thing to her children. It was good to be able to pass on the research data to her social worker and clarify that it says nothing of the sort!

Caring for Children in Distress

Children who come to the attention of social workers will include those received into care, those who have been found to be the victims of physical, sexual or emotional abuse and others whose parents may be unable or unwilling to care for them. They will include children from all sections of society, from every racial and cultural background, as well as children with physical or learning disabilities. Some children may have appeared in court. Children in distress will have particular needs which include the following.

Security
Children who have had difficult experiences are likely to feel anxiety and fear. This anxiety may concern their very survival, so that the provision of a safe environment, food and warmth are primary concerns. Things familiar to the child should be present: one of Mum's scarves, photographs, any cherished item, may help to give the child a sense of security. Anxiety will stem from several sources: the crisis left behind, the unknown future and separation from parents and significant others. Being both afraid and separated from those who usually provide security is an extremely threatening experience for a child; this explains why moves in care are so frightening and why some children who have been abused by their parents may not want to be separated from them.

It follows that everything which supports a distressed child's sense of security should be maintained. According to the child's circumstances, this security may best be available in his or her own home, so long as some changes are made, or it may be available in a range of other settings: with relatives, neighbours, foster carers or in residential care. It is now accepted that every effort must be made to enable brothers and sisters to remain together, and that children coming from a particular racial or cultural group should be cared for by people from a similar background.

If children do have to leave their homes, it is crucial that as much contact as possible be maintained with familiar settings and routines, such as attending the same school and the same youth club. Older children may be able to say what their priorities are in this respect; young children cannot, but it seems likely that maintenance of contact with some members of their extended family is essential to their well-being. These requirements are built into the Children Act 1989.

Emotional support

Many children in distress may have lost, or lost trust in, those who cared for them formerly. Some will have been bereaved; some will have been abused by parents or other caretakers; some will have been neglected; yet others will have been rejected. In such circumstances (of threat) children, like all human beings, are likely either to fight back or withdraw, that is, they are likely either to behave aggressively or to distance themselves from others. What they cannot do is to transfer the trust which they had formerly placed in their parents or other carers to new people within a few weeks or months. The lesson that people are not to be trusted can go so deep that it may take years of consistent care before the seeds of a new trust begin to flower.

Such children need to be given emotional support, conveyed by expressions of interest, empathy, encouragement and understanding. In a supportive environment, children's resilience can come to the fore, and their coping strategies can find expression. Carers may feel rejected and undervalued during this time; they need support too.

Understanding what has happened

Children and young people in distress are dealing not only with confused feelings, but with difficulties in understanding what has happened to them. Some of their questions may have answers: 'Why did my mother say she couldn't look after me any more?', 'Did I get ill before or after my dad left?'; but others are likely to be unanswerable: 'Why did this accident happen to me and not to my sister?', 'Why did my mum die?'. Attempts to answer with honesty and gentleness, acknowledging that we have no answers to some questions, will be least confusing for the child.

Devising life story books and genograms are invaluable ways of helping children and young people make sense of the fragmentary and sometimes inaccurate memories that all of us have of our early lives. As Fahlberg (1988) suggests, the life story book, which children can re-read at their own pace, can help to:

- organize past events in the chronological schema;
- aid in children's ego development;
- increase self-esteem;
- share in an orderly fashion their past with selected others;
- build a sense of trust in the worker who aids in compiling the book;
- help children to accept their own past;
- facilitate bonding.

Retaining control

Several studies, such as *Lost in Care* by Millham *et al.* (1986) showed that children were all too likely to have little information about their families after only a brief time in care, and that clear plans for their return to their parents or other caregivers were seldom made at the time of reception into care. The Children Act 1989 is intended to correct this situation by maintaining parents as responsible for their children, and by emphasizing the rights of children and young people to be consulted about plans for their future. These provisions will at least give those whom the legislation is designed to protect clearer voices in the decisions about their future.

The needs of each child or young person require individualized assessment so that clear and realistic plans for the future can be devised with him or her. Almost certainly the planning will not work out as intended, but in the light of events, a revised plan or set of objectives can be devised, which in turn will need revision. The involving of children and young people in planning for their own futures is crucial, as it gives them some sense of control over their own destinies.

Children as Witnesses

As more and more children disclose the events of child abuse and child sexual abuse, so they are called upon to appear in court to give evidence about these events. Until very recently, there has existed across legal circles the assumption that children were inevitably less reliable and less accurate witnesses than adults, and that their testimony was less to be believed than that of adults.

The glare of publicity thrown upon child sexual abuse both in the UK and in the US has triggered a rush of research by psychologists and others into the accuracy of these assumptions. This brief section will draw upon the review of the field by Spencer and Flin (1990), who examined the evidence under several headings: the reliability or otherwise of children's memories; their egocentricity; their suggestibility; their difficulties in distinguishing fact from fantasy; their tendency to make false allegations; and their failure to understand the importance of telling the truth in court.

The reliability of children's memories

Reviewing empirical studies which bear upon the reliability of children's memories, Spencer and Flin concluded that the evidence suggests that this depends upon how children are questioned; for example, how soon after an incident they are able to give an account of it. The most accurate account is likely to be that taken as soon as possible after an event and which is told as a simple narrative.

Children's 'egocentricity'

Regarding children's 'egocentricity', that is, their alleged lack of concern for the effects of their behaviour on others, Spencer and Flin confirm that very young children (four and under) are not readily able to take the point of view of other people. They stress, however, that this is a separate issue from whether children attempt to tell accurately what they experienced.

Children's suggestibility
Spencer and Flin draw upon a range of sophisticated research studies which indicate that, like adults, children can be suggestible; this risk is reduced if careful precautions are taken by the interviewer. These include that the interviewer:
- explicitly tells the child that the interviewer does not know what occurred;
- gives the child unambiguous and comprehensible instructions at the start of the interview;
- explicitly instructs the child to say 'I don't know' if unsure of the answer to a question;
- avoids repeating questions;
- generally avoids leading questions, but if these are necessary, knows how and when to use them;
- interviews the child 'on home ground' if possible.

Children from ethnic minority communities should be interviewed where possible by a worker from their own community.

Children's inability to distinguish fact from fantasy
Spencer and Flin found only limited empirical research material to suggest that children cannot distinguish fact from fantasy. They stress though that young children cannot readily imagine accurately and in detail sexual activity which they have not experienced. They again emphasize the importance of careful interviewing, so that imagined experience may be distinguished from reality. Concerning ritualistic abuse, they report that as yet few specific indicators of accuracy exist and comment that 'professionals who deal with children are keeping an open mind'.

Children's tendency to make false allegations
Jones and McGraw (1987) who examined 576 reports of suspected sexual abuse concluded that 'of the 439 cases where there was sufficient information to judge whether or not sexual abuse had occurred, only 2 per cent of reports were fictitious reports made by children'. Other studies confirm this very small percentage of false accusations, both in the UK and in the US.

Children's understanding of the importance of telling the truth in court
Several studies suggest that children as young as five or six do understand the meanings of such terms as 'telling a lie', even if like many adults, they cannot define the nature of 'truth'. Other studies report that children from six to ten years also understand the importance of telling the truth in court, in terms of the implications of falsehood for innocent people.

The overall message of the review of empirical research material by Spencer and Flin is that, given sensitive interviewing soon after the event, a child's evidence is likely to be accurate. Other studies, using different paradigms, lend support to this conclusion. For example, Davies (1991) reports two differing ways of examining the accuracy of children's statements. In the first, indicators of accuracy were found to be:

- reference to the setting and circumstances of the incident;
- reference to explicit detail of sexual acts;
- a strong emotional reaction by the child.

The second approach for testing the validity of allegations is Statement Validity Analysis, developed by workers in Sweden and Holland. This procedure examines statements for certain key features which are typical of true statements. Davies reports that, for example, true statements typically include detail apparently irrelevant to the main account.

Happily, the courts are beginning to take notice of this evidence, and as video-links permit child witnesses to give their evidence in a separate room, an increasing amount of confidence may be placed in what they have to say.

CHAPTER 6

Crisis Intervention and Counselling

At times of tragedy and major difficulty social workers are much in demand as people who understand crisis and crisis responses. There is however a shortage of research in this field, although the 'post traumatic stress syndrome' has now been recognized as a distinct syndrome (Diagnostic and Statistical Manual of Mental Disorders III Revised, 1987). Crisis intervention is a familiar concept to many social workers and its practice is common to social workers, psychologists and others in the helping professions.

What do We Mean by Crisis?

The original word, from the Greek, was *krisis*, meaning 'decision', but the word nowadays usually indicates difficulty or distress. Glenys Parry (1990), a psychologist who has made an extensive study of the experience of crisis, gives this definition:

The word crisis *really means a point of a time for deciding something; the turning point, the decisive moment . . . We use the word when we are faced with an urgent stressful situation which feels overwhelming. Crises happen to individuals, families, organizations and nations.*

Most social workers will have experienced crisis – perhaps in their own lives but, if not, then certainly in the lives of other people. Although we are expected to be good at handling crises – social workers are called upon at times such as the Zeebrugge ferry disaster or the Lockerbie air crash – how well do our two year courses leading to the social work qualification equip people to deal with crises of this proportion or, indeed, lesser proportions?

Key features of crises (Parry, 1990) are:
- a triggering stress event or long-term stress;
- the individual experiences distress;
- there is loss, danger, or humiliation;

- there is a sense of uncontrollability;
- the events feel unexpected;
- there is disruption of routine;
- there is uncertainty about the future;
- the distress continues over time (from about two to six weeks).

There is no universal list of events constituting a crisis, but there are certain events which would pose a major threat to most human beings. The Life Events Scale devised by Holmes and Rahe (1967) lists the following as being major sources of stress to most people: death of spouse or life partner; divorce; marital separation; jail term; death of close family member; personal injury or illness; marriage; loss of job. Other crises which people with whom we work may have experienced include: racial abuse; discrimination; breakdown of close relationships; accusation of serious crime: child abuse, child sexual abuse.

As we see from Parry's analysis, crisis may strike anyone at any time. A person may lose a close relative in a car accident or through sudden illness. This is often known amongst friends and acquaintances and help and support are offered. Sometimes, however, people may not know about the trauma, and those concerned may not wish it to be known, as may be the case for the person who discovers that his or her spouse or partner is having an affair, or for the parents who discover that a grandparent has abused their young child while babysitting. The trauma is no less real.

Medical social workers are probably particularly familiar with the phenomenon of 'broken identity' – of people whose sense of self is shattered when an especially significant part of themselves is, in some way, damaged. Much publicized is the musician or artist who loses, in a car crash, the use of her hands, or the footballer whose untimely accident leaves him unable to play again. Such people can suffer disorientation and deep despair as they struggle to rebuild a sense of identity without its former cornerstone. Less dramatic, but in considerable numbers, are women who find a mastectomy totally destroys their sense of being a woman, or people whose loss of employment shatters their sense of worth as human beings.

Response to Crisis

Parry emphasizes that crisis is an *enduring* response, that is, it is one which persists over time (she suggests at least two weeks), and the person experiencing it feels that it is *uncontrollable*. People respond very differently to major life changes. Two people might experience the same event, such as being made redundant, but one, with another job to go to, might feel totally in control while the other might be overwhelmed. Similarly, two people may be suddenly bereaved, but one, who has a network of family and friends, may come through as a result of much support, while another, whose life centred almost entirely around the dead person, may feel that his or her sense of identity has been lost. According to

Parkes (1985), the manner of death, characteristics of the relationship and the personal circumstances of the bereaved person all affect the vulnerability of those who survive. A common feature is that the crisis poses a massive *threat* to those concerned.

Anxiety

Anxiety has been the focus of extensive research by psychologists. It arises in essence from a subjective appraisal by the person concerned that there is a threat to the physical or psychological self. Just as one person may be exhilarated by a roller coaster ride and another terrified, so one person might find moving to a new locality a challenge and an opportunity, while another might find it a cause of great unhappiness. There are some events however, which most people perceive as deeply distressing and which are inevitably accompanied by profound anxiety. It is now known that there are four separate systems which mediate the anxiety response, and which interact with each other.

1. *The physiological.* The person's response via the autonomic nervous system. Because the crisis is perceived as a threat, adrenalin is secreted to prepare the person for emergency action. Adrenalin increases heart rate and muscle tension, and overall vigilance and arousal rise. Yet the point of all these changes, intense physical activity, is often inappropriate or impossible.

2. *The emotional.* The person's private emotional experience. He or she may experience intense fear to the point of terror. There may be waves of misery and despair or feelings of panic. In panic the essential feature is a compelling desire to avoid the feared situation, but in a crisis the object of fear cannot be avoided, the terrifying event has already happened.

3. *The cognitive.* The person's thoughts and self-statements. Often the person is unable to comprehend what has happened. This may last for several days or more. The response may be seen by others as denial, but it seems to be common for people to need time to assimilate what has happened. Later the person's capacity to concentrate or plan may be impaired, and he or she may experience flashbacks or nightmares as the mind attempts to integrate the event with previous experience.

4. *The behavioural.* The person's observable behaviours. Often he or she is extremely restless and hyper-vigilant to further threats. Sleep is disturbed, and sleepless nights may be one of the most distressing parts of the crisis experience.

Post traumatic stress

If people are denied the opportunity of assimilating the reality of what has happened to them (such as being mugged or raped or in an accident or disaster), they may experience acute stress subsequent to the event. This is now recognized as a specific syndrome, or group of associated symptoms, which may include numbness and a feeling of estrangement from others, unexpected flashbacks of the event, panic attacks, nightmares and hyper-vigilance. The terrifying events often happen without any warning – too fast for the brain to process fully what is occurring. This means that people cannot assimilate the *meaning* of the event, so flashbacks and nightmares are in essence re-runs of the trauma, as the brain tries to accommodate huge amounts of crucial information by re-enacting the scene. As Parry (1990) indicates, talking repeatedly about the events to a supportive listener helps to facilitate the process of accommodation and recovery.

Response to bereavement

It is now generally agreed (see Parkes 1980, 1985) that there are a number of stages that people go through following bereavement, *although these are not invariable and frequently overlap.*

Table 6.1 Stages or components of the grief response (Parkes, 1972; Bowlby, 1979)

1. *The initial shock and sense of unreality.* This lasts for a variable length of time, perhaps days or weeks.

2. *A phase of anxiety, agitation, crying, going over what happened in an attempt to make sense of things.* This will be affected by whether the death was or was not anticipated, and the relationship with the dead person.

3. *Disorganization and despair.* This may be compounded by a sense that life is not worthwhile. Much support, both for the bereaved person and for relatives and caregivers of the bereaved person is needed at this time.

4. *The beginnings of recovery.* If there is adequate support, there is gradual readjustment and acceptance. For many people, however, there may be a desperate sense of missing the person who has died, and of great loneliness.

People do not, of course, pass smoothly through the above stages. There is inevitably much individual variation, dependent upon the implications of the loss, the coping resources of the person concerned and the levels of support available. In my own experience of being bereaved, the stages were all jumbled up together. Rather than being aware of stages, I experienced waves of tension which rose to a climax every few days, and had to be released in weeping and calling out. This brought some relief, but soon the tension began to increase again. Over the months, the intensity of the waves and their frequency decreased slightly. I feel it may also be helpful for those supporting bereaved people to know that I found I had to cope with two separate trauma: first, the loss or bereavement itself, and all its implications; and second, the grief response which accompanies it and which incorporates an acute experience of pain, disbelief and intense anxiety.

Many people experience a moving forward and back according to personal circumstances, a recapitulation of stages only partially completed, and often a resurgence of the original pain at anniversaries and at other reminders of loss. In addition, however, there are blocks to the grieving process which may sometimes be culturally imposed and sometimes imposed by the person him or herself. Some children are actively brought up to inhibit signs of emotion and to regard such behaviour as weak or upsetting to others. Other people, because of mixed emotions towards the person who has died, do not express *any* emotions in case, for example, they find their grief for the lost person mixed up with anger towards him or her.

I recall well a young mother whose husband had died suddenly from a heart attack, leaving her with three young children to bring up. She felt that her husband would expect her to carry on as usual, so for a while she did so, preventing herself from grieving 'because it would upset the children', but also preventing them from talking about their daddy. The children became withdrawn, did not want to go to school and began to show great anxiety. It took several long talks, in which this pattern of adjustment was gently questioned, before the mother began to give way to grief, to allow photographs of her husband to be set out again and to talk to the children about their father. Gradually, the usual pattern of grieving took its course.

Drawing upon tradition and rituals

Bereavement is a crisis which we all experience, yet in the western world it seems to be far from adequately handled. Holmes and Rahe (1967) have shown that major bereavement, especially the death of a spouse or long-term partner, is the most severe of all the crises which befall people – in all the many communities which they studied. Yet in the West, this event seems often to be accorded only fleeting significance. In some communities, a bereaved person wears a special flower or token which carries multiple significance: a symbol of the persisting attachment between the bereaved person and the one who has died, an indication to other people that the bereaved person is suffering emotional pain, and a sign that he or she should be treated with extra consideration. We have abandoned the black armband in the West; it is a pity that we have not replaced it with another symbol carrying the same message.

Audrey Gordon (1975) describes the stages of mourning within the Jewish community, which parallel those developed in many other cultures. She writes that Judaism enjoins bereaved people to express grief and sorrow openly. In the funeral itself there are several signals for the full outpouring of grief. The year following bereavement is organized into three days of deep grief, seven days of mourning, 30 days of gradual readjustment and 11 months of remembrance and healing. The mourner is thus gradually reintegrated into the community in a way which acknowledges the different levels of grief he or she is experiencing.

During this period specific customs are expected of members of the community which provide a ritual broadly adapted to the needs of people in crisis. In essence both the immediately bereaved and the wider community are given a structure in which to grieve and respond to grief.

Supporting People in Crisis

Parry (1990) emphasizes that professional workers should act to support and mobilize the person's own coping resources, and should avoid encouraging dependency. She writes that, in her experience, there is no rigid set of rules to follow when helping others. She does however isolate three qualities which distinguish effective helpers:

- they have an internal 'map' of the psychology of crisis;
- they understand how help from professionals can complement the person's own resources;
- they have great empathy with the person's situation.

Parry likens the experience of helping someone through a crisis to a journey: there are many ways to help people resolve crisis, not one, and equally, there are many ways of getting lost. She suggests that there are two main dimensions upon which people in crisis have to adjust: coping with feelings and coping with practicalities.

Coping with feelings

People in crisis often report that they 'feel as if their world has fallen apart'. This may be a literal representation of their experience; our sense of identity and sense of security are often profoundly shaken by crisis. Familiar routines and patterns of life are disrupted so that the very nature of reality is called into question. Parry acknowledges the importance of being listened to when in crisis and writes:

We are fundamentally social animals and when in distress there is great value in expressing our feelings to a sympathetic listener. In most crises there is a need to talk about it over and over again, in order to do the mental work necessary for the information to be assimilated. With each telling the feelings are re-experienced, so that they gradually become less frightening.

People in crisis need the support of other people, particularly those close to them. Sometimes support may involve simply sitting in silence with someone who wants companionship – it is not always necessary to talk. The literature has shown that grief has to be worked through, that is, allowed to take its course; if not, problems will continue to arise. The needs of some people, however, may be neglected or even denied. People with a lesbian or gay sexual orientation may feel inhibited about expressing grief for the loss of a partner when the relationship has never been openly acknowledged or because relatives have not accepted the relationship. It is beneficial, even essential, for bereaved people to give way to grief and the other emotions which flood them at such times. One elderly man finally lost control when his dog died. He had 'coped' earlier with the death of his daughter, but his further loss was in one sense a 'blessing' as it enabled him to let go and grieve as he had not hitherto.

Other forms of emotion may need to be allowed free rein. These include, in particular, anger, which may be very difficult to express. Facilitating its expression can give enormous relief. People who have undergone trauma such as sexual abuse in childhood, rape or personal violence, may have been so powerless at the time that their fear and anger lie very deep. The recognition of the extent of child sexual abuse in this country and elsewhere has enabled many people, mainly women, who suffered in this way to seek help by talking of their experiences – often for the first time. Jehu (1988) has reported that enabling women to talk of their experiences, to allow memories to surface and to re-experience the fear, anger and other emotions associated with the abuse, are crucial features of the therapeutic help offered. This emotional release was supplemented by extensive cognitive therapeutic approaches, in which survivors were helped, for example, to see themselves as the victims of abuse not as equally responsible (and therefore blameworthy) participants therein.

People may be prevented from releasing their emotions when others do not accept their feelings or are frightened by the intensity of emotion. This extract from an article by Davis and Choudhury (1988) illustrates the benefit of facilitating emotional release.

On first meeting, Mrs B. appeared bewildered, lonely, distraught, and unable to cope with the problems facing her, including: the recent sudden death of her husband; her daughter's Down's syndrome; her own ill-health; her inability to speak English; her fear of leaving the flat; her enforced separation from her other children in Bangladesh; the absence of a support system (family or friends); and extreme poverty . . . Mrs B. agreed to see the Parent Adviser, who began visiting weekly. At first, Mrs B. cried constantly and described many of the problems listed earlier. She had no one with whom to share the shock of her husband's death. She felt isolated and her feelings flooded out when she met the Parent Adviser.

After some time had passed:
Mrs B. described how different she felt now compared with how she felt before having a Parent Adviser, when nobody seemed to listen, understand, or help. This is not to say that nobody tried; various professionals had visited her, She perceived her own needs as having been totally unmet. The problem was not just one of language, but a failure to understand her feelings, her culture and her situation.

Here is a woman with multiple disadvantages whose coping skills were mobilized by support from a Parent Adviser. The first step, however, was allowing Mrs B. the opportunity to confide in a trusting and understanding listener to whom 'her feelings flooded out'.

Coping with the situation

While accepting that there are bound to be feelings of great intensity, there are usually also a range of adjustments and decisions to be made at, or soon after, a crisis. Parry (1990) points out that people who have been accustomed to coping with challenges in their lives, who have overcome previous difficulties, may bring to a crisis resilience and resourcefulness which are unavailable to people who have lived quiet and sheltered lives, largely dependent upon others. There is increasing recognition of the importance of these 'coping skills' in facing crises of all kinds: severe illness, broken relationships, business difficulties as well as major disasters like fires and plane crashes.

A key principle seems to be *to enable people to feel in control of events* as much as possible – since the crisis may well have robbed them of that feeling, so important to a sense of well-being. This is a clear example of empowerment.

There are two bodies of ideas which are relevant here. The first, derived from social learning theory, was developed by Seligman (1975) and concerns 'learned helplessness'. It suggests that if a person repeatedly experiences events as being out of control and that actions on his or her part have no effect upon events or situations, that person gradually learns that he or she is helpless and gives up trying to exert an influence. This can be seen when apathy develops among people who constantly experience deprivation and disadvantage.

The second, complementary, set of ideas is associated with Bandura (1977), also writing from the standpoint of social learning theory. Bandura proposed that 'self-efficacy' (the sense that one is oneself the agent of change and can bring it about, or can contribute to change by one's own efforts) is a primary feature of mental health. An extension of this idea is that one is in control of events, not powerless or a victim.

It can now be seen why empowerment is such a central concept in all forms of work with people weighed down either by social deprivation or by life events. In these, and other settings, we seek to strengthen their sense of having some measure of control over their destinies. The opportunity to make their own decisions, rather than having decisions made for them, will strengthen people's sense of control.

Ways of empowering people in crisis:
- Being ready to listen empathically.
- Giving them 'permission' to be preoccupied with themselves.
- Helping them say what help they want, and providing it.
- Helping them care for their health: sleeping, eating, etc.
- Providing encouragement: thinking of past occasions when they coped with adversity.
- Taking 'a day at a time', as advised by Alcoholics Anonymous.
- Helping them think through what plan or action would make them feel better: for example, seeing a particular person, going to a particular place.
- Supporting them in implementing that plan.

Counselling

As we have seen, people in crisis need other people. It is to be hoped that they can usually find this support in their families or immediate social circle, but this is not always the case. More and more people are turning to counsellors in the hope of finding help for their difficulties. According to Hopson (1986) counselling helps people to help themselves, or, as the British Association for Counselling (1985) more formally states:

People become engaged in counselling when a person, occupying regularly or temporarily the role of counsellor offers or agrees explicitly to offer time, attention and respect to another person or persons temporarily in the role of client. The task of counselling is to give the client an opportunity to explore, discover and clarify ways of living more resourcefully and towards greater well-being.

Carl Rogers (1958) proposed that helpful relationships show certain specific features: unconditional positive regard towards clients; congruence (being open and consistent); genuineness (being honest and sincere); and being empathic (entering into the reality of another person's world of feeling).

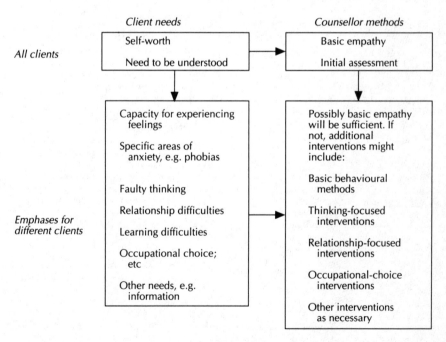

Figure 6.1 A model of counsellor methods in relation to client needs (Nelson-Jones, 1982)

The 'client-centred' school of counselling established by Carl Rogers has become very influential. Other writers, such as Gelso and Carter (1985) who emphasize the importance of the 'therapeutic alliance', seem to be drawing on the same concepts, but using different terminology. Some counsellors claim, as did Rogers, that the client-centred approach offers the 'necessary and sufficient' conditions for people to benefit substantially. Others, including myself, see the warm, genuine and empathic relationship as an essential component, which will sometimes be sufficient to help people, but which will often need to be supplemented by the counsellor's drawing upon a repertoire of knowledge, skill and resources, both his or her own as well as those of the client. *Figure 6.1* illustrates some of the methods used by counsellors.

Towards demystifying counselling

Hopson (1986) is among the many researchers who are trying to demystify counselling (see *Table 6.2*). I quote him below, as I agree with his point of view entirely. He writes:

Training courses can sometimes encourage the mystification. They talk of 'counselling skills' and may, by implication, suggest that such skills are somehow separate from other human activities, are to be conferred upon those who attend courses, and are probably innovatory. In fact , what 'counselling' has done is to crystallize what we know about how warm, trusting relationships develop between people.

Table 6.2 The counselling process (after Hopson, 1986)

The counsellor		
	uses	*helps the client*
Relationship Building Skills	respect genuineness empathy	to feel valued, understood and prepared to trust the counsellor
Exploring and Clarifying Skills	contracting open questions summarizing focusing reflecting immediacy clarifying concreteness confronting	to talk and explore to understand more about how he/she feels and why to consider options and examine alternatives to choose an alternative
Skills of supporting people to resolve difficulties	objective setting action planning problem-solving strategies	to develop clear objectives to form specific action plans to do (with support) what needs to be done

What happens in counselling?

Readers will be aware that there are many different schools of counselling and therapy, and that there is often conflict between them. Atkinson and colleagues (1990) have distinguished the crucial variables which appear to help people in distress, and which are generally common to all the schools.

❑ There is a relationship of warmth and trust in which the counsellor attempts to understand the person and to convey this understanding and respect for the person.
❑ The person is offered support by the counsellor: this may be support in coping with a distressing or crisis situation; support in terms of acceptance and respect as an individual; or support in facing past events or traumas.
❑ The person experiences a release of tension or reduction in anxiety which allows him or her to face or talk about a particular problem or problems.
❑ The adaptive responses of the person are reinforced. In learning to understand more about themselves and any self-defeating patterns of thought or behaviour, the person is given an opportunity of solving particular problems, improving relationships, etc. The counsellor shares any skills or knowledge which may be appropriate.

The Counsellor's Repertoire

Counselling gives people the opportunity to speak freely about their feelings and, as we saw earlier in this chapter, can enable people to discover and experience emotions they didn't know they had. An accepting relationship in which people can talk of their fear or pain will provide great relief and should lead to a reduction in anxiety and tension. However, the effective counsellor will be able to take the process further.

Dealing with depression

A great many people who come to counsellors are depressed, and it is vital that the interacting causes of this are investigated in order to make an effective intervention. Many of those to whom social workers and community workers offer supportive counselling need money. According to Livingston Bruce *et al.* (1991), people with incomes at poverty level are at increased risk for a number of psychiatric disorders.

Other assessments, however, reveal different causes of depression. One study of elderly people found that acute loneliness was seen by them as the main cause of their depression, while a seminal study of depressed women by Brown and

Harris (1978) found that being at home with young children, unemployed and with no one to confide in, was virtually a recipe for depression. Here the accuracy of the assessment is crucial. While counselling may offer relief for depression, it is vital that the counsellor should be able to identify whether the main sources of stress are linked to a 'private sorrow' or a 'public issue' such as access to appropriate services and resources.

Counselling should also enable people to explore the implications of different courses of action: for example, a woman experiencing violence at home from a partner with alcohol-related problems can be supported in her decision about whether to leave him or not. The counsellor can help her explore the range of possible actions she could take, and the implications of each. In essence the fine details of the cost-benefit analyses for each course of action can be weighed up. Other approaches for dealing with depression are discussed in Chapter 7.

Support in times of crisis or long-term stress

As already mentioned, counsellors need to support people to face distressing events of the past, as well as to deal with current problems and crises. Practitioners in health settings, for example, attend to the needs of sick people in life-threatening situations and to the needs of their relatives, offering them emotional support, a listening ear and practical help. For example, a Vietnamese family whose child was involved in a road accident was distraught as they witnessed their beloved little girl losing, day by day, the struggle for life. The social worker, working through an interpreter, was able to help them to ask questions, to support them in their grief and to prepare for the funeral according to the customs of their community.

The problem-solving approach

This method of working has been successfully applied to a number of different situations, with particular success in the field of mental health. Nezu (1986) and Nezu and Perri (1989) used this approach to help people with non-psychotic depression and Falloon *et al.* (1984) used it when working with families with a schizophrenically ill member. Those families trained to use problem-solving techniques in managing day-to-day difficulties fared far better than families in which the person was given individualized help.

According to Spivack *et al.* (1976), problem-solving can be divided into a number of stages (which also follow the ASPIRE sequence).

1. Pinpoint the problem.
2. Gather all the relevant facts about the problem.
3. Formulate the difficulty in terms of a problem-to-be-solved.
4. Generate potential solutions by means of a 'brainstorm': any ideas may be put forward; criticism is deliberately withheld.

5. Examine the potential consequences of each solution. How well does each one solve the problem? Agree on the best strategy/solution.
6. Plan how to implement the strategy.
7. Put the plan into action.
8. Review and evaluate the effectiveness of the plan.

A worker might use the approach in the following way:

Assessment

1. *Pinpoint the problem.* In the course of the assessment, it may emerge that the central difficulty is that the person concerned feels very lonely.

2. *Gather all the relevant facts about the problem.* Perhaps the person concerned has lost self-confidence as a result of recent redundancy and difficulties with personal relationships. He or she may have had friends formerly, but has now lost touch with them.

3. *Think in terms of a problem-to-be-solved.* The worker should help the person to state each difficulty in the form of problem which may have a solution. 'I feel very lonely' may become 'I want to make two new friends to go out for a drink/walk with'.

Planning

4. *Generate potential solutions by means of a 'brainstorm'.* Some examples are to:
- join a women's group;
- join an interest group in a local community centre;
- join a political/religious group;
- join a walking/music/art/sports group;
- become a volunteer in an area of interest, such as conservation.

5. *Examine the potential consequences of each suggestion.* How well does each one solve the problem? Agree on the best strategy.

Implementation

6. *Plan how to implement the strategy.*

7. *Support the person in putting the plan into effect* by negotiating an easily attainable goal – one for which success is virtually inevitable.

Review and evaluation

8. *Review, monitor and evaluate the effectiveness of the plan;* if need be, reassess.

A problem-solving approach is extremely useful in many situations. Recently I met with a young couple having destructive arguments so frequently they were contemplating separating. Neither wished to do so, and yet they were unable to see a way out.

Once a positive working relationship had been established between the three of us, and after the couple had been given an opportunity to voice their exasperations with each other in separate sessions, it was agreed that the desired outcome was to reduce the number of rows per week to one. Together we explored possible strategies for dealing with the situation. These include 'separate', 'refuse to speak to each other', 'go for a long walk whenever a row broke out', and so on. To my interest and surprise, the strategy they eventually chose was to:

- note the precise topic of the argument they were having;
- write it down;
- agree not to argue any more about it (so that the rows did not carry over into other areas and spoil all their time together);
- bring the agenda of topics about which they disagreed to a 'business meeting' each Friday night and talk calmly about how to resolve each disagreement in a formal way.

This strategy proved extremely effective, and was working well at our last follow-up meeting.

CHAPTER 7

Working for Mental Health

Mental health is a field where the boundaries between who may be regarded as sane and who insane are becoming increasingly blurred. Many of us at times experience distress of a marked and sometimes disabling degree, and counsellors and social workers know that concern about our own mental health is a common experience. How then are we to begin to distinguish between the 'normal' and the 'abnormal'?

Psychologists, such as Hetherington (1991), point out that normality may be seen as a matter of degree: that is, rather than there being an absolute distinction between the 'normal' and the 'abnormal' there is a *continuum* between states. Everyone experiences anxiety, but there is a continuum between ordinary anxiety, uncomfortable but common, and panic, totally disabling but more rare. Atkinson *et al.* (1990) suggest that when all four of the following criteria are present, we may feel justified in using the term 'abnormal' in matters of mental health.

❑ *Deviation from a statistical norm.* Statistically infrequent behaviours have been considered abnormal. This would imply, however, that small numbers of people, such as those who never experience stress, would be seen as abnormal. It is therefore an inadequate definition.
❑ *Marked departure from social norms.* While recognizing the variability of social conventions, some behaviours, such as the signs of acute depression, are uncommon in all known cultures.
❑ *Maladaptiveness of the behaviour.* The well-being of the person and/or his or her group is affected, for example, by severe and persistent self-harming behaviour.
❑ *Personal distress.* The people concerned describe themselves as being unhappy or distressed.

Mental health then, is not a feature of people who experience no distress or conflict, but of those who can cope with the demands made upon them (see *Table 7.1*). Just as different people find differing situations stressful (one person

Table 7.1 Some characteristics of people with positive mental health (National Mental Health Association, 1987)

1. They feel comfortable about themselves.
- They are not bowled over by their own emotions – by their fears, anger, jealousy, guilt or worries.
- They can take life's disappointments in their stride.
- They have a tolerant, easy-going attitude towards themselves as well as others.
- They neither under-estimate nor over-estimate their abilities.
- They can accept their own shortcomings.
- They have self-respect.
- They feel able to deal with most situations.
- They get satisfaction from the simple, every day pleasures.

2. They feel right about other people.
- They are able to give love and to consider the interests of others.
- They have personal relationships that are satisfying and lasting.
- They respect the many differences they find in people.
- They can feel they are part of a group.
- They feel a sense of responsibility to their fellow human beings.

3. They are able to meet the demands of life.
- They do something about their problems as they arise.
- They accept their responsibilities.
- They plan ahead but do not fear the future.
- They welcome new experiences and new ideas.
- They make use of their natural capacities.
- They set realistic goals for themselves.
- They are able to think for themselves and make their own decisions.

will find being alone much of the time restful and desirable and another will find it intolerable), so people's coping strategies differ. There is no 'right' way to maintain mental health; but there are a number of differing strategies which can be used to help people in difficulties. Certain factors seem to make people vulnerable to mental health difficulties. A report of the National Mental Health Association of America (1987) notes:

We know that some types of life experiences and circumstances mean increased risk from mental–emotional disorders. These known risk factors include having a parent with mental illness, childhood experiences of separation and loss, mental retardation, foster home placement, chronic physical illness, early difficulties in school, physical or sexual abuse, divorce, bereavement, repetitive and long-term unemployment, poverty and racial or other discrimination . . . Those who experience multiple stressors are most at risk. The risk is not for a specific disorder but for a spectrum of disorders, including depression, behaviour problems, schizophrenia, anxiety, drug or alcohol abuse, physical illnesses or accidents.

Stress and its Management

'Stress' is a word which is very loosely used. In some cases it refers to the experience of being tense, worried and aroused, when a more accurate word might be 'anxious', and in others to the event or person causing the stress, 'My boss is a stress to me', when the more accurate word might be a 'stressor'.

An individual's stress reaction depends on how the person consciously or unconsciously interprets a harmful, threatening or challenging event (see *Figure 7.1*). The crucial point is that the judgement is *subjective*: what is anxiety-provoking to one person is perceived by another as a stimulating and thrilling event. To free fall from an aeroplane, to drive at 150 miles per hour, or to climb the north face of the Eiger may give intense satisfaction to one person; to her neighbour it may be frightening even to watch such things on television.

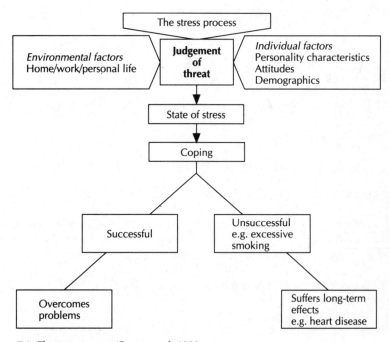

Figure 7.1 The stress process (Cooper *et al.*, 1988)

Figure 7.2 shows that when people are anxious, their bodies become physiologically aroused. Under the influence of the hormones adrenalin and noradrenalin, which prepare the body to deal with emergencies, there is a level, at the top of the inverted 'U' curve, which represents very efficient performance; people feel in control and thinking is clear. When arousal goes higher than this, performance diminishes. Very anxious footballers score fewer goals, very anxious students do not do themselves justice in examinations and very anxious actors forget their lines.

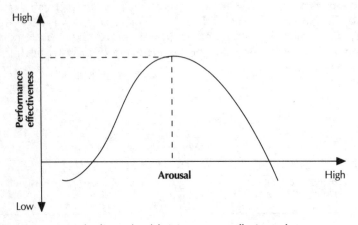

Figure 7.2 Levels of arousal and their impact upon effective performance

Major sources of stress

Atkinson *et al.* (1990) have grouped these as follows:

Traumatic events. We have already touched upon these in Chapter 6 when we considered crisis intervention and bereavement. Studies of survivors of concentration camps in Nazi Germany found that a large number still experienced anxiety associated with the experience decades later. Experiences such as being sexually abused, raped or violently assaulted also give rise to feelings of fear and apprehension which can persist throughout life.

Life events. Holmes and Rahe (1967) devised a list of events ranked from most stressful to least stressful (*Table 7.2*). This table has been standardized with many groups and communities, though not with Asian, African-Caribbean or Chinese people in Britain. While it has been criticized (for example, because items on the scale may be the result, rather than the cause, of illness), it can be a useful resource in practice. Holmes and Rahe found that high life event scores over the previous year (that is, over 300) were associated with increased physical and psychological ill-health. People with high scores may be well advised to avoid situations which make yet further demands.

Table 7.2 Life Events Scale: measures stress in terms of life changes (after Holmes and Rahe, 1967)

Life event	Value
Death of spouse	100
Divorce	73
Marital separation	65
Jail term	63
Death of close family member	63
Personal injury or illness	53
Marriage	50
Fired from job	47
Marital reconciliation	45
Retirement	45
Change in health of family member	44
Pregnancy	40
Sex difficulties	39
Gain of new family member	39
Business readjustment	39
Change in financial state	38
Death of close friend	37
Change to different line of work	36
Foreclosure of mortgage	30
Change in responsibilities at work	29
Son or daughter leaving home	29
Trouble with in-laws	29
Outstanding personal achievement	28
Wife begins or stops work	26
Begin or end school	26
Change in living conditions	25
Revision of personal habits	24
Trouble with boss	23
Change in residence	20
Change in school	20
Change in recreation	19
Change in religious activities	19
Change in social activities	18
Change in sleeping habits	16
Change in eating habits	15
Vacation	13
Christmas	12
Minor legal violations	11

Difficulties of everyday life. These refer to happenings which affect us all: lost keys, missed buses, arguments with family members or friends. It has been found that the extent of minor daily aggravations constituted an even better predictor of people's physical and mental health than the major events in their lives.

Strategies for coping with stress

Social support

There is a good deal of evidence that social support, in the form of regular contacts with friends, acts to buffer the effects of stress upon the individual. Brown and Harris (1978) carried out a major investigation into the factors contributing to women having a depressive breakdown and distinguished the following 'vulnerability factors':

- loss of mother before the age of 11;
- three or more children in the family under the age of 14;
- the lack of someone to confide in;
- the lack of paid employment.

Women who had a confiding relationship showed only 25 per cent of the incidence of depression demonstrated by those with high stress but little support. The way in which social support protects people against stress is shown in *Figure 7.3*. Social support is essential not only for those with whom we work, but for ourselves. We need friends and family members to confide in; people who listen, enable us to give vent to our frustrations and feelings and who offer understanding and empathy.

Stress analysis

This refers to the exercise of pinpointing very precisely the causes of the stress which you, or people whom you are trying to help, are experiencing. Most people have a general idea of what is causing them difficulty, but that idea needs testing. To do so try writing down in exact terms what you yourself believe causes you most pressure, for example:

- never having enough time to do a piece of work adequately;
- people who are late for an appointment and then continue beyond the time available;
- my line manager's critical manner – hasn't he heard of positive feedback?
- the expectation that I will take all the child sexual abuse work because I've been on a course;
- the way we waste time at meetings because Tom doesn't know how to chair meetings properly.

It should be possible to do something about some of these stressors. It might be embarrassing for Tom to hear that he needs to learn how to chair meetings more effectively, but without this information he will have no incentive to do anything about it. If people receive no feedback, they assume that what they're doing is all right.

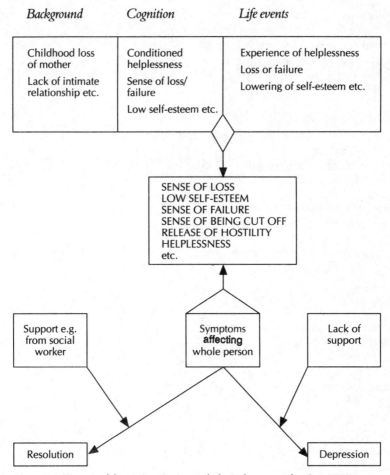

Figure 7.3 Genesis of depression: Socio-psychological aspects (after Cox, 1988)

It is helpful to ask people with whom you are working: 'Within the limits of what you think is possible, what could we do which would most relieve the stress you are under?'. You can't, of course, enable them to win the pools, and you probably can't do much to lift them up the housing list, but if money is the main problem, then you can ensure that they are receiving all their financial entitlements, and you can approach charities and trusts on their behalf. Sometimes, though, the stressors pinpointed are matters you *can* do something about: enabling an isolated child with disabilities to join a youth club; arranging a holiday for an exhausted caregiver; developing a playgroup with parents who are desperate for other adults to talk to.

Reducing arousal

If successfully managed, stress diminishes; if not, it intensifies. Strategies to reduce arousal are of three kinds: those which use up adrenalin, those which reduce its secretion and those which employ arousal in creative ways. Smoking and heavy use of alcohol are ineffective methods of reducing stress in the long-term.

Active strategies to use adrenalin:
- sport, running, swimming, tennis, football, boxing, squash
- dancing, fencing
- mountaineering, climbing, fell–walking
- jogging, aerobics

Calming strategies to reduce the flow of adrenalin:
- ventilating or 'unloading' problems by talking
- relaxation
- meditation
- caring for animals
- taking a bath
- listening to soothing music

Creative strategies to divert arousal into alternative channels:
- making music or singing
- acting, drama
- painting
- creative dance
- writing one's feelings
- sculpture and pottery.

Women and Mental Health

Women use the mental health services more frequently than do men. This seems to reflect the fact that more women than men live to an advanced age, and that many of those who care for elderly or needy relatives are women. In a male-dominated society, women are not merely discriminated against; domestic and other violence against women is common, and social workers will frequently need to deal with this in their work with individuals and their families.

Mental health needs

Perkins and Rowland (1991) in their study of rehabilitation services for people with mental health problems have recently drawn attention to the neglect of the needs of women with long-term mental health difficulties by comparison with men. They found that the women had been in contact with services for longer, but had received a less intensive and a less comprehensive range of provision than did men. Women aged over 45 received a particularly poor service.

A recent supplement of the *British Journal of Psychiatry*, entitled 'Women and Mental Health' (1991), has focused upon the needs of women. Subotsky (1991) stresses the importance of effective services for women. In addition to family planning services, support is needed for premenstrual tension and for the many women who have to deal with infertility, miscarriage or stillbirth (see also Hunter, 1994).

The needs of older women must also be addressed. Here Subotsky highlights the different *meanings* which women attach to the menopause and to major surgery such as mastectomy and hysterectomy, stressing the necessity for these subjective responses to be taken into account. She reports on the value of the social work contribution towards the relief of much emotional, social and family stress. She concludes her paper by stressing the need for more individualized services for African-Caribbean women, for women with mental health difficulties and in particular for those women, themselves under strain, who care for ageing relatives.

The needs of girls and young women
Studies by Rutter (1978) which compared ten-year-old children in the Isle of Wight and Inner London found 12 per cent of the former and 25 per cent of the latter to be displaying some form of disorder. These consisted mainly of emotional disorders such as anxiety or depression and conduct disorders such as aggressive or destructive behaviour. Other studies, for example Rutter (1986), have shown that depression is twice as common among boys as among girls before puberty, but twice as common in girls after puberty.

Subotsky (1991) reports that despite increased awareness of child sexual abuse and the fact that it is mainly girls who are the victims of abuse, about twice as many boys as girls are referred to child guidance and related services. She questions why girls are apparently receiving an inadequate service, and draws attention to two main areas where young women are particularly in need of mental health services: eating disorders and self-harm or parasuicide. She writes that it is now thought that sexual abuse may be an important predisposing factor in both circumstances, and stresses the urgency for follow-up services after discharge.

Alcohol consumption among younger women in the UK has been found to have risen significantly, with the heaviest drinkers being single, employed women under 25. There is evidence that people who consume a considerable amount of alcohol experience greater stress in their relationships with their partners and/or children.

Depression in women
Paykel (1991) has carried out a review of studies of depression in women, finding that twice as many women as men sought help for depression. He acknowledges that such a discrepancy may be accounted for by social conventions which make it difficult for men to ask for help for depression, but highlights the evidence that the group most frequently seeking help are women with children, in the 25 to 45

years age group. This data confirms that of Brown and Harris (1978), who estimated that depression amongst urban mothers with young children may be as high as 30 to 40 per cent. This can have an impact on children and lead to increased family stress. Subotsky (1991) reports the incidence of severe post-natal depression as one in 600 pregnancies and stresses the severity of this disorder and the urgency with which it must be diagnosed and treated.

In an excellent book, *Working with Depressed Women*, Alison Corob (1987) analyses women's depression from a feminist perspective. She suggests that women may be vulnerable to depression for three main reasons:

• their socialization into subordinate roles may result in a diminished sense of their own worth and power;
• the roles and behaviour they have been trained to adopt may make them vulnerable in times of stress;
• they are usually encouraged to aspire to goals defined for them by others: for example, body shape, size and appearance.

Ethnic Minority Groups and Mental Health

Members of ethnic minority groups seem to have fared badly in terms of mental health provision. In a field where there is little certainty concerning diagnosis, and even less concerning treatment, provision and services for people from ethnic minority groups remain fragmentary and piecemeal. In what follows I wish to address three issues: the experience of black people within mental health services; the over-representation of black people as patients under the Mental Health Act; and the lack of provision of much needed services.

The experience of black people within mental health services
The loneliness, distress and fear experienced by people with major mental health disorders such as schizophrenia is well-documented. People from ethnic min-ority communities, however, have an additional burden to cope with: the prejudice and racism shown towards them solely on grounds of skin colour. Westwood and colleagues (1989), in a study of black people's experience of mental health provision in Leicester, examined characteristic reports of people who participated in their study:

Elroy, recounting his life experiences through the courts and in hospital, repeatedly asked: 'Why do they do these things to me? Is it because I am black? White people hate black people'. At his first court appearance the magistrate referred to him as a 'black menace'; later, in secure units and in hospital he was called a nigger, Sambo and a black bastard . . . His experiences led him to reflect on his status as a black man and suggested to him that what happened in his life was bound to his colour.

Such accounts have led researchers such as Fernando (1988) to suggest that racism may be a contributory factor in mental illness among black people. It has been found that racism generates depression and a loss of self-esteem, as well as placing people in a position of helplessness.

The over-representation of black people in psychiatric hospitals

There is much evidence pointing to the disproportionate numbers of black people who are patients in psychiatric hospitals in Britain (see for example, Littlewood and Lipsedge, 1989). The debates continue about why this should be so. Reasons suggested for the over-diagnosis of schizophrenia among people of African-Caribbean origin include lack of knowledge on the part of white professionals of the impact of prejudice, poverty and disadvantage, as well as tendencies to misinterpret as signs of major mental illness the patterns of behaviour which people under acute stress may exhibit – such as disinhibited and unusual behaviour.

There is further research giving grounds for concern. Several studies have demonstrated a disproportionate number of compulsory admissions to psychiatric hospitals for patients of African-Caribbean ethnicity in Bristol (Ineichen and colleagues, 1984) and in Birmingham (McGovern and Cope, 1987). Other studies have shown an over-use of section 136 of the Mental Health Act 1983, which gives the police considerable powers to detain those thought to be suffering from major mental disturbance. The publication, *A Place of Safety* (Rogers and Faulkner, 1987), provides evidence that this section of the Act is used proportionally more against members of the black community than white. It raises concern about the role of the police in using this section.

The lack of appropriate services

There seems to be a particular shortage of supportive resources for black and ethnic minority people who experience difficulties. In view of the many negative experiences which people have had within mainstream psychiatry and the associated services, it is natural that minority groups should seek alternative services sensitive to their particular needs. Developments such as the Mansangathan Project in Southall are making a contribution to meeting such needs.

In particular there seems to be a shortage of counselling and psycho-therapeutic services – or even of people who have time to listen. Instead, there is a heavy reliance upon medication and, in some instances, upon electroconvulsive therapy (ECT). As Westwood and colleagues (1989) write:

People talked to us because they felt a desperate need to talk to someone whom they regarded as sympathetic. Therapy, of course, is crucially bound to talk but no one in this group had ever been offered therapy. Drugs, injections, pills cannot tackle the issues . . .
and we have to start thinking about what can – otherwise we are left with the damning and chilling comment made by Elroy's mother, 'My boy, he just wanted someone to talk to and they electrify him'.

Table 7.3 Variables differentiating [children's] diagnostic categories (Rutter, 1975)

Diagnostic Groups	Variables						
	Age of onset	Sex	Reading difficulties	Organic brain dysfunction	Family discord	Response to treatment	Adult state (if impaired)
Emotional	any	=	–	±	–	++++	neurosis/depression
Conduct	any	male	++	±	++	+	delinquency/personality disorder
Hyperkinetic	<5 years	male	+++	+	+	+	personality disorder/psychosis
Autism	<2½	male	+++	++	–	+	language and social impairment
Schizophrenia	>7 years	=	+	±	±	+	relapsing or chronic psychosis
Development	infancy	male	+++	+	–	++	educational difficulties

Classification of Mental Disorders

There have been many attempts to classify the disorders which people experience, both children and adults. *Table 7.3* shows one such attempt concerning children by Rutter (1975) and *Table 7.4* one concerning adults by Shapiro (1986). Both are simplified forms of classification devised by the World Health Organization upon data gathered from international sources.

If we consider *Table 7.3*, it *suggests* – as such classifications are only provisional and may be improved upon – that six main groups of disorder are experienced by children. 'Hyperkinetic' may be loosely equated with 'hyperactive'). The table also shows variables which are often associated with a given disorder. For example, emotional difficulties (such as anxiety, fearfulness, and depression) can occur at any age; both boys and girls are affected to a roughly equal degree; they are not associated with reading difficulties or family discord; they may or may not be associated with brain dysfunction (such as brain damage); they respond very well to intervention, but if the condition persists into adulthood it may manifest as neurosis or depression.

Table 7.4, devised by Shapiro (1986), shows the main groupings of adult disorder: neuroses, psychoses, personality disorders and organic syndromes. We shall consider each one briefly.

Neuroses

Neurotic disorders are those in which the person retains the ability to function more or less well in the day-to-day world, but whose life is often overshadowed by anxiety, fear, guilt, phobias, obsessions or rituals. The normal level of anxiety, common to all human beings, is intensified to the point where it disables the person concerned. People with neurotic disorders tend to show the following characteristics:

❑ They retain links with 'reality'; that is, they interpret external events in broadly the same ways as other people.
❑ They can manage their lives – though often at the cost of much distress. For example, people with compulsive behaviours arrange their lives so as to be able to complete their washing or checking rituals.
❑ They understand that they have difficulties which others do not; that is, they have insight into their problems.
❑ Their behaviour can be seen as an extension of ordinary behaviour. For example, a person with a phobia of fire is experiencing an intensification of everyone's natural fear of fire.
❑ They are able to recall events which precipitated or intensified the difficulty; that is, they are able to gain an understanding of the problem, which makes them amenable to intervention.

Table 7.4 The medical model of mental disorders (Shapiro, 1986)

Major category	NEUROSES (milder disturbances)				
Illustrative syndromes	Anxiety state	Obsessive-compulsive disorders	Phobias	Conversion reactions	Neurotic/reactive depression
Characteristic symptoms	Palpitation, tires easily, breathless-ness, anxiety, nervousness	Intrusive thoughts, urges to acts or rituals	Irrational fears of specific objects or situations	Physical symptoms, lacking organic cause	Hopelessness, dejection
Major category	PSYCHOSES (severe non-organic disturbances)				
Illustrative syndromes	Affective disorders	Schizophrenia			
Characteristic symptoms	Disturbances of mood, energy and activity patterns	Reality distortion, social withdrawal, disorganization of thought, perception and emotion			
Major category	PERSONALITY DISORDERS (anti-social disturbances)				
Illustrative syndromes	Psychopathic personality	Alcoholism and drug dependence			
Characteristic symptoms	Lack of conscience	Physical or psychological dependence			
Major category	ORGANIC SYNDROMES				
Illustrative syndromes	Epilepsy	Severe mental handicap			
Characteristic symptoms	Increased susceptibility to convulsions	Extremely low intelligence social impairments impairments			

There is abundant evidence that the best way of helping people with such anxiety-based disorders is by using behavioural approaches, that is, strategies based upon social learning theory. One particularly effective approach is desensitization, whereby the person concerned, having been taught practical skills of physical relaxation, learns to tolerate very gradual increases of the anxiety-provoking situation. As I have outlined elsewhere (Sutton, 1987), it is essential that there is skilled assessment, goal-setting agreed between the worker and the sufferer, and rigorous evaluation of progress. It is also essential that attempts to relieve acute anxiety, such as that underpinning ritualistic or compulsive behaviour, are carried out under the supervision of an appropriately qualified practitioner, usually a clinical psychologist.

Sometimes these behavioural interventions are appropriately supplemented with counselling, brief psychotherapy and/or cognitive approaches, but the empirical evidence suggests that it is the trying out of new *behaviours*, and finding that these bring about positive rather than negative outcomes, which is responsible for the improvement.

Neurotic or, more accurately, reactive depression can be seen as a reaction to some distressing life circumstance, and is often associated with loss: for example, bereavement, redundancy, a broken marriage or relationship. Counselling is often beneficial, but a range of interventions used together has been found to be particularly helpful.

Psychosis

Psychotic disorders, of which the most well-known and extensively studied is schizophrenia, are those in which the personality of the sufferer is markedly changed – at least during the period of the illness. Characteristics of people with psychotic disorders include:

❑ A loss of touch with reality in that they are often unable to manage their day-to-day lives; hallucinations and delusions are likely to be experienced.
❑ The 'whole' person is usually affected: behaviour, speech, interaction with others, patterns of living.
❑ There is often a marked change of personality; the person who existed before the onset of the disorder seems changed.
❑ They usually do not appreciate that they are having unusual experiences; that is, they do not have insight into their problem.
❑ There are no *apparent* events which precipitated the difficulty, though closer examination often reveals that increased stress is often implicated.

As can be seen from *Table 7.4* the major syndromes constituting the psychoses are affective disorders (that is, disorders of mood and feeling) and schizophrenia.

Affective disorders
These refer mainly to forms of depression. Catalan (1988) has listed the main

features of a major depressive episode and has shown how it tends to affect people's moods, patterns of thinking and their ability to cope with the demands of living.

❑ Abnormalities of mood:
  – sadness,
  – tearfulness,
  – anxiety,
  – worthlessness, hopelessness, self-blame,
  – loss of feeling.

❑ Abnormalities of speech and thought:
  – slow speech, poverty of thought,
  – agitated speech,
  – pessimistic thought content,
  – suicidal ideas,
  – impaired attention and concentration,
  – mood congruent delusions,
  – other delusions.

❑ Abnormalities of bodily functions:
  – early waking, restless sleep,
  – lack of energy,
  – psychomotor retardation or agitation,
  – loss of appetite,
  – loss of weight
  – reduced sexual interest and activity,
  – constipation, menstrual problems.

❑ Perceptual abnormalities:
  – illusions,
  – mis-interpretations,
  – hallucinations.

❑ Abnormal behaviour:
  – avoidance of social interaction,
  – impaired work performance,
  – self-neglect,
  – neglect of responsibilities,
  – actions in preparation of suicide.

Schizophrenia

The following list of symptoms is drawn from the *Diagnostic and Statistical Manual of Mental Disorders* (DSM-III-R) of the American Psychiatric Association.

❑ Features of the active stage present for at least one week.
  1. Two of the following:
     – delusions,
     – prominent hallucinations,
     – incoherence,
     – catatonic behaviour (that is, rigid postures),
     – flat or inappropriate emotions: for example, laughing on hearing of an accident.
  2. Bizarre delusions (that is, involving factors that most people would see as implausible, such as being controlled by a dead person).
  3. Prominent hallucinations; for example, hearing voices commenting on the person's behaviour, or discussing the person concerned.
❑ Marked reduction in the person's capacity to function in, for example, social or work settings.
❑ Major depressive or manic features.
❑ Continuous signs of disturbance for at least six months.
❑ Not due to any organic mental disorder.
❑ If autistic behaviour was previously diagnosed, additional delusions or hallucinations are present.

Research into the origins of schizophrenia has taken place within three main fields: the contribution of genetic factors, the role of family pressures and the neuro–chemical factors associated with schizophrenia. The study of genetic factors used data from twin studies and adoption studies. There is increasing evidence that people inherit a *vulnerability* to schizophrenia, although this notion has been disputed.

Research has also been carried out regarding the suggestion that parents of a child with schizophrenia are frequently in conflict with each other and in competition for the child's loyalty, but no empirical evidence in support of this idea has been found. There seems to be increasing consensus among leading researchers in this field that schizophrenia arises from a genetic predisposition interacting with environmental 'triggers'; frequently the trigger appears to be stress.

Finally, research into neuro–chemical factors associated with schizophrenia lends weight to the view that a biochemical irregularity is the basis of schizophrenia. In short, it appears as if there is an excess of a chemical known as dopamine in the brains of people with this disorder.

Treatment

Both schizophrenia and major depression are typically treated by medication. The tranquillizers which have helped to cut short the episodes of acutely disturbed behaviour of schizophrenically ill people are called phenothiazines. These are not cures for the disorder, and they do have some unpleasant side effects, but they may enable people who could not otherwise care for themselves to do so. It is important to note that people experiencing psychotic disorders are not usually markedly helped by counselling and similar therapies. They should always be referred, usually via the general practitioner, for skilled psychiatric diagnosis and intervention.

It is desirable for people who suffer from schizophrenia to avoid major stress, and to consider their illness as something which, like diabetes, needs *managing*. Falloon and colleagues (1984) have developed a problem-solving approach for supporting families who are caring for a schizophrenically ill person (see Chapter 6). Whatever the intervention, however, it seems important for people with this disorder to remain in touch with health and social services resources such as out-patient clinics, for as long as they remain at risk of breakdown.

Other models of intervention for schizophrenia include 'milieu therapy' and therapeutic communities. Researchers such as Mosher *et al.* (1975) compared the effects of giving schizophrenically ill people treatment based upon medication, which required a two-month stay in hospital, with the effects of strong, positive support in a therapeutic community over an average of five to six months. Six months after discharge, only four per cent of the former were able to live independently, compared with 60 per cent of the latter. The great difficulty associated with this intervention is its expense.

The major depressive disorders are also characteristically treated with medication. The drugs given are usually tricyclics which have an effect upon centres in the brain which influence mood. Although some have unpleasant side effects, they can counter profound depression.

A further treatment for the most severe depression (which can sometimes lead to attempted or actual suicide), is electroconvulsive therapy (ECT). Despite understandable public fears concerning this, there is consistent evidence of the helpfulness of this approach for a small number of profoundly depressed people (for example, Rosenhan and Seligman, 1984).

Personality disorders

These are far from clearly understood. According to Atkinson *et al.* (1990), personality disorders are 'long-standing patterns of maladaptive behaviour that constitute immature and inappropriate ways of coping with stress or solving problems'. Terms such as 'psychopathic personality' or 'sociopathic personality' tend to be used loosely and in ways which stigmatize people. Such terms should be employed with caution and used only where there are clear-cut characteristics present. Intervention is difficult as people with personality disorders frequently show minimal guilt or awareness of the effects of their cruel or impulsive behaviour. They tend to show a lack of concern for others, a failure to learn from past experience and an inability to form and maintain close, warm relationships.

Unhappy early family relationships, together with parental modelling of anti-social behaviour and a lack of, or inconsistent, discipline have been seen as possible explanations for this disorder. Especially when people are in trouble with the law, intervention needs to be tightly structured. It often takes the following forms:

- establishing very clear goals for work together;
- pinpointing triggers to violence; for example, real or imagined criticism, brooding on past or current frustration;
- working on impulsiveness as a source of difficulties; for example, teaching anger-management.

Organic syndromes

These are disorders which arise from disease or damage to the structure of the brain, such as brain tumours or degeneration. Many instances of dementia, though not all, fall into this category. Some instances of severe learning disabilities are sometimes included in this category. Reality orientation (see p.71) can be used to help people with these complaints to manage their lives more effectively.

Provision of Mental Health Services

When trying to develop health and mental health services for different communities, use is often made of various scales of material deprivation (for example, Townsend *et al.*, 1988). The case has been made (Campbell *et al.*, 1991) that *rates of unemployment* in a locality are 'a simple, up-to-date marker for deprivation and consequent need for health service provision'. So, if you are a community worker or a social worker wanting to offer preventive mental health services, you should consider first those neighbourhoods where there is high unemployment. There is a patchwork of provision in the field of mental health. Statutory sector and voluntary sector organizations attempt to work collaboratively in a field of great complexity.

Statutory services
Table 7.5 shows a range of preventative and post-discharge care offered by some authorities. These are resourced by a very limited number of daycare centres, drop-in centres and mental health 'shops'.

The voluntary sector
There have been major initiatives by national organizations such as MIND and by local organizations such as Shanti, a black women's counselling centre in South London, to offer services tailored to the needs of individual users. Organizations such as the Black Mental Health Shop in Leicester attempt to meet the mental health needs of members of the community in culturally sensitive ways.

Table 7.5 Models of care offered by teams in the community in the UK (Gelder *et al.*, 1989)

Preventive care
- *Primary health care teams,* involving, for example, general practitioners and their colleagues, offer supportive help in the community to those experiencing disabling distress.

- *Community mental health teams,* involving workers from a range of disciplines including psychiatry, community psychiatric nursing, social work and others, provide care in the community. A concerted attempt is made to avoid hospital admission.

- *Specialist mental health teams,* targeted towards a particular area of difficulty, offer help to those coping with a particular disorder, for example, the dementias.

Post-discharge care
- *Mental health workers* who may be social workers, community psychiatric nurses, workers from voluntary or specialist sectors (such as black mental health groups), offer on-going support to those who have received in-patient care.

- *Community mental health teams* offer support to people discharged from hospital following treatment for acute disorder. Such teams are often multi-disciplinary involving psychiatric, social work, occupational therapy and other services.

- *Rehabilitation mental health teams* offer support to those discharged from hospital after a prolonged stay. Such teams are usually multi-disciplinary, as above.

- *Specialist mental health teams,* for example dementia teams, offer tailored help to people in need and their carers.

Mental Health Promotion

Mental health *promotion,* as distinct from the *prevention* of mental health disorders, is a concept attracting increasing attention. It is grounded essentially in a community development approach, and a review of the relevant literature by Ketterer *et al.* (1980) suggests five major strategies employed by workers.

Assistance to natural support systems. Social support provided by an individual's primary group plays a significant role in reducing mental disorders. The community development worker should identify people who enjoy supporting others – natural neighbours – and assist them in this support by providing resources and information.

Community network/coalition building. This is another community development approach, in which the worker seeks to bring together participants from a range of agencies or projects in a locality to foster mental health initiatives by promoting for example campaigns against racial harassment or to lobby councillors to grant funding for, say, a rape crisis centre.

Support for caregivers. This is a major development, where carers come together to call for the setting up of specialist teams and networks: for example, dementia teams.

Mental health education. Here strategies include:
- informing the general public about mental health issues;
- empowering users of mental health services; for example, supporting them in making complaints;
- supporting those who have crucial, but often under-recognized roles in caring for people in crisis: clergy, funeral directors, teachers.

Influencing policy makers. Keeping people with decision-making power informed about issues concerning mental health and its promotion.

Approaches in Mental Health Work

The central issue here is that of which approach offered to whom, by whom works best, under which circumstances? This section will focus primarily upon depression as a means of assessing the effectiveness of various approaches. Clearly, however, each individual will have his or her own special needs and requirements.

Scott and Freeman (1992) compared the effectiveness, costs and levels of personal satisfaction obtained from four methods of intervention with 121 clinically depressed people, between the ages of 18 and 65.

1. Medication: amitriptyline prescribed by a psychiatrist.
2. Cognitive behaviour therapy offered by two clinical psychologists, including problem-solving approaches.
3. Counselling and case work offered by two social workers; this included 'encouragement and listening, help to understand feelings, . . . advocacy on the patient's behalf, arranging social support or holidays and marital or family meetings if appropriate'.
4. Routine care offered by a general practitioner; this might include referral to other agencies.

Measures of levels of depression were made before intervention and after four and 16 weeks. The results are reported in the abstract as follows:

Marked improvement in depressive illness occurred in all treatment groups over 16 weeks. Any clinical advantage of specialist treatment over routine general practitioner care were small, but specialist treatment involved at least four times as much therapist contact and cost at least twice as much as routine general practitioner care. Psychological treatments, especially social work counselling, were most positively evaluated by patients.

This is clearly a very encouraging outcome for social work – one in line with earlier studies, for example, by Corney (1984). It is the comparative costs which are discouraging; any intervention which costs twice as much as another is likely to be unpopular with managers. There is good evidence to support the view that those wanting to help depressed people should use a variety of strategies. According to the individual assessment, specific interventions can be used separately or together. These may include:

- offering social support, or ensuring that it is offered;
- using a range of approaches selectively: for example, counselling, cognitive approaches, problem-solving (see Chapter 6);
- drawing on a range of other services; for example, advocacy, support services, respite care for dependents, and so on.

Group work

Group work is a popular approach within social work and community work, but there is still a shortage of empirical evidence to evaluate its effectiveness. (The major forms of group work are explored in Chapter 8.)

From an ethical standpoint, it is essential that anyone undertaking to work with people experiencing mental health difficulties should be professionally qualified, competently supervised and have knowledge of current research. The dangers of, for example, parasuicide or suicide by members of groups of depressed people are real, and it is therefore essential that practitioners should seek professional support from, say, psychiatrists before convening such groups.

Cognitive-behavioural approaches

According to Trower *et al.* (1988) there are three main assumptions underlying cognitive-behavioural counselling:

1. that emotions and behaviour are determined by thinking;
2. that emotional disorders result from negative and unrealistic thinking; and
3. that by altering this negative and unrealistic thinking emotional disturbances can be reduced.

People often unwittingly rehearse negative thoughts and statements about themselves, such as, 'How stupid I was to do that . . .'; 'They must have thought I was a fool . . .'; 'I've never been any good at . . .'; 'If only I'd . . .'. These thoughts become a habit which over time can seriously undermine the emotional well-being of the person concerned; they can cause profound depression.

Trower *et al.* have set out the stages involved in working to combat this self-defeating cycle of thinking. In cognitive-behavioural counselling the client is taught to:

- monitor emotional upsets and activating events;
- identify maladaptive thinking and beliefs;
- recognize the connections between thinking, emotions and behaviour;

- test out maladaptive thinking and beliefs by examining the evidence for and against them;
- substitute the negative thinking with more realistic thinking.

There is a large body of evidence supporting the helpfulness of this approach for depressed people. Dobson (1989) carried out a review of studies which compared this cognitive intervention with other approaches to helping people, including medication. Among the conclusions were that cognitive therapy achieved markedly better outcomes than offering people no help at all, and substantially better ones than offering them medication. Although this form of intervention would not suit all depressed people, it seems to have much to offer.

It has been suggested that helping people to escape from the vicious spiral of self-defeating thinking is intrinsically empowering. It enables people to understand the way in which they have, unintentionally and unwittingly, become their own enemies, and to move towards greater freedom of action. A child neglected by her parents who has heard herself being described as 'unlovable' may, by exploring and questioning her past, be helped to realize that many people do indeed love her, enabling her to develop a completely new view of herself.

Assertiveness training

There is accumulating evidence that assertiveness, the ability to state one's own views, needs and opinions in a forthright and clear way, is directly linked to self-esteem – a central concern both for ourselves and for those with whom we work. Corob (1987) has shown the effectiveness of assertion training in helping depressed women. Sanchez *et al.* (1980) compared the results of randomly allocating 32 women to one of four therapy groups, two employing traditional psychotherapy and two employing assertion training. Measures taken pre-intervention, post-intervention and at one month follow-up showed a statistically significant difference in favour of the assertion groups.

This view is supported by Pattenson and Burns (1990) who make a strong case for assertiveness training in promoting women's health. Trainees learn to identify situations in which being non-assertive leads to feelings of depression; they also learn to handle these situations and social interactions more confidently via modelling and role-play. This enables them to deal with negative comments from others, intimidation, 'put-downs' and criticism – which in turn enables them to deal effectively with stress. Here is an area where social workers and community workers, once they have received appropriate training themselves, can make a major contribution to women's health and general well-being.

CHAPTER 8

Working with Communities and Groups

The ability to work with and in communities, always the distinguishing mark of youth and community workers, is now becoming a skill required of many social workers and probation officers as well. As society becomes ever more diverse and the gap between the rich and the poor widens, many professional groups find themselves called upon to work on a broader range of issues and with an increasing range of people.

What do we mean by 'community'? There are literally dozens of definitions, some based upon geographical neighbourhoods, some upon social networks and yet others upon the notion of a tightly knit group of people with a common interest – political, social or economic. When I use the term 'community' in this chapter, I base my definition on that of the Oxford Dictionary: an organized political, municipal or social body; a body of people living in the same locality; a body of people having a religious or other identity in common.

Community work is grounded upon a number of values. While there are inevitably differences of emphasis about these values, the following list of propositions from *Current Issues in Community Work* (Community Work Group, Calouste Gulbenkian, 1973) is probably subscribed to by most people who work with and in communities.

❑ People matter, and policies, administrative systems and organizational practices should be judged by their effect on people.
❑ People acting together develop their capacities as human beings. A society
   should give the maximum opportunity for the active participation of people
   in every aspect of the environment: social, economic and political.
❑ The pursuit of greater social equality and justice is possible through the sharing
   and redistribution of power.

Whatever form of professional practice is undertaken, and whoever undertakes it, *all* work is located in a community context. As we have seen in earlier chapters, many of those with whom we work are profoundly disadvantaged people, and their difficulties are frequently those which accompany unemployment: low income, poor housing, poor health and limited educational opportunities. It is vital then that practitioners are able to place their work in the context of the community in which they practise, and are familiar with the issues affecting people's lives.

Getting to Know your Community

Workers are usually appointed to a specific locality: a particular estate, geographical area or recognized neighbourhood. This makes sense; one human being can get to know the issues in only a limited 'patch'. He or she should become a familiar figure in that locality, greeted by passers-by and trusted by the young people.

Understanding power and influence in the community

It is important to identify and, if appropriate, make contact with as many key people in the community as possible. Whether you are employed as a community worker, or as a social worker or probation officer with opportunities to practise community development, there will be people who hold power, formally or informally, within local systems and hierarchies whom it is important to know.

It is valuable to build links with elected representatives, with people in the statutory or voluntary sector as well as with community leaders representing under-privileged people: ethnic minorities, people who are disabled, older people. If you listen and respect confidences, you may not only understand the workings of your patch, but also win goodwill from people who can help you do your job better. More specifically, it is important to:

❑ Learn as much as you possibly can about different communities: their cultures, beliefs and practices.
❑ Attempt to build individualized and trusting relationships with elders and respected people of different communities.
❑ Develop codes of conduct for occasions when people meet together and there is the possibility of serious intergroup differences of opinion. Some particularly helpful guidelines have been developed by the Black Section of the National Association of Local Government Officers.
❑ Be seen to be even-handed; that is, avoid using your own power and influence to favour one group more than another.

Carry out a community profile

Right from the start it is important to glean as much information as you can about the neighbourhood in which you work. This does not mean knowing only the relevant councillors and MP; workers need to compile a detailed community profile of the locality: a basic map of housing, industry, schools, GPs, health centres, community centres, churches, temples and mosques, together with

service agencies like drop-ins. Each newly appointed worker can add a contribution: for example, updating a description of the age profile of the locality, or
visiting parent and toddler groups and playgroups to see what provision they
make for children with disabilities. Walking round neighbourhoods, seeing
where the empty buildings are, where unemployed people go, what the transport system is like, whether the library is accessible to people with wheelchairs or
pushchairs, what condition the public loos are in and where young people meet,
will all inform your understanding of your patch.

Identify the needs of the community

The only sure way of finding out what people need is to ask them. So community workers need skills of gathering and presenting evidence and data. They
need to be able to devise simple questionnaires (see Chapter 9 and the example in
Appendix E), to analyse the results and to compile a case based on evidence.
Whether workers are attempting to address the needs of elderly people within
the Asian community or the needs of travelling people who have difficulty in
enrolling with GPs, any good case will have to be based upon hard evidence. As
groups compete for an ever-dwindling supply of resources, the skills of workers
in community settings in making strong cases on behalf of disadvantaged people
are crucial. Such cases have to be made both verbally and in report form.

If people cannot immediately state their needs, perhaps because they are
unaccustomed to being consulted, it can sometimes help to offer a number of
realistic possibilities, encouraging them to state priorities. For example, if a
worker wants to help young black people with disabilities to develop their
interests, it may be helpful to offer a preliminary list of activities from which they
can choose: for example, black history, assertion training, health issues, visits to
other youth groups, camping, drama, international youth exchanges and so on.

Forms of Community Work

Those who work with communities typically address *issues*, that is, major causes
for concern which affect a great many people: unemployment, homelessness, the
needs of people from ethnic minorities, women caring for young children or
other people in isolation at home, people with disabilities, and older people. The
primary strategy of community workers is likely to be the *campaign*.

There are many forms of activity recognized as community work, three of
which will be mentioned here (see Armstrong *et al.*, 1974)

Community organization. This refers to fundamental forms of community work
such as good neighbour schemes, involving volunteers in meeting social need,
and organizing self-help groups. It also includes community education and
encouraging participation in local initiatives. Strategies employed include publicizing services available, developing liaison between community groups and the
promotion of positive relationships among members of different communities.

Community development. This involves more long-term work than community organization. It is concerned primarily with issues, such as housing, health and unemployment, but attempts to educate people in terms of their rights and entitlements; for example, unemployed people are encouraged to take a political, not personal, view of their circumstances so that they see that they are victims of a situation not of their making. Working strategies include the raising of awareness regarding issues such as the right to continuing education, as well as campaigning for change in matters of deprivation and disadvantage.

Community action. This is a more overtly political approach, challenging the existing sources of power where these are oppressive. Campaigns focus on a range of social, economic, political and environmental issues, such as low pay, racism, sexism, the right to housing and access to services. Similar strategies are used as those mentioned under community development, but community action focuses more on challenge and conflict where it is thought that these will achieve the desired results more effectively than working through consensus and negotiation. Social workers tend to be involved more in community organiza-tion and development, but may ally themselves with those taking community action. Community workers employ all three approaches, selecting the best strategy for any given situation.

Organizing a campaign

It was noted earlier that the focus of practitioners in community work is typically the issue, and that the strategy is frequently the campaign. Table 8.1 shows the detailed stages of using a campaigning approach within communi-ty work. The table was devised by Mark Smith, and has parallels with the steps of the ASPIRE process.

Participating in community groups

When people hear about a community group which bears upon their interests or circumstances, they assess it in terms of its benefits and costs to themselves *as they perceive them.* I once encountered an enthusiastic group which decided that there was very little provision for women in a locality with a large Asian community, so they arranged a morning 'drop-in' for mothers and children at the neighbouring community centre. They prepared well, including advertising in local shops and putting leaflets through doors. When the appointed morning came, seven workers and volunteers appeared but not one Asian mother. The group had neglected to find out whether the 'drop-in' met the needs of Asian mothers as they, the mothers, perceived them. They had not ascertained whether the time of day, the day of the week, and the location were appropriate, nor whether the very activity of 'dropping-in' was something that mothers in that community did. Drawing on a range of pros and cons, the mothers' cost–benefit calculation about attending the 'drop-in' had clearly suggested that it would *not* be to their overall advantage to attend.

Table 8.1 Organizing a campaign (with acknowledgements to Smith, 1984)

Successful actions are usually based on:
- a clear idea of what you want to achieve;
- setting realistic objectives;
- the use of a number of tactics;
- getting access to the resources you need;
- making allies;
- doing the unexpected thing/keeping the initiative.

Step 1: Anticipate	• Build up goodwill, and make links with possible allies.
Step 2: Get clear on the issue	• Get your facts and evidence right. • Be clear why you want to change things.
Step 3: Know what your membership thinks	• Recruit more people who are concerned about the issue.
Step 4: Find out where the power lies	• Who makes the decisions on the issue? • Who or what influences those decisions?
Step 5: Test your thinking	• Put together a 'case', and try it out on sympathetic people.
Step 6: Plan your campaign	• Use several tactics to achieve your objectives. • Never assume agreement: being listened to does not mean support. • Plan but be flexible. • Be on the look out for possible allies.
Step 7: Get the resources you need	• Check your financial situation. • Check access to telephone, secretarial help, etc.
Step 8: Use the 'normal channels'	• Don't alienate people by neglecting/abusing relevant officials or councillors.
Step 9: Lobby/mobilize public support	• Decide whether to work publicly or quietly.
Step 10: Review	• How far have you come, and what do you do next?
Step 11: Take further action	• Work on a number of different fronts.
Step 12: Look at what has happened	• Evaluate your progress against your objectives.

Workers should always bear in mind the cost–benefit analysis (see Chapter 3) and the individual factors which contribute to it. When I state that people all 'maximize their benefits and minimize their costs', this does not refer solely to the selfish pursuit of material or personal advantage. Other factors to take into account include people's values, the well-being of those they care about, as well as personal beliefs and aspirations such as hope of life hereafter or release from the cycle of rebirths. It follows that you should use this understanding when supporting groups.

Group Work

Community workers, probation officers and social workers are increasingly undertaking group work. The term 'group work', however, applies to a great many different forms of activity. These can be usefully seen as falling into four main categories, according to the respective levels of power of the workers and the participants – though there are of course substantial overlaps. This chapter addresses issues pertinent to all these forms of group work.

Therapeutic groups. Here the worker or workers take a leading role, plan the composition and programme of the group and take the main responsibility for devising the objectives and structuring the work of the group. The participants are relatively passive. Examples are groups for bereaved people and for survivors of sexual abuse in childhood.

Support groups. In these the professionals take a less central role. They may initiate the group by bringing people with a common concern together, but workers act primarily to assist participants in exploring their concerns by offering a listening ear and by putting participants in touch with existing services. Examples are groups set up to support those caring for elderly relatives and groups for parents looking after children with a disability.

Self-help groups. Here professional workers may or may not be involved. While many such groups originate with people who have a shared concern or interest coming together, they often find it useful to enlist professional workers to supply information, to put them in touch with influential people and to indicate where pressure might be usefully applied. 'Gingerbread' is such a group.

Self-directed groups. Here the express aim of the professionals is to enable the participants to take over the work of group and to move it forward. These are essentially social action and campaigning groups. A major aim is to facilitate the development of leadership from within a group or community. Such groups have been excellently described and discussed by Mullender and Ward (1991) in their book, *Self-Directed Groupwork*.

— ASPIRE: group work —

Assessment
- What are the concerns/needs/issues?
- Who are likely to be the participants? If you are setting up a group to address a particular issue, there may be some strongly motivated individuals, but you may have to go 'door-knocking' to win further allies.
- Why have these concerns/needs/issues arisen?
- What are the participants likely to expect of such a group?
- Do we have the skills to support or mobilize the group?

Planning
Plans need to take address of a range of concerns:
- The location of the group; consider issues of access, etc.
- Eliciting participants' views on, and agreeing on, the objectives of the group.
- Publicizing the group: the publicity needs to appeal to the people you wish to attend the group. Do some 'consumer research'.
- Financing the group.
- What was learned from past experiences of similar groups?
- How often the group will want to meet.
- Issues of equal opportunity: how will the needs, for example, of deaf people be met? or people who use wheelchairs?
- Gather resources; for example, structure plans/teaching aids.

Implementation
- Welcomes: negotiate ground rules: for example, people should listen to each other without interrupting.
- Discuss the rationale for the group; adapt in light of feedback.
- Negotiate practicalities; for example, time for the group to start and finish.
- Implement the programme, and work towards clear objectives. Ensure that the group aims at simple objectives so that its members are not disillusioned. These objectives can contribute to long-term goals, but should be achieved in the early life of the group. Always offer encouragement and personal appreciation to group members and provide positive feedback.

Review and evaluation
- Encourage participants to review group progress and to evaluate it at a previously agreed date against the written objectives.
- Use this feedback to monitor your own performance.
- Apply the learning from this experience to planning the next group. If necessary support members of the group to take their own initiatives so that the group eventually becomes self-sustaining.

Understanding group dynamics: within-group processes

Group dynamics have been a major focus of research and features such as the emergence of hierarchies within a group and the development of norms and alliances between members have been the focus of intensive study. Newly formed groups often pass through a series of stages which have been delineated by Tuckman (1965):

1. *Forming:* characterized by anxiety, looking for a leader, uncertainty about the task and the situation.
2. *Storming:* marked by conflict between individuals and subgroups, challenge to the leadership and resistance to both the rules and the tasks of the group.
3. *Norming:* marked by greater stability, with the development of a group structure, leading to the recognition of norms and the growth of cohesiveness.
4. *Performing:* marked by increased attention to the task, and the constructive solution of problems.

Forming

Members of new groups, be they student social workers, self-help groups or tenants planning to develop a tenants' association, all experience uncertainty. This uncertainty arises because of the strangeness of the situation. Have they come to the right place? Where should they sit? Have they come on the right day? Is there anyone else here they know? *Who's in charge?* People come to groups with certain expectations which may or may not be met.

The worker's first task is to reduce uncertainty and insecurity. He or she should have prepared the room beforehand, and should be available to meet people at the door. People who come alone, those from ethnic minority groups or those with disabilities need particular consideration in that they may feel isolated or vulnerable. Providing advance information is helpful. For example, preparing a leaflet or flip-chart display for people to read as they wait is useful, and if the size of the group allows it, people can be introduced to each other. The loos and the creche should be clearly indicated.

Storming

If the group is one which meets frequently, conveners should be alert to what may happen early in the meetings if members are left to their own devices; some people can be disconcerted by the intensity of the conflict which may develop. Since people usually attend groups on a voluntary basis, they may be alienated by conflict and stop coming. In a formal group, the chairperson should anticipate and manage conflict; in an informal group, someone who takes this role usually emerges sooner or later.

Dominance hierarchies develop within almost all groups. Argyle (1983) writes that a struggle for status within the group occurs during the early meetings. Once this has been established, senior members can be distinguished from low status members in terms of how much they speak and the notice that is taken of what is said. The hierarchy works by non-verbal as well as verbal means. Note not only the number of contributions by dominant members, but also tones of voice, facial expressions and body language.

Once established, the dominance hierarchy is hard to change, as dominant members resist challenges to their influence. However, less dominant members can achieve change by working together, supporting each other, and insisting that their voices be heard and their views taken into account. In some larger groups, containing ten people or more, alliances or cliques may emerge, especially between people who know each other well. In other, more formal groups, such as local authority committees, the alliances almost inevitably coincide with the groupings of political parties, that is, between people who hold similar views.

If the community worker plays a central role in the group, then it is his or her responsibility to ensure that all members' views and expectations are voiced, including those of people lowest in the hierarchy. If the worker's role is one of facilitator, he or she can act as a source of support and information to the whole group. He or she will know how the group should be organized – with an elected chair, secretary, treasurer and so on – and will also know details such as where meetings may be held, costs involved and transport.

The worker should ensure that democratic principles are adhered to in the group: for example, taking and checking minutes, devising a constitution, calling an Annual General Meeting, and writing an Annual Report. Of course, such responsibilities should ideally be held by members of the committee or group.

Norming

The term 'norm' means a convention or customary behaviour. In group settings, norms develop about group tasks, such as who takes the minutes; about interaction in the group, such as whether first or surnames are used; about attitudes, which tend to be those of the dominant members of the group; and about style of dress, such as formal or informal. Social pressure to conform to group norms is often powerful. Several well-known studies demonstrate the unease which many individuals experience when dissenting publicly from a majority judgement. It is for this reason that secret ballots have been instituted.

The worker can contribute by ensuring that the norms which develop are genuinely anti-discriminatory; for example, by ensuring that power is not continually being exercised by those at the top at the expense of those at the bottom of the hierarchy. He or she should intervene to support people who seldom enjoy power: women, people with disabilities and quieter members who rarely summon up the courage to speak. The worker may pick up cues that there are those who disagree with a decision, but need support in voicing their concerns.

Norms often 'creep up' on groups, so that things are done in certain ways 'because they've always been done that way'. Workers can challenge such norms. Men in therapeutic groups can be encouraged to experience the relief of tears; people with learning disabilities may be helped to make their own decisions for the first time.

Performing

This is the stage when the group becomes productive, and settles down to the task for which it has come together. There may be conflicts, but for the most part these are likely to be storms in teacups, which pass quickly. By now group members who, remember, are still conducting their individual cost–benefit analyses about the value of belonging to the group, are beginning to want some return on their investment of time and effort. If there is still no sign of settling down to business and getting results, there will be further defections from the group.

A certain amount of *cohesiveness* is essential if a group is to work together to achieve its tasks. There are dangers however in too much or too little cohesiveness. If a group is too inward-looking or too long-established, it is likely to be inefficient due to stagnation. By contrast, one which is too fragmented, where there is much mistrust or rivalry between members, is unlikely to be able to give sufficient of its time and energy to meeting group tasks.

This is a very important stage for the group worker, who should support the group, now if not before, in clarifying and writing down its aims and objectives, especially when these may be indistinct. The worker can help group members to prioritize their objectives, from the most easily to the least easily attainable. This enables the group to achieve the simplest of its objectives very swiftly – and, as we know from social learning theory, the positive feedback of success is rewarding and acts to reinforce the behaviour.

The worker acts as motivator to the group, helping members clarify what they want to achieve, supporting it through its frustrations and encouraging it to further achievements. He or she avoids taking over the group, but, drawing on experience, enables the participants to work towards the group's goals despite disappointments and setbacks.

Finally, some community groups may need help in 'coping with political realities'. In times of frustration, group members are in danger of venting their feelings upon the individuals whom they see as having blocked or frustrated their plans. This may be counter-productive. If, say, a local councillor is accused by group members of neglecting their cause or failing to back it sufficiently, and if these accusations are made on a personal basis, then the councillor may well refuse to have anything further to do with the group. Workers may need to explain that failure to support well-made cases on the part of local authorities usually stems from political rather than personal considerations and that local government, under enormous pressure from central government, is often prevented from providing the services it wishes to offer.

Understanding group dynamics: between-group processes

Intergroup processes refer to the changing patterns of relationships which occur between groups, or between subgroups of a main group. Sometimes they are strongly established, as in the shifting tensions between political parties or between religious communities; sometimes they are less noticeable, but spring into prominence when a particular event occurs or debate arises – for example, those who are in favour of, or opposed to, abortion.

In-group and out-groups and the forming of cliques

'In-groups' and 'out-groups' are terms which convey the tendency of groups to polarize when they take opposing views on an issue. Each subgroup develops a distinctive identity based upon one or more dimensions, such as belief system, profession, religious or political creed and so on – and so constitutes an 'in-group'. It distinguishes itself from others who have a different identity, belief system or profession, or who follow a different religious or political creed – who constitute the 'out-group'. The relationship is reciprocal: each group is an in-group to itself and sees those whom it categorizes as different on its own distinctive dimensions as the out-group(s). There are plenty of examples: Catholics and Protestants, capitalists and communists, conservatives and social-ists, even field social workers and residential social workers.

There have been several major researchers in the field of intergroup relation-ships. Sherif (1958) conducted a series of studies about allegiance to the in-group and the growth of prejudice towards the out-group, and also about ways in which cooperation between mistrustful groups can be promoted. Tajfel, himself a Jew incarcerated by the Nazis in a concentration camp, devoted the rest of his life to the study of intergroup relationships. Tajfel and Turner (1979), from their extensive studies, concluded:

The mere perception of belonging to two distinct groups . . . is sufficient to trigger intergroup discrimination favouring the in-group. In other words, the mere awareness of the presence of an out-group is sufficient to provoke intergroup competitive or discriminatory responses on the part of the in-group.

Arthur Koestler (1978), writing of this phenomenon, and the horrors to which it can lead, wrote ruefully and amusingly of his own boyhood experience:

On my first day at school, aged five, in Budapest, Hungary, I was asked by my future class-mates the crucial question: 'Are you an MTK or an FTC?' These were the initials of Hungary's two leading soccer teams . . . as every schoolboy knew – except little me, who had never been taken to a football match. However, to confess such abysmal ignorance was unthinkable, so I replied with haughty assurance: 'MTK, of course!' And thus the die was cast; for the rest of my childhood in Hungary, and even when my family moved to Vienna, I remained an ardent and loyal supporter of MTK; and my heart still goes out to them . . . Moreover, their glamorous blue-and-white striped shirts never lost their magic, whereas the vulgar green-and-white stripes of their unworthy rivals still fill me with revulsion . . . I may laugh at myself, but the emotive attachment, the magic bond, is still there . . . Truly, we pick up our allegiances like infectious germs. Even worse, we walk through life unaware of this pathological disposition, which lures mankind from one historic disaster into the next.

Characteristics of intergroup conflict

The experimental studies by Sherif and his colleagues have been confirmed by other researchers, and there is broad consensus that the phenomena described by Stoner (1978) (see *Table 8.2*) are features of conflict between groups, and of situations where an in-group feels threatened by an out-group.

Table 8.2 Typical developments when groups polarize (Stoner, 1978)

1. *A rise in internal cohesion.*	Group members tend to set aside former disagreements and to close ranks in the face of a real or perceived threat from another group.
2. *The rise of leaders.*	As intergroup conflict increases those people who are more aggressive, able or articulate are given power by the group – in the expectation that they will lead the group to victory.
3. *Distortion of perception.*	Group members' perceptions of their own in-group, and of the out-group, become distorted. Each in-group tends to regard the skill and characteristics of their group as superior to those of the out-group.
4. *Rise of negative stereotypes.*	As each group belittles the other's ideas, the differences between the groups are seen as *greater* than they actually are, while the differences within each group are seen as *less* than they actually are.
5. *Selection of strong representatives.*	Each group selects representatives who, it believes, will not capitulate under pressure from the other side. Each group tends to view its own leaders positively and the opposing leaders negatively.
6. *Development of blind spots.*	Strong identification with the in-group develops, and this tends to obscure clear thinking and the resolution of differences.

Psychologists such as Gilbert (1989) have explained the phenomena associated with intergroup conflict as a response to perceived threat. If threat (real or only perceived) is detected, people become preoccupied with safety. As Stoner (1978) suggests, people who feel threatened by outsiders, be they people of another skin colour, another nationality or just another football team, tend to close ranks; they seek safety in group solidarity. If the threat seems to persist, the more able or aggressive members are given power by the group and the dangers of discriminating against non-group members intensify. People become more tense, more aroused, uncertain whom to trust in the out-group, and the quality of communication deteriorates into rumour. The differences *between* the groups seem to be greater than they actually are, while the differences *within* each group seem to be less than they actually are.

As social workers and community workers, we are probably already familiar with intergroup conflict, and with the way it can work to the detriment of those whom, ultimately, we exist to serve: members of the community. The processes just described lead to prejudice and discrimination, and to the exclusion of minority groups – poor people, black people, gay and lesbian people, disabled people – from positions of influence. The Equal Opportunities legislation has been introduced to check dominant groups' tendencies to assume power for themselves. It does seem, however, that there exists a strong need for safety and survival which, together with learned stereotypes and the pursuit of power and influence, can lead to the rejection and dehumanization of others.

Social workers and health visitors, or community workers and social workers are themselves at times increasingly distanced from each other, unable to communicate with trust across professional boundaries. One solution seems to lie in developing strong relationships with *individuals* in other groups.

Worchel's (1979) review of the research on the reduction of intergroup conflict suggests three conclusions. First, that the effects of bringing people together, *per se*, is as likely to intensify conflict as to reduce it. So if your team of social workers or community workers seem to be increasingly out of sympathy with another professional group, don't take it for granted that simply having lunch together once a month is going to resolve your differences. Second, negotiation by representatives is also unpredictable, in that even if the representatives achieve agreement, the groups they represent may reject the terms; these clearly need to have been talked through beforehand. Third, and more encouragingly, there is substantial agreement among researchers that bringing groups together in a *series* of situations to work towards goals which both want but which they cannot achieve separately, does reduce intergroup conflict. For example, bringing two youth groups who are bitter rivals together to play sport is as likely to increase tension as to reduce it, but drawing on both club memberships to represent the neighbourhood against another neighbourhood is likely to reduce hostilities between them. Most encouraging of all, both real world and experimental evidence suggests that open and consistent efforts at conciliation can make for more trusting and cooperative relations.

Group Care and Residential Settings

Let us be clear what is meant by group care. It has been defined by Ainsworth and Fulcher (1981) as 'those areas of service – institutional care, residential group living (including but not necessarily requiring 24 hour, seven days per week care) and other community-based day services . . . that supply a range of developmentally enhancing services for groups of customers'. Thus residential care, family centres and day centres for elderly people are all examples of group care. Group care is a fairly new field of research, and there is space here to address only a few areas. In some instances, researchers come from disciplines other than psychology.

Children in residential care

The publication *Patterns and Outcomes in Child Placement* (Department of Health, 1991) contains an impressive amount of research concerning children in the care of local authorities. The information presented here is based on the findings of this report. I shall focus on promotion of children's welfare, partnership with parents and carers, and planning.

Concerning *children's welfare*, the authors report clear evidence that most children and young people needing placement are already disadvantaged: almost three-quarters of the families, for example, needed income support and over half were living in 'poor' neighbourhoods. Many have health problems and educational deficits which typically are not rectified while they are in care. Young people leaving care are particularly vulnerable, and there is evidence many of the homeless and destitute young people who are to be found in our cities have been in the care of local authorities.

It is reported that local authorities have not typically kept information about the numbers of children from black and minority ethnic groups with whom they are concerned, so they cannot provide appropriately for them. In an earlier publication, *Child Care Now*, Rowe *et al.* (1989) found that while the proportion of African and African-Caribbean children in care in the preschool and primary school age is higher than white children of the same age group, teenagers from African-Caribbean communities enter care at only slightly higher rates than their white peers. There is however, a high proportion of children of mixed racial parentage in care, especially of preschool age, and these children are likely to have multiple admissions to care during childhood. The authors note some disturbing experiences of black children and young people being looked after in a largely white orientated care system.

Concerning *partnership with parents*, studies show the vital importance of maintaining strong links between the child admitted to care and his or her birth family. This principle is now, of course, enshrined in the Children Act 1989. Concerning the 'leaving care curve', the report notes:

Whereas it used to be thought that children who were still in care after a few months were likely to remain a long time, it is now clear that it is a matter of weeks not months. Most of those who remain after six weeks are destined for a long or very long stay.

Both British and American studies show that family contact is the 'key to discharge'. The emphasis in the Children Act 1989 is towards avoiding taking compulsory measures as far as is consistent with meeting children's needs. The authors of this report consider this a desirable step, but are aware of research which has found few examples of social workers and parents reaching an agreement on the nature of the difficulties being encountered and working together to try to resolve them. Studies found little evidence of partnership with parents. Written agreements are unusual, and it is reported that even where these are used, they seldom appear to specify exactly what is expected from parents during the placement.

Concerning *planning for children's futures*, there is some evidence that the necessity to prepare for the future with children and their parents is now beginning to inform practice in many local authority social services departments. Farmer and Parker (1991), however, found that case files in their sample lacked details about goals and changes which would be necessary before a child could go home. They noted that this could lead to prolonged stays in care. Stock Whitaker *et al.* (1984) confirmed that lack of clear objectives for each child retarded progress and recommended that both long-term goals (for example, fostering) and short-term and situation-specific goals should be identified for all children in residential care.

Selected findings relevant for social work practice
❑ Most children are admitted to care from backgrounds of deprivation.
❑ The level of family fragmentation is so high that practical help is likely to be insufficient, and help with family relationships is necessary.
❑ Young care leavers experience great loneliness and many problems. This calls into question the notion of ever younger independence and suggests rather that these young care leavers urgently need networks of support.
❑ Monitoring of ethnicity is an essential pre-requisite to the provision of services for black and minority ethnic children.
❑ Special attention should be directed towards the situation of children of mixed racial parentage who are at present in care in disproportionate numbers.
❑ Visiting and contact enhances the welfare of placed children and does not increase the risk of breakdown.
❑ Open adoption and permanent fostering should be considered as forms of planning for children's long-term welfare.
❑ Relatives are an important source of family contact, and the possibility of placements with them should always be explored.
❑ Real partnership with parents or carers is based on a shared perception of what has gone wrong and what needs to be done. Practitioners will need to develop their capacity to empathize with the feelings and concerns of parents and carers.

❑ Written agreements are crucial for partnership work.
❑ Attendance of parents at reviews, case conferences and planning meetings should become a normal part of policy and practice.
❑ Continued emphasis is needed on the importance of planning for individual children.
❑ Good planning requires specifying in writing what needs to be done, by whom, how, and within what timespan.
❑ Everyone involved in making placement decisions should be familiar with the research evidence on outcomes: for example, it is better to avoid a child being placed in a foster or adoptive home where there is a child of a similar age.
❑ Better decisions would result from giving more attention to the past history of the child and family.

Many of these recommendations advocated in *Patterns and Outcomes in Child Placement* (1991) were anticipated by the 14 young people and four adults who grew up in care and who compiled *Who Cares?* (Page and Clark, 1977). They devised a statement of 'Things we want to change', which include:

❑ Give us a chance to find a voice and to speak and mix with ordinary people so that public attitudes about care can be changed for the better.
❑ Give all young people in care a chance to attend their own six-monthly review. Give us a say in who attends . . . Give all children in care a voice in their life.
❑ Do away with the order book and special voucher system for buying our clothing.
❑ Help residential workers and field social workers to find ways of working more closely together.
❑ Bring pocket money and clothing allowance into line nationally.
❑ Help us to have a realistic approach to sex education and personal relationships.
❑ Help us to sort out our education while we're young.
❑ Make sure every young person in care really understands his situation and why he cannot live with his family.
❑ Ask local authorities to decide whether or not corporal punishment is allowed in their children's homes.
❑ Find ways of letting us help children younger than ourselves. Give us something to work for while we're in care.

— ASPIRE: a residential care context —

The Children Act 1989 attempts to ensure that parental responsibility for their children is maintained. Evidence that children are in danger of 'drift' while they are in care, makes it likely that efforts to enable children in care to return home as soon as possible, but in a carefully planned manner, are likely to increase.

Let us consider the circumstances of Delroy, a 13-year-old boy with an African–Caribbean father and a white mother, who was admitted to care in a residential setting some eight months ago. His father died when Delroy was three. When his mother became seriously ill and was admitted to hospital for a long-term stay, she requested that Delroy should be received into care, as she had no one in a position to care for Delroy. This was agreed. As no homes with black or dual heritage foster parents were available, Delroy was placed in a white foster home where there were two boys, one older and one younger than Delroy. This placement was not successful. The two boys closed ranks against Delroy despite the best efforts of the foster parents. After a month, it was agreed by all concerned that the placement should be brought to a close.

As it was anticipated that Delroy's mother would soon be returning home, Delroy was placed in a residential children's home. Unfortunately, his mother made a very slow recovery, and it was nearly a year before she felt ready to care for him again. During that time, she met Mr Williams, a friend of Delroy's father, who was now living with her. Although research shows that it is difficult for children to return to families whose composition has changed, plans were made for Delroy to return home.

Assessment
WHAT *are the major considerations?*
Delroy, Margaret Blake, his key worker at the residential home, and Joseph Winter, his field social worker, have a preliminary meeting about the proposed return home. This is to prepare for a meeting with Mrs French, Delroy's mother, and Mr Williams. They pinpoint the following considerations:

- Delroy wants to go home as quickly as possible.
- He has been away from home for almost a year, and during that time he has changed. When asked how he has changed, he says: 'I can stand on my own feet now!'.
- Mr Williams has moved into the household, but last time Delroy met Mr Williams he thought he was 'all right'.
- Delroy wasn't enjoying his school, and he now has to go back there.
- The things Delroy did like at his school were science and computing.
- He didn't like being called racist names at school.
- Delroy quite often 'skived' (truanted) from school.
- Delroy thinks he has fallen behind in his school work, and is upset at missing out on science and computing.
- Delroy liked the foster parents he lived with, though the two boys were 'scum'.
- His mum doesn't have much money, while Delroy has hopes of buying a computer of his own.

WHICH *are the priority considerations?*
1. Delroy wants to go home as quickly as possible, and stay there.
2. Mr Williams and Delroy may not get on.

3. When Delroy goes back to school, he is worried about:
   – being called racist names,
   – having fallen behind in science and computing,
   – how easy it will be to skive from school.
4. Delroy wants to work towards getting his own computer.

WHO *is involved / affected?*
Delroy French, aged 13
Rosemary French, his mother
Roland Williams, now living with Delroy's mother
Margaret Blake, key (residential) worker to Delroy
Joseph Winter, field social worker to Delroy
Mr Mason, form tutor

WHY *have the concerns arisen?*
Delroy's mum became ill, and couldn't look after Delroy.
The arrangement for Delroy to be fostered didn't work out, so Delroy came
to live at the Crescent – the children's home.

Planning

There is a good deal of evidence that children and young people moving out
of care benefit from the devising of agreements with those concerned when
they move back home. A careful plan is worked out between Delroy,
Margaret Blake and Joseph Winter.

Joseph undertakes to work with Mrs French and Mr Williams, exploring
with them whether they foresee any difficulties in Delroy's returning home,
and Margaret Blake undertakes to continue as Delroy's key worker. She
thinks he may feel more anxious than he admits about going back home to a
changed situation, and returning to a school where he hasn't been very
settled.

HOW *are we together going to manage the situation?*
Joseph carries out his part of the plan and talks with Mrs French and Mr
Williams. They are both keen to have Delroy home, and his mother is aware
that he is now 13 and no longer a child. The relationship between Mrs
French and Mr Williams seems stable, and when Joseph raises the topic of the
relationship between Mr Williams and Delroy, Mr Williams says he will 'play
it by ear'. He says he will not put up with nonsense from Delroy and that
Delroy must not be rude to him. Joseph explains that he will be visiting
Delroy's school to talk to the form tutor, and invites them both to a meeting
at the Crescent the following week when all concerned can discuss the
arrangements and come to an agreement about details.

At the family meeting, Joseph explains that they want to enable Delroy to
return home and to school as smoothly as possible. The policy of the Social

Contracts in One-to-one or Family Work

This form to be completed by the worker in discussion with the client and the family. It is all-purpose and can be adapted to a wide range of situations.

A. The agreement

This agreement is drawn up between:

1. Delroy French   3. Roland Williams

2. Rosemary French (mother) 4. Margaret Blake (key worker in residential setting)

and Joseph Winter (field) worker from: ....

Agency: Middleshire Social Services Dept.

Address: Park House, Southampton Road, Middleton   Telephone no: 24719

B. What we are trying to do together

We have talked about what we can work towards together, and agree that our goals are to:

1. To enable Delroy to live at home on a permanent basis.

2. To develop a positive relationship between Delroy, his mother & Mr Williams.

3. To ensure that Delroy attends school daily.

4. To ensure that Delroy is not subjected to racism/bullying.

5. To support Delroy's interests in science & computing.

C. To work towards these goals

The worker (Joseph) agrees to:

1. meet with Delroy each Tues. at 5 p.m. & with the whole family fortnightly.

2. talk to Delroy's form tutor about Delroy's return to school.

3. talk to the science/computing teacher about Delroy's interests.

The following members of the family agree to:

First person (name) Delroy

1. meet Joseph each Tues. at 5p.m. at a place Delroy chooses.
2. attend school daily, and to remain there after registration.
3. note any instances of bullying or racist remarks & report them.
4. say hello to Mr williams each day & not ignore him.

Second person (name) Rosemary French (mother)

1. tell Delroy she is pleased with him each day he attends school.
2. give Delroy money weekly for his personal expenses (not food).
3. read any homework Delroy asks her to & say what she likes about it before suggesting improvements.

Third person (name) ROLAND WILLIAMS

1. say hello to Delroy each day.
2. speak calmly to Delroy when he asks him to do something.
3. thank Delroy if he does what he is asked, for example, helps clear up.

Fourth person (name) Eric Mason (the form tutor)

1. spend a few minutes each day looking at Delroy's work with him.
2. take up with the Head any instances of bullying or racism, and see they are dealt with.
3. encourage Delroy to take further his interests in science and computing.

D. Other points to be noted

The above agreement is to be reviewed every ....2.... weeks.

The above agreement can be changed if everyone agrees. Margaret Blake, Key worker at the Crescent, will send a card to Delroy each week & keep in touch.

Signed: Delroy French   Signed: R. Williams

Signed: Rosemary French   Signed: Eric Mason

Date: March 21st

Services Department is to encourage any child who had been in care for more than a few weeks to make some introductory visits before returning home. Everyone seems agreeable to this arrangement but Delroy says he wants to get things settled as soon as possible.

Joseph and Margaret then introduce the idea of drawing up a written agreement to make it clear exactly what everyone was trying to do, and what their personal contribution will be to making things work. Mrs French looks a bit bewildered, but says she will go along with anything to make things work. The agreement on page 174 specifies the objectives, based on Delroy's needs, which were negotiated.

Implementation

As the objectives for Delroy's move home and each person's contribution towards them have already been agreed, implementation is relatively straightforward. It is agreed that Delroy shall spend two consecutive weekends at home before making the full move.

The plan is put into action. After the second weekend, Delroy is very reluctant to return to the Crescent. At the third weekend, he moves permanently. He starts school, first for a day at a time, then for two days consecutively and finally full time. When he meets Joseph the first Tuesday, he is still unsettled, but says he is trying to keep to the agreement. Over the next three weeks, Joseph supports all those involved to keep their parts of the bargain. There are some problems, and some tensions between Delroy and Mr Williams, but Joseph gives support and encouragement to them both, and reminds them that Delroy's future is at stake. Two months later, Delroy is still at home, and still attending school.

Review and Evaluation

All those cooperating in Delroy's move come together on the agreed date, two months after the initial contract was signed, to evaluate progress. They have been meeting fortnightly with Joseph Winter, as agreed. They use the original objectives as the basis for the evaluation.

Objective	*Evidence of attainment – or not*
1. To enable Delroy to live at home on a permanent basis.	Delroy is still living at home. He went missing one weekend, when he went to Blackpool with some mates without telling anyone, but got back before the alarm was raised.
2. To develop a positive relationship between Delroy, his mother and Mr Williams.	A record of family arguments shows three big arguments (lasting more than five minutes) in the first month, but only one in the second month. Things are moving in the desired direction.

3. To ensure that Delroy attends school on a daily basis.

Some difficulties here. Delroy missed school for two days, after being involved in a fight.

4. To ensure that Delroy is not subjected to bullying or racism.

The fight was caused by Delroy being called names. The form tutor took this up, and the name caller was dealt with by the Head. Delroy is now back in school.

5. To support Delroy's interest in science and computing.

Good success here. Delroy has joined the computer club.

A plan is made for a further meeting in two months' time.

Young offenders in residential and community settings

Research both in the United States and in Britain has shown extremely disappointing results concerning the therapeutic treatment of young offenders in residential settings. There have been no significant differences in reconviction rates between those in therapeutic communities and those subjected to a more paternalistic regime. In fact there is little evidence at all that residentially-based intervention, including short, sharp shocks in penal institutions, achieve the goal of deterring young people from offending (Thornton *et al.* 1984).

Romig (1978), in an early review of effective and ineffective interventions with young offenders, devised the following lists.

Summary of approaches that have consistently failed to rehabilitate:
- Casework.
- Direct services.
- Diagnosis and recommendations only.
- Discussion groups.
- Use of behavioural approaches for performance of complex behaviours.
- Manipulating what teachers expect of their pupils.
- School attendance alone.
- Job placement.
- Vocational training.
- Occupational orientation and work programmes.
- Field trips: camping.
- Group counselling.
- Individual psychotherapy.
- Family therapy.

Summary of approaches that consistently achieved favourable rehabilitation results:
- Behavioural approaches for simple behaviours.
- Involving the youths in setting their own goals.
- Differential reinforcement.
- Specificity for rehabilitation goals.
- Education when it utilized:
  - individualized diagnosis;
  - specific learning goal;
  - individualized programme based on relevant material;
  - basic academic skills;
  - breaking complex skills into simpler ones;
  - rewarding attention and persistence initially;
  - differential reinforcement of learning performance.
- Job training with supportive educational training.
- Training in job advancement skills.
- Training in systematic career decision-making skills.
- Educational programmes that culminate in a qualification.
- Follow-up help after job placement.
- Group therapy with a teaching focus.
- Individual counselling that included the following ingredients:
  - counselling to get input from youths on problems;
  - diagnosis of the problem and the problem setting;
  - setting behavioural goal;
  - practising new behaviour in the problem setting;
  - the staff member who provided the counselling directly observing the youths in the problem setting.
  - evaluating and modifying goals in subsequent counselling sessions.
- Family treatment that focused on improving the communication skills of the family.
- Parent training in problem-solving and disciplining skills.

It is apparent from these lists that the approaches which Romig found to be consistently effective can in many cases be described in terms of social learning theory and a behavioural approach. This has clear implications for practice. It is hard to understand why, rather than persist with methods of dealing with offending which have been demonstrated as ineffective, such as locking up young people at an ever earlier age, politicians do not base intervention on methods of working with offenders which have research support. The findings reported by Romig have not been systematically implemented, and yet more recent studies support the relevance of approaches based upon social learning theory for the prevention of offending.

In the Cambridge Study of Delinquent Development, Farrington (1990) followed up 411 London males from age eight to age 32. Offending showed strong continuity from childhood to adulthood. The most important predictors of offending at age eight to 11 were: socio-economic deprivation; poor parent-ing; family deviance; school problems; hyperactivity-impulsivity-attention deficit; anti-social child behaviour.

Farrington concluded that the most helpful methods of preventing offending were behavioural parent training and preschool intellectual enrichment programmes. Although modest steps are being taken to develop methods of working with young children based on the Highscope nursery programme found to be effective in Canada as a means of preventing delin-quency, behavioural parent training has barely begun to be recognized. None of these approaches is at odds with attempts to improve the socio-economic circumstances of deeply disadvantaged people; the approaches are complementary.

Recent research efforts in the field of offending have focused upon analysing large numbers of studies designed to discourage young people from offending – an approach called 'meta-analysis'. The best known, that by Lipsey (1992), analysed the data from over 400 studies. From this type of large-scale analysis, conclusions can be drawn about whether intervention works, and about what type of intervention works best in what setting. Hollin (1993) has summarized the findings from Lipsey's work; the list below outlines the factors that character-ize intervention programmes that show a substantial effect in terms of a reduction in offending.

1. Indiscriminate targeting of treatment programmes is counterproductive in reducing recidivism: important predictors of success are that medium to high risk offenders should be selected, and that programmes should focus on criminogenic areas (variables concerned with the crime, not those concerned with the offender).
2. The type of treatment programme is important: more structured and focused treatments (e.g. behavioural, skill-orientated) and multimodal treatments seem to be more effective than the less structured and focused approaches, e.g. counselling.
3. The most successful studies, while behavioural in nature, include a cognitive component in order to focus on the 'attitudes, values, and beliefs that support anti-social behaviour'.
4. With respect to the type and style of service . . . some therapeutic approaches are not suitable for general use with offenders. Specifically, psychodynamic and nondirective client-centered therapies are to be avoided.
5. Treatment programmes conducted in the community have a stronger effect on delinquency than residential programmes.
6. The most effective programmes are carried out by trained staff and the treatment initiators are involved in all the operational phases of the treatment programmes.
7. Effective programmes include work with the families of young offenders.

Group homes for people with learning disability

Much effort is being devoted to attempts to 'normalize' the lives of people with learning disabilities, that is, to enable them to live full and 'ordinary' lives. It has been accepted that most people with learning disabilities have far greater potential for development and self-direction than they often attain, and one major step has been the development of group homes in the community for those with learning disabilities. For example, the authors of the influential publication, *An Ordinary Life* (King's Fund, 1980) have demonstrated how a range of forms of group care for people with learning disabilities can be offered according to the 'core and cluster' principle (see *Figure 8.1*).

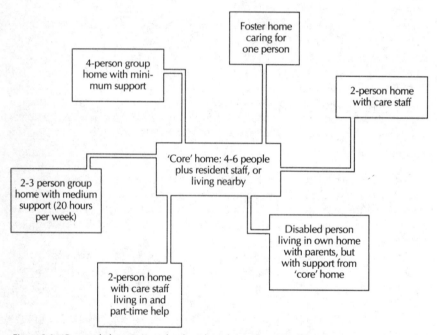

Figure 8.1 'Core and cluster' principle of residential provision (King's Fund, 1980)

Psychologists have made two particular contributions to enabling people with learning disabilities to undertake independent or semi-independent living. The first has been in the area of assessment and individualized skills training, and the second in that of the evaluation of different types of group care regimes. In terms of assessment, psychologists, working with other colleagues, have made a major contribution in enabling people with learning disabilities to acquire repertoires of the skills needed for independent living: self care, cleaning, shopping and independent travel. These can be taught by means of individually tailored programmes within a social learning theory framework.

In terms of evaluation studies, Malin (1983) compared the progress of 24 residents living in six group homes, who received only part-time support from home helps and social workers, with that of 24 others who lived with care staff in local authority hostels. Residents in both settings were assessed on a range of measures at the start of the study and again at the end. Results indicated that group home residents scored higher than hostel residents in several areas: handling money, budgeting, language and concept development and self-care skills. Previous residential placement did not prove to be a decisive influence; several residents who made the most progress had spent ten or more years in hospital.

Group homes for elderly people

There is space here to consider only two contributions from psychology: *reality orientation therapy* and *goal planning approaches*.

Reality orientation therapy has emerged from substantial research evidence that many elderly people lose, or apparently lose, some of their cognitive faculties through lack of appropriate stimulation and activity, both in group care settings and at home. Holden and Woods (1988) have shown in their work that many confused elderly people can, with carefully devised materials appropriate to their needs, regain significant command of their cognitive faculties and that this improvement persists. For example, several confused elderly people in a group care setting were able to discuss lucidly their memories of and feelings about the Second World War when photographs and newspapers from that time were brought out. Other strategies of orienting them to reality proved effective in both the short and long-term, and psychologists are now advising a number of group care institutions upon ways of maintaining the cognitive faculties of elderly people.

Other psychologists have been addressing the task of maintaining elderly people's skills in group care settings. Care staff, with many people to care for, may not have the time to help people dress themselves; it may be more convenient to dress them instead. The contribution of workers like Barrow-clough and Fleming (1985) has been to devise means of setting goals *with* elderly people about skills which they would like to regain, such as preparing a simple meal for themselves rather than eating all their meals in a communal dining room. Again, the approach is individually tailored to the needs of the particular person.

Group Care: A Systems Perspective

To conclude, it is appropriate to point out that a group care setting is essentially a system with complex inter-relationships. It may be useful to recapitulate so that those who choose to work in group care may not be surprised or distressed when difficulties occur.

❏ *Hierarchies*, both formal and informal, develop. Alongside the formal hierarchy of the institution, the line management, there may well be informal hierarchies with a dominant individual at their head. If hierarchies clash, conflict ensues.
❏ *In-groups and out-groups develop*. This could be a problem in settings in which teams of staff work in rotas. Ensuring that the well-being of residents remains the priority calls for superb management and/or staff members with great self-discipline.
❏ *Powerful norms develop*. In group care certain ways of doing things are bound to emerge and these are likely to be hard for a newcomer to change. People become set in their ways, and only a powerful person who is prepared to insist on change and see this through will have a significant impact.

Community Care

This is *not* a form of community work, but is introduced here deliberately in order to distinguish it from all the other terms using 'community'. The National Health Service and Community Care Act 1990 introduced legislation which requires local authorities to rethink their approach to arranging and providing care.

Care management and assessment constitutes one integrated process for identifying and addressing the needs of individuals within available resources recognising that these needs are unique to the individual concerned. For this reason, care management and assessment emphasise adapting services to needs rather than fitting people into existing services.

'Community care' then is about looking after people's personal needs in the context of the community – a very different concept from 'community work'. *Figure 8.2* shows the process of care management and assessment.

The needs-led approach

The whole thrust of assessment in community care is that it should be needs-led – as perceived by users in consultation with caregivers and other relevant agencies rather than services-led – as perceived by those who offer the service.

As noted by authors of the materials on care management and assessment (Department of Health/Social Services Inspectorate, 1991), need is an individual and changing concept, the definition of which will vary over time as legislation, policies, patterns of demand and resources change. Thus, while a 'needs-led' approach is constantly advocated, the term is never defined – indeed it is acknowledged that the concept of 'need' is essentially personal, impossible to fix! This opens the door wide to bitter rivalries for resources, not least between those leaving institutional care and their families and those already struggling to cope in the community.

In an attempt to clarify the term, the authors assert that need is a multi-faceted concept which can be sub-divided into six broad categories:

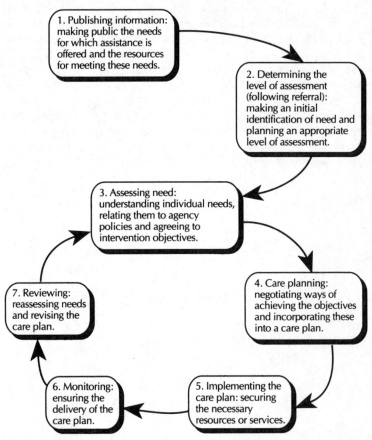

1. Publishing information: making public the needs for which assistance is offered and the resources for meeting these needs.

2. Determining the level of assessment (following referral): making an initial identification of need and planning an appropriate level of assessment.

3. Assessing need: understanding individual needs, relating them to agency policies and agreeing to intervention objectives.

4. Care planning: negotiating ways of achieving the objectives and incorporating these into a care plan.

5. Implementing the care plan: securing the necessary resources or services.

6. Monitoring: ensuring the delivery of the care plan.

7. Reviewing: reassessing needs and revising the care plan.

Figure 8.2 The process of care management (Department of Health/Social Services Inspectorate, 1991)

- personal/social care;
- health care;
- accommodation;
- finance;
- education/employment/leisure;
- transport/access.

The new procedure should consist of two stages: assessment of need, and relating assessed needs to resources. These two stages will be coordinated into an *individual care plan*, of which each user is to be given a copy. This will specify:

- the needs to be met;
- the services to be provided and who will pay for them;
- the outcomes to be achieved;
- the means of measuring outcomes.

While one can only approve of the intention to provide this individualized service, major flaws are already emerging, in addition to those arising from the imprecision of the concept of 'need'. First, the rules and responsibilities of purchasers/commissioners and providers of services are not clearly defined or differentiated; this can lead to acute conflict, along in-group/out-group lines, as care assessors and care managers dispute the boundaries and responsibilities of their roles. Second, there are large numbers of people, for example, people with learning disabilities and some older people, who may not be in a position to make informed choices; they may receive services which *others* think suitable for them. Third, as demand increases, who is to provide the money to pay for all the highly individual interpretations of need?

CHAPTER 9

Continuing Professional Development

The characteristic course of education and training in social work in Britain lasts two years. About half that time is rightly devoted to practice in the field; this leaves about one year in university or college for the formal teaching of the syllabus in law, sociology, psychology, social policy and social work studies. To be sure, this is supplemented by the teaching of practitioners in field settings, and by students' own reading and writing, but the situation is all too clear: it is impossible to cram more than a small proportion of what students need to know into their programmes of study and work. No doubt each profession makes the same claim: as knowledge and understanding of issues proliferate, as legislation becomes tighter and as resources diminish, so the demands upon practitioners become ever greater. Just like lawyers, doctors and pharmacists, social workers must take active steps to take forward their own professional development.

We saw a concerted attempt to advance professional training with the publication of the Children Act 1989 and its implementation. Social workers all over the country undertook further training to bring themselves up-to-date with the Act and its implications. What is needed are regular up-dating sessions for social workers in each of the contributory disciplines – not just in law.

The particular contribution of psychology has been in the field of research; there is almost no field of practice within social work where research by psychologists has not been undertaken. Results from research in chemistry, physics, engineering and the 'hard' sciences are being published in hundreds of journals which are read by workers in those fields all over the world. The same is certainly true of sociology and psychology and is beginning to be true of social work. In furthering our professional development, we are responsible for keeping abreast of the work of researchers in the UK and abroad.

To illustrate the central importance of research within social work, let me highlight the part played by the publication *Social Work Decisions in Child Care* (DHSS, 1985) in influencing the form of the Children Act 1989. This publication drew upon nine inter-related studies which highlighted how children received into care tended to 'drift' and to lose contact with their families. The Children Act 1989 was framed in part so as to prevent this loss of contact, and to emphasize the continuing responsibility of parents for their children.

Becoming Research Oriented

To think in a research-oriented way is a skill, like any other, to be acquired with practice. Social workers and community workers are turning more and more to evidence to support their own work; local authorities are beginning to keep detailed records of their clients in terms of their number, gender, ethnic background, as well as the nature of the services offered. Far more detailed records are being kept of the numbers of children in care, and in what form of care.

There was a time when using scales, numbers and records as the basis for activity within counselling or social work, or even as an adjunct to these skills, was unacceptable to many practitioners. Even now, many workers shirk or mistrust data collection, regarding the gathering of evidence about, for example, the effectiveness of their work as a deliberate attempt to devalue their practice – rather than an attempt to *demonstrate accountability*. The general public are now far more familiar with scales, checklists and gathering numerical information than was formerly the case. Who has not filled in a chart or questionnaire in a popular magazine to assess your personality characteristics, assertiveness or creativity?

Whether workers are comfortable with numbers or not, the time has come when practice must take account of *evidence*. Using simple scales and counts of activities in no way devalues practice: it enhances it by grounding it in evidence. Sometimes workers will need to set up more formal studies in order to solve particular problems or to enhance their own body of knowledge.

Research in Psychology

Psychology, despite being a young science, has been able to make use of the methods of investigation developed by the older, mathematically based sciences, and is having considerable success in introducing a disciplined way of looking at our world and ourselves. The aim of science is to provide new and useful information in the form of verifiable data: data obtained under conditions such that other qualified people obtain the same results under the same conditions. The task calls for orderliness and precision in investigating relationships.

In an attempt to be as accurate as possible in their research, psychologists need to convey exactly what they mean when they use a term. They are trained to be aware that a simple word such as 'learn' may be understood in many different ways, and that bitter disputes and factions can arise from such misunderstandings. Thus within experimental psychology, terms and concepts are often given an 'operational definition', that is, an exact description of the phenomenon under investigation, how it is to be recognized and how it is to be measured – so that there shall be as little room as possible for confusion.

For example, it is not uncommon to find people described in case records as 'aggressive'. This is a very general term, and might refer to the fact that the person concerned is reported to have hit another person, that his vocabulary contains many swear words, or that he spoke in a raised voice on a particular occasion. In order to reduce the number of possible interpretations, a definition of

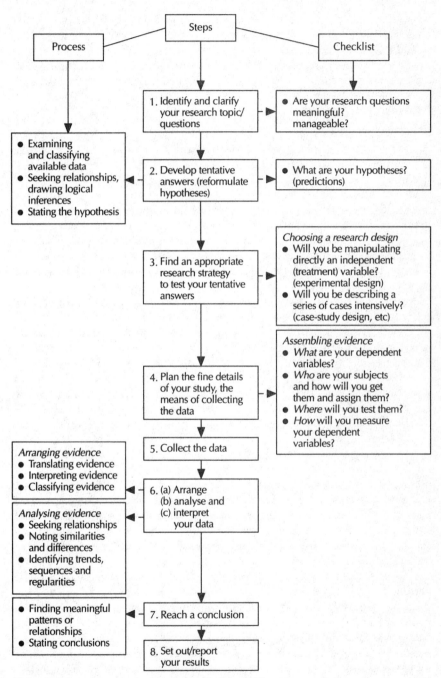

Figure 9.1 Flow chart of research processes (Herbert, 1990)

'aggression' might be: that the person in question is seen to *hit, push, punch, or head-butt another person* – and only this. Only these behaviours and no others, would serve as evidence for aggression in this study. This is the kind of precision which courts are increasingly looking for from social workers and probation officers. It allows *counts* or *measurements* of instances of aggression to be made.

The research process

Herbert (1990) has written an accessible guide to doing research in the helping professions. It will not be possible here to examine this process fully, but a brief description of the basic stages (see *Figure 9.1*) and problems concerned with research will be given.

Before embarking on any study, you need to identify clearly your research question. Only then can you begin to generate hypotheses for your study. A hypothesis is a statement about the relationship between two or more variables, a proposition or assumption whose accuracy has not yet been tested. For example, your hypothesis might be that boys are more likely than girls to become ill in childhood. The study you are about to embark on should provide evidence which either supports or does not support your hypothesis.

You then need to choose an appropriate strategy to address your specific research problem. There are a number of different types of research design. The hypothesis that boys are more likely than girls to become ill in childhood would be grounded in descriptive research in order to provide accurate quantitative information about the numbers of boys and girls who do in fact become ill.

Other methods are grounded in an experimental approach. The studies described by Hollin (1993) where the data was subjected to meta-analysis by Lipsey (1992) (see Chapter 8) were experimental studies, in that each study described an experiment to examine whether a given type of intervention with young offenders was likely to discourage them from reoffending.

Increasingly, the behavioural and social sciences use the common currency of mathematics to report their findings ('quantitative' data) – although they may use other verbal or written accounts as well ('qualitative' data). They employ a range of statistical techniques to examine the significance of these findings. When planning a research study it is important to consider beforehand what forms of statistical analysis will be undertaken. For example, there are specific techniques appropriate to situations where the effects of several variables and possible interactions between them are being investigated.

If the data and the statistical analyses performed thereon warrant it, it may be possible to draw some provisional and tentative conclusions as to whether the evidence does or does not support the original hypothesis. Such evidence is then compared and contrasted with other evidence found in similar fields in the literature, and implications discussed. It is customary to acknowledge the weaknesses of one's research and to be open to informed criticism. Such honesty is, or should be, part of the scientific or empirical approach. The constructive criticism of one's own work, and that of others, is to be encouraged.

Some research methods

The experimental method

The aim is usually to test the impact of a particular variable, the independent variable, on a particular situation. Such an impact can be measured by noting changes in other features of that situation: these are called the dependent variable(s). Put differently, we test the hypothesis by seeing what happens to the dependent variables when we manipulate the independent variables (see *Figure 9.2*). Psychologists use this method frequently. Sometimes they work in labs but increasingly, together with sociologists and social workers, they work in natural settings: the home, playground or shopping centre.

An interesting study appeared in the *British Medical Journal* (Thomas, 1987) which illustrates the usefulness of the experimental method and has direct relevance for social work practice. Two hundred people visited the same GP with symptoms for which no physical abnormalities could be found. These patients were randomly allocated to one of four consultations:

	Positive consultation	*Negative consultation*
With treatment	Person given firm diagnosis and told he/she would be better in a few days. Placebo was given.	Person told that doctor could not be certain what was the matter. Placebo was given.
Without treatment	Person given a firm diagnosis, but told he/she did not require treatment.	Person told that the doctor could not be sure what was the matter, and therefore the doctor would give no treatment.

Patients were followed up two weeks after visiting the surgery, and asked for details of their health and satisfaction levels after seeing the doctor. Thomas reported that there was a significant difference in patient satisfaction between the positive and negative consultations but not between the treated and untreated groups. Sixty-five per cent of those receiving a positive consultation got better within two weeks, compared with 39 per cent of those who received a negative consultation – a significant statistical difference. There was no significant difference, however, between those who were treated and those who were not treated.

Thomas claims, therefore, that there is indeed a point in being positive when meeting with sick people, and that the practitioner's style of interaction itself contributes significantly to the person's speed of recovery. Social workers and community workers are likely to have a similar positive or negative personal effect upon those with whom they work.

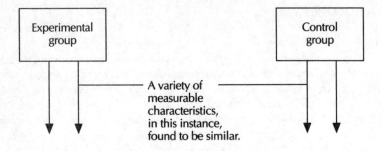

A. *Pre-test situation:* two matched samples, chosen to be as similar upon as many different variables as possible: e.g. age, sex.

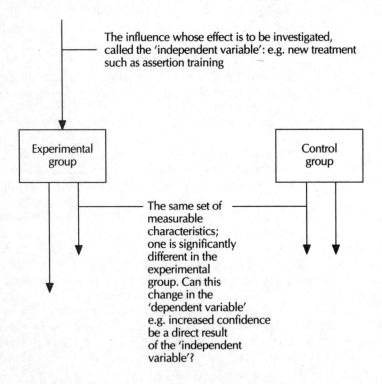

B. *Test situation:* the same matched samples tested following the application of a specific influence e.g. a new drug, or a new form of treatment.

Figure 9.2 Independent and dependent variables in a controlled experiment (Sutton, 1979)

The observational method

One of the most direct ways of measuring behaviour is through observation. This approach, which includes studies of the same group of people over time, as well as surveys and field studies, characteristically considers much larger samples and does not set out to examine particular variables. One of the best known British observational studies is that which is being carried out by the National Children's Bureau on all the children, some 16,000 of them, born in one week in March, 1958. The children's progress in terms of their physical development, health, family circumstances, school experience and life events has been monitored for all traceable children ever since, and many excellent short research reports, named 'Highlights', are available.

Advantages of the observational method include the desirability of minimal interference in a natural system such as a playground or classroom. Disadvantages include 'selective perception', that is, observers may see what they hope to see. It is increasingly the custom to employ more than one observer to reduce this problem. Many studies have taken place in educational contexts, such as classrooms; we may anticipate more in social work settings, such as residential homes for children or day centres.

Questionnaires

Social and community workers can use questionnaires (see Appendix E) in order to identify needs such as support for caregivers, facilities for disabled people, counselling services for particular groups, as well as to identify people who are willing to contribute to fulfilling these needs. *Table 9.1* provides guidelines for the use of questionnaires (Herbert, 1990).

Difficulties in human research

Problems of sampling. It is rarely possible to measure all aspects of a phenomenon. For example, you cannot interview every member of a community to ascertain the incidence of a particular problem, such as loneliness, in that community. Instead you would interview a sample of people from the community and infer the incidence of the problem in the whole community from the incidence in the sample. The smaller the sample, the more unrepresentative of the community it will be.

Problems of validity. There are great difficulties in being sure that your test or questionnaire actually measures what you intend it to measure. For example, if your test purports to measure depression, the items making up your test should reflect your operational definition (see earlier) of depression. The issue of validity is complex and the validity of a particular measure is frequently open to debate: for example, can IQ tests measure intelligence?

Problems of reliability. Reliability refers to the stability and dependability of the method you are using. A reliable test, say, for depression, will give broadly the same result whoever administers it and in whatever circumstances. Such reliability is very difficult to attain.

Table 9.1 The questionnaire method (Herbert, 1990)

Range of types	Advantages	Disadvantages/biases	Safeguards
Close-ended (range of possible answers specified with the question)	Can be given to large numbers of people simultaneously and who may be widely distributed geographically	Respondents may not be able to reply because the questions do not use the concepts, the constructs or the vocabulary that mean something to them	Preliminary study to determine relevance of questions and vocabulary
Semi-open-ended (prespecified answers, with encouragement for open comments; or some questions open-ended)	Standardized wording and order of questions means responses can be compared	May be filled in under widely different (non-standard) conditions	
	Anonymity for respondents	May be low percentage returned	
	Can be filled in respondent's own time	No way of checking whether respondent has understood questions in way intended	'Back-translation' – ask sample people to go through their own questionnaire explaining their answers
	Relatively speedy way of collecting data	Biasing responses by choice of questions and range of prespecified answers	
Open-ended (each question represents a topic and the respondent is asked to comment freely on it)	Respondents can answer from their own point of view, selecting what is relevant to them	Mass of data difficult to analyse	
		Difficult to compare with other other respondents	
		Researcher bias most likely at data analysis stage	Analysis done independently by several different individuals who then develop a common framework
		Respondents may be put off by open format which provides few cues to the answers	

Remember too that your observations may be distorted by your previous experience, needs or motivations, and people may react differently when being questioned or when they feel under scrutiny. All these factors may alter your test results and need to be taken into account when embarking on (or when reading) any research.

Evaluating interventions by gathering data

Why not gather data in order to evaluate your work? Anyone who has tried to lose weight, take regular exercise or stop smoking will find that monitoring progress is a useful way of helping to achieve one's goals. Imagine that you are working with a woman who feels she is drinking too much but is being persuaded by her friends to drink when in their company. There are many ways to deal with this problem, and you may wish to use the ASPIRE process to work through the various issues that are involved. But is there a concrete way of evaluating the progress the woman is actually making in refusing drinks during the course of the intervention? In this case, a standard chart can be used by your client to monitor her own progress (see *Table 9.2* and Appendix D for a blank copy).

Using charts in this way may not seem to be 'research', but in that it provides both the person with whom you are working and yourself with *evidence* as distinct from general and vague information, this approach has much to offer. It can be adapted to a wide variety of goals such as:

● Practising a new skill: relaxation, assertion, using a word-processor.
● Working towards improving a relationship (see Chapter 5).
● Gaining control over the tendency to attend only to one's shortcomings by reminding oneself of strengths instead.
● A disabled person regaining a former skill: for example, aspects of self care.
● A person experiencing agoraphobia gradually venturing further from base.

Professional skills

Negotiation skills

According to Argyle (1983), negotiation is a process of joint decision-making between representatives of two sides who are in conflict, although both sides wish to reach a settlement. Social workers and community workers are likely to need negotiation skills in a range of situations; for example, when trying to obtain resources for people with whom they work. Studies have shown that strong, active and dominant people are usually chosen to represent groups in negotiation situations in preference to people who are seen as constructive and helpful. This seems to suggest that such situations are perceived as implicitly threatening, which may cause difficulties in communication.

Table 9.2 Monitoring progress towards goals

Client's name: **Maria**

Worker's name: **Nancy**   Date: **17 may**

Record whether you personally feel that you are making progress towards your goal, or are getting further away from it, on average, each week.

Goal

to: **be assertive in refusing pressure to drink alcohol.**

Where +10 represents total success in behaving assertively and −10 represents very serious deterioration in the ability to be assertive

Perceived threat may best be managed through:

The avoidance of insult. People who deliberately insult those with whom they are bargaining have been found to obtain less favourable outcomes. That is, those who are insulted take personal offence and are unwilling to make the concessions made by people who are not personally attacked. The implication is that any attack should be at the case presented – rather than at the person presenting the case.

The enhancement of trust. An effective way of increasing understanding between groups in conflict is to ask each side to summarize the case made by the opposition. This ensures that the case is heard and understood.

Fisher *et al.* (1983) have set out a list of principles found to be helpful in constructive negotiation:

❑ Separate the people from the problem. Treat those with whom you speak with personal respect.
❑ Avoid seeming to threaten those whom you are approaching – either verbally or non-verbally.
❑ Prepare your advocacy well beforehand, with a few clear points; avoid getting into an argument.
❑ Have all the details of the case or circumstance (dates, correspondence, etc.) to hand, so that you are seen to be fully prepared.
❑ Demonstrate that you appreciate the difficulties faced by the other party; that is, let the other person explain the problems he or she is facing in responding constructively to your position and do not ride roughshod over them.
❑ Adopt a problem-solving approach. Can a solution be found so that everyone gains something?
❑ If you have a good case but are not successful, try to enlist senior people to support your case, for example, MPs.
❑ If you are unsuccessful on this occasion, anticipate future successes on other occasions.

It is very important that those who represent others in negotiations should not allow themselves to raise false expectations; that is, they should clarify with those they represent the *range* of possible outcomes which would be acceptable. Otherwise there is a danger of a negotiator failing to meet the group's expectations and returning to the group, crestfallen and embarrassed. For example, if a community worker representing a group at a meeting of a funding body has assured the group, 'I'll get the money for you. Leave it to me!', and then fails to achieve the desired objective, he or she may be ridiculed and rejected by the group when the outcome is known.

Asserting and challenging
There are times when you will need to assert yourself and this is especially so if you are a woman. It may be that you wish to express an opinion when it is being

intentionally or unintentionally ignored, or actively to reject or expose another person's racist or sexist views. These skills, in increasing order of combativeness, include: refusing to accept another person's point of view; disagreeing with another person's point of view; asserting one's own point of view; questioning a view; challenging a view; contradicting; confronting; accusing another person.

Clearly those towards the end of the list are more provocative and more threatening than those at the beginning and, tactlessly expressed, will undoubtedly elicit the fight, flight or freeze response from the person on the receiving end! The skill probably lies in selecting the level of assertion or challenge most likely to elicit the response you are hoping for; for example, a willingness on the part of a colleague to reconsider and change an opinion.

Advocacy and self-advocacy

The responsibility to speak on behalf of another person may frequently fall to a social worker or community worker who is seeking to promote the rights or well-being of those who lack the experience or confidence to speak for themselves. For example, social workers may act to support people with learning disabilities who may not be in a position to act on their own behalf. Whatever the situation, it is essential that there shall have been pre-liminary discussion between all those concerned to clarify the objectives of their shared action.

Brechin and Swain (1988) have written with insight about the principle of 'normalization' as it applies to people with learning disabilities. The term refers to a range of activities which enable people with such disabilities to live as 'normally' as possible, but Brechin and Swain claim that too often professionals 'normalize' people's lives according to *their* view of how people should behave. Against this, they highlight the development of the self-advocacy movement, and write:

Self-advocacy is in essence about a process of self-actualisation. It is about people coming to identify and express personal feelings, wishes and circumstances . . . It is about opening up the range of choices which could and should be available to them.

In the light of this, Brechin and Swain make the case for a 'working alliance' between professionals and people with learning difficulties, in which profession-als facilitate the self-determination of those with whom they work (see *Table 9.3*).

In facilitating self-advocacy, the role of the worker is to support clients in developing their own case, often to people with considerable power over them. Clients usually know what they want to say, but are inhibited by lack of confidence or experience in presenting their case. There are some pointers to assist workers in this role (Howard, 1991):

Table 9.3 Gains from self-advocacy and features of support offered (Brechin and Swain, 1988)

Gains from self-advocacy	Features of support offered
● Growth and confidence	Enhancing mastery and control
● Trust	Learning to be on their side in seeing problems
● Self valuing/pride	Learning to enjoy and know people
● Identity	Believing in people
● Determination	Commitment
● Responsibility	Accentuating positive qualities
● Ability and knowledge	Shared skills and information
● Sensitivity to others	Monitoring own communication
● Developing a voice	Learning to assist without control or power

❑ Help the person concerned to clarify the issues or problems he or she wishes to represent; for example, accommodation, plans for the future, finance, etc.

❑ Help the person prepare the case beforehand, with three or four main points to be presented.

❑ Help him or her to think through the *range* of acceptable outcomes – from most preferred to least preferred.

❑ Help the person to rehearse the case to be presented – at least twice, so that confidence is gained.

❑ Stress the importance of *seeming* calm and confident.

❑ Remember that your role is to empower and support clients; for example, you might provide information or remind them of something they wished to say. Your role does *not* involve speaking on their behalf.

❑ Have all the details concerning the case to hand, so that you are fully prepared to help the client.

❑ Help the person use a problem–solving approach. Can a solution be found in which everyone gains something?

❑ After the meeting, go through what happened, what the implications are, and how the person felt and feels about it all.

Once the goals of shared action have been agreed between workers and those they are supporting in advocacy, there will be many occasions when the latter are able, with support, to move forward 'under their own steam'. There will be times, however, when workers are called to speak on behalf of those with whom they work. In these circumstances, the research already quoted in the area of negotiation will be relevant.

Educational skills

Social workers and community workers are often called upon to act as formal and informal educators. For example, social workers may be required to teach foster parents aspects of inclusive fostering work, that is, work which involves the natural parents; and one of the main skills of community workers and youth workers is seen as informal education in a social and political context.

Preparation

Think through your overall objectives for the whole series of sessions; this is a priority. Unless you have decided what you want to achieve, you cannot work effectively. This preparation will help you to be realistic about how much can be attained in the time available; usually people attempt too much.

Write your objectives on a postcard and prepare the teaching material. Having objectives will help you to stay on target, especially if you refer back to them in the course of the session to monitor how you are doing. Prepare your material for teaching: handouts, visual aids, flip charts, video or audio-tapes.

Assess the existing level of understanding of the audience. This is important: if you pitch the teaching too low it will annoy those who have prior knowledge or skill; if you pitch it too high, it will upset those who don't. For example, if foster parents have their own children, and have been approved as foster parents, you should assume a basic knowledge of child development. You will, however, have to highlight particular needs of children who may be fostered with them; for example, the need for special hair and skin care for African-Caribbean children.

Discuss your plans and preparations with the participants and obtain their views, making changes where appropriate. Agree when and where the sessions will be held, how long they will last, who will attend, the form of the sessions and so on.

Conducting the sessions

Tell the participants how you intend to use the time. This prior information is important, and enhances motivation all round. Give a straightforward, clear presentation; avoid jargon words; use a range of resource material; involve your participants actively in exercises or discussion of the main ideas. Take account of the following factors which can help people learn (Shepherd, 1992).

- provide training objectives;
- provide advance organizers (that is, an overall plan or structure);
- give explanations;
- provide opportunities for practice;
- control practice;
- motivate the trainee;
- build confidence;
- give feedback on performance, knowledge of results is important.

Finally, it is important to carry out an evaluation by enabling participants to give *you* constructive feedback.

Decision-making

In the past, social workers had far more autonomy than they do now. They could decide, with only the approval of their immediate seniors, whether to take a child into care and, once in care, what to do, or not to do, about that child's future. Sadly that autonomy led in many instances to situations of 'drift' (Millham *et al.*, 1985).

Sinclair (1984) undertook an important study of decision-making in statutory reviews on children in care, and found that a high proportion of these decisions were recorded in a vague way, thereby making effective monitoring of intervention difficult. She writes, however, that 62 per cent of decisions were put into effect, although this figure drops to 50 per cent in residential homes. The two main reasons for failure to implement the decisions were lack of cooperation of those involved and lack of resources.

There have been two main ways in which Departments of Social Service have attempted to ensure that crucial decisions are both made and implemented. First, manuals of procedures have been developed which have built into them 'decision points' which actively require social workers and their managers to hold case conferences, statutory reviews and panels whenever certain crucial sets of circumstances occur. These have gone a long way towards minimizing uncertainty concerning the welfare of individual children or adults. Moreover, the guide *Working Together Under The Children Act 1989* (Home Office, 1991) indicates how agencies may collaborate in making decisions, for example in Area Child Protection Committees. Second, the Children Act 1989 requires that each child or young person in care has an Assessment and Action Record, which is itself a means of monitoring his or her progress and welfare. This contains detailed plans for the future of each child, with specific aims to be achieved and the names of those responsible for seeing that the work is done.

Once *any* decision is made, it should be recorded indicating:
- the specific goals to be achieved;
- the specific actions to be taken;
- the named persons who will take them;
- the date by when the actions will be taken;
- how the actions will be monitored: for example, by reporting back to a chairperson.

Record keeping

Many social work departments and all probation departments use case records with at least two separate means of recording information: one for 'running records', with very brief details of phone calls made or letters sent, and one for 'case summaries'. The latter typically summarize in about one or two paragraphs the events of a fixed period of time, say three months.

We should be extremely cautious in our judgements of others and in what we commit to paper. The ideal to which we should aspire, though which we can seldom hope to attain, is that we should *agree with those concerned* the content of anything that we intend to put on paper. This ideal has been achieved in part by probation officers by sending a copy of the probation report submitted to the court to the person concerned. The task of recording involves a filtering process on the part of the recorder. The emphasis should be on the recording of *facts* rather than of opinions. If opinions are recorded, they should be reported as such; for example, 'In my view . . .'.

Memory is extremely unreliable. We therefore have the dilemma of whether to write notes as we proceed with our interviews – generally considered to be a disagreeable experience by those about whom they are written unless they are shown the notes – or trust to our all too imperfect memories important information. The skill of writing brief notes which can be shared with those about whom they are written comes with practice, as does the skill of recording differing points of view, for example about a family row. We might note:

'Mrs H's view of the incident was such and such . . .'.
'Mr H's view was rather different and was such and such . . .'.

One of the foundation stones of our work must be honesty: better to be straight (which is different from being blunt) with people early in our contact with them, than to mislead them for the sake of a 'good' relationship – only to have to undeceive them later.

Of course when we have completed our interviews, we shall probably need to make supplementary notes to fill in the outline as soon as possible. The message from the research in psychology is very clear: much information which we hear and which enters our short-term memory decays very fast (certainly within minutes) unless it is rehearsed. A strategy to minimize loss of information is to write it down as soon as possible after the meeting or interview.

Writing reports

Social workers and community workers all have to write reports of many different kinds: for example, social workers write regular reports of children's progress between case reviews; community and youth workers and workers in voluntary organizations report regularly to their management committees; and probation officers and social workers are frequently required to submit pre-sentence reports to a court. There are considerations common to all report-writing.

Preparing to write the report
1. Consider to whom the report is addressed. Who are the readers? This will affect your content and style.
2. Clarify the objectives of the report. To give information? To persuade with arguments? To fulfil a court requirement?

3. Plan the task and outline a provisional format.
4. Work out your time plan for the production of the report. Pinpoint the deadline by which the report must be complete and work backwards from this date, noting deadlines for the completion of key tasks; for example:
   – gathering the necessary material,
   – completing the draft,
   – submitting for typing,
   – checking the final format,
   – posting it to the specified recipients.
5. Decide the approximate length of the report. The aim should be to be as brief as possible, while leaving out no key information. Reports to court are often only two or two-and-a-half sides of A4 paper.

Language and content

The recommendations made for the language and content (and appearance) of reports by the authors of the document *Reports to Courts: Practical Guidance for Social Workers* (Department of Health and Social Security, 1981) are relevant to almost all kinds of report. The authors write:

It is essential that the author of a report aims for 'a concise, objective and interesting report for the court'. The report should communicate effectively and plainly to a wide range of readership, e.g. children, parents, magistrates, judges and lawyers, bearing in mind that the essential task of the report is to assist the court. Overlong sentences with several sub clauses should be avoided.

Material to be included in a report should be tested against several criteria:

Relevance: Is what is included pertinent to, connected with and bearing upon the matter in hand?

Reliability: If two or more people collect the same information and come independently to the same conclusion, then the information may be regarded as reliable.

Validity: Is the information provided an appropriate indicator of what is claimed? For example, if it is claimed that there has been 'an improvement in relationships' between two people, what is the evidence of this, and how long has it lasted? The more rigorous the evidence provided, the better.

Accuracy: It is vital to check very carefully all information offered in a report.

Administrative Skills

Before you can organize your own working life, you first need to understand the organization in which you work. If you work within an organization, however small, you are working within a system – probably several interacting systems. It is important to understand the workings of these systems, how the different levels of power and responsibility are interlinked, and who are the key people with influence at each point. Who sits on the various boards and committees? Who has power? Who holds the purse strings? These are all key questions for workers if they wish to influence the course of events in today's increasingly political society.

Next, you need to be clear about the objectives of the larger organization and of your own particular group. With Departments of Social Service under increasing pressure to provide more and more services, and to be increasingly cost-effective, it is important for each person within a team to be specific about his or her objectives and how they mesh with those of the larger organization. Stoner (1978) has outlined the requirements of an effective objective-setting approach:

❑ Realistic goal-setting and planning towards their attainment.
❑ Setting of individual unit goals by members of units in relation to the broader goals of the organization.
❑ Consultation with group members to ensure that goals are attainable.
❑ Considerable freedom in the methods employed to reach the goals.
❑ Frequent review of performance as it relates to objectives.
❑ Commitment to the approach at all levels of the organization.

Time management

Time is a fixed resource. Human beings, if they are to remain effective, need to use that time not only to work, but also to sleep, eat, spend with families and friends and to 're-charge their batteries'. There is never enough time for all that social workers and community workers have to do, and as their work seems to move increasingly towards meeting a series of emergencies, the emphasis must always be upon determining priorities.

Repeated demands upon us make us feel out of control. This causes feelings of anxiety which can lead to panicky thoughts – further undermining our coping capacities. Making a plan restores, in some measure, the crucial sense of being in control. This is valid both for ourselves and for people we are trying to help. Planning requires a consideration of priorities, and the allocation of time to competing demands. List-making underpins much planning, and acts as a means of controlling anxiety.

When you feel swamped by an array of commitments, professional and personal, make a list of them all – excluding things you would do anyway, like eating. Then, go down the list, placing an 'A', 'B' or 'C' against each item, with 'A' representing top priority commitments, 'B' the next level and 'C' the least pressing. Start each day with the most pressing tasks and work your way down, breaking large tasks into several smaller ones (Hicks and Gullett, 1981).

For forward planning and long-term responsibilities, it is vital to work out a time plan. Using a diary here is essential. For example, in order to run a training course, you may need to allocate time to printing leaflets, receiving applications, making and confirming bookings, etc. All these activities require precise time management and forward thinking. Always be sure to build in enough time for others to respond.

Looking after Yourself

Practice in social work and community work settings becomes ever more demanding, under increasing statutory responsibilities and increasing public claim upon resources. It is vital that we look after ourselves if we are to remain well and able to function in situations of stress. Cooper *et al.* (1988) undertook a major study of the levels of stress experienced by over 100 workers in 13 different occupations. Each group was assessed on a ten-point scale, with social workers emerging with a rating of six, indicating a very stressful job.

People can cope with emergencies if they are occasional, but if the level of demand is maintained for too long, workers experience the phenomenon of 'burn out'. This is associated with having to respond repeatedly to crisis – often in those most exacting of tasks, the investigation of child abuse and child sexual abuse.

Recognizing stress

The following features have been associated with burn-out in the helping professions:
- loss of concern for the people with whom one is working:
- physical exhaustion or illness and increased absenteeism;
- emotional exhaustion, leading to lack of empathy or respect for those with whom one is working, and a sense of detachment from work and clients;
- a dehumanized perception of people: they may be labelled in a derogatory manner, or seen as deserving of their problems;
- cynicism and negativity;
- inflexibility and rigidity in thinking;
- paranoia – the view that colleagues and administrators are deliberately trying to make life difficult;
- psychosomatic complaints and illness.

In an investigation of the particular circumstances leading to burn-out, Edelwich (1980) found that the following were most frequently reported by his respondents:
- too many work hours;
- a 'dead-end' career;
- too much paper work;
- insufficient training for the job;

- not paid enough money;
- not appreciated by clients;
- not appreciated by superior;
- no support at work.

While it is clearly very difficult to bring about changes in some of these factors, others, such as the issue of support at work, can and should be addressed. Edelwich concludes by highlighting the fact that many people seem to enter the helping professions with unrealistic expectations, for example: that the services they provide will drastically improve the lives of their clients; that they will be appreciated by their clients and their agency; that they will be able to bring about change in bureaucracies; and that there will be opportunities for rapid advancement within their career.

Supervision

In professional settings, most workers are expected to turn to their line manager for professional support, but he or she may not always be the ideal person. Sometimes it is the line manager who is causing the stress, for example, by always being critical of what you do. In these circumstances, many workers develop arrangements for 'collateral supervision', that is, they find a colleague to supervise them who knows the nature of their work, but who is not personally involved in it. This person should be trusted to maintain confidentiality and should offer a listening ear to allow for the release of frustration and emotion. This form of supervision is an invaluable form of social support to workers who often carry great responsibilities. Supervisor and supervisee should together complete a contract before embarking on their sessions. *Table 9.4* can be adapted to a range of practice settings.

Working as a member of a supportive team

Virtually all social workers, probation officers and community workers practise as members of teams. This can be a source of support and satisfaction or one of frustration and tension. In successful teams, meetings are held regularly and they are chaired in a disciplined way. The objectives of the team's work are explicit, and progress towards them is monitored in an open and honest way. What can an individual do to gain from and contribute to the working of a team? Some suggestions are to:

❏ Attend team meetings; send an apology if you cannot attend.
❏ Favour formality rather than informality: for example, brief minutes should be taken and referred to at the following meeting.
❏ Fix the time for ending the meeting right at the outset, and adhere to it.
❏ Take your turn of duties: taking minutes, chairing the meeting.
❏ Keep your own contributions brief and succinct.

Table 9.4 A contract for supervision (Sutton and Herbert, 1992)

Supervisor's name: _____

Worker's name: _____ Date: _____

On the part of the supervisor
I undertake to carry out the following supervisory responsibilities to the best of my ability during the next _____ months.

1. To meet with _____ once a week or fortnight* for at least one hour:
   - to offer encouragement and support to the worker;
   - to give feedback upon performance – positive before negative;
   - to discuss necessary actions concerning practice;
   - to discuss issues arising from practice;
   - other_____

2. To prepare an agenda for our sessions.

3. To devise objectives with him or her concerning development and progress as a worker.

4. Other_____

5. Other_____

On the part of the worker
I undertake to carry out the following responsibilities to the best of my ability during the next year.

1. To attend supervisions at the agreed time.

2. To bring records of work up to date the day before the supervision so that the supervisor may read them beforehand.

3. To prepare an agenda for supervision sessions.

4. To bring any matters which cause me professional concern to the attention of the supervisor.

5. Other_____

6. Other_____

This agreement may be renegotiated at the request of either party.

Date: _____   _____ (Worker)

                                _____ (Supervisor)

*Delete as applicable.

❑ Try to avoid putting people down or interrupting them. This is discourteous and humiliating for those on the receiving end.

❑ Try to keep the meetings light–hearted and enjoyable. Give positive feedback to those who have had some success since the previous meeting – however slight!

❑ Try to build in something to look forward to: a team visit to a show, going out for a meal together, a visit to an ice rink.

The team meeting at least should be seen as a small oasis of good communication, support and satisfaction for people often stretched to breaking point.

Being Alert to Potential Violence

This section is included not because there is a high probability that you will encounter violence, but because it is important to have given some prior thought to potentially violent situations. These demand considerable skill on the part of the worker (see *Table 9.5*).

Table 9.5 Verbal and non-verbal factors in potentially violent situations (from Davies, 1990)

Non-verbal considerations	Verbal considerations
Acting to avoid violence:	
● Convey respect. Use your body language to demonstrate confidence but not threat.	● What are the appropriate forms of address, for example, to married or older people? If you do not know, it is usually fitting to ask. For example, 'Please tell me how I should address you'.
● Try to be authoritative, but not authoritarian.	● Say, 'I would like to sit down. May I sit here?' Choose a seat near an exit.
● Do not take actions without prior agreement.	● Say 'I should like to turn the TV off. Is that all right?
● Avoid standing in a way which might be seen as confrontational. Standing or sitting at an angle is appropriate.	● Show empathy towards people in a difficult situation. For example, 'This must be an upsetting time for you . . .?'.
● Do not write things in a notebook without showing your notes.	● Explain that there is an open recording system.
Acting to handle anger:	
● Attempt to defuse the anger.	● Avoid provocative statements like 'Just calm down . . .'.
● Keep as calm as you can yourself.	
● Try to sound confident even if you don't feel it.	● Some ways of talking have a more calming effect than others. The expression, 'The situation we are in is that . . .' brings you alongside an angry person, and emphasizes the 'togetherness' aspects.
If the person does become violent:	
● Speak strongly, firmly and loudly.	● 'Take your hands off me!'.
● Make a rapid exit and get help.	

In order to predict situations in which violence may occur, Davies (1990) recommends that you think about:

❑ *Precipitating situations common to all people:*
- situations of great frustration or anger: bad news, for example, about a court decision; refusal of parole;
- a direct threat to someone's well-being: news of a tragedy; perceived or real accusation of having abused/sexually abused a dependent.

❑ *The person's past history.* This is especially relevant if the situation is similar to one where the person was violent in the past.

❑ *Physical factors.* These include pain, being under the influence of alcohol.

❑ *Feelings of humiliation or powerlessness.* A person may have been denied rights or entitlement to benefit.

If you feel that a particular situation may lead to violence, Davies suggests taking the following precautions:

❑ Find out if the person or family is known to your agency.
- If so, has he or she ever shown violence in the past?
- If not, are the circumstances of your visit ones in which a person might be expected to be violent, for example, frustration because of long delayed services?

❑ Clarify agency procedures for visiting unknown situations.

❑ Inform your colleagues of exactly where you are going.

❑ Give them an estimated time for your return/phoning in.

❑ Ask a colleague/police to accompany you if you feel fearful.

❑ Check beforehand the location of the place you will visit. Is it a street with easy access, a block of flats, a cul-de-sac?

❑ If travelling by car, check where you can park safely, with easy access and outlet.

CHAPTER 10

Values and Ethics

The words 'values' and 'ethics' are used freely in everyday conversation, but their meaning is seldom discussed or defined. The term used by the Central Council for the Education and Training of Social Workers is 'values', and these can be understood as the 'principles for practice' guiding the conduct and actions of social workers. These values, and their implications for the practice of social work were set out explicitly in the Introduction. The term used by The British Psychological Society is 'ethics'; this refers to the set of principles governing conduct and practice. The Code of Conduct of The British Psychological Society (1993) reads:

In all their work psychologists . . . shall value integrity, impartiality and respect for persons and evidence and shall seek to establish the highest ethical standards.

These organizations, then, are concerned to establish principled practice among their members towards members of the public, whose value and dignity as individuals they are required to respect.

The Complexity of Social Work

Social work is an extraordinarily complex and difficult field of practice. Below I address four of the factors which contribute to that complexity: the exceedingly demanding nature of the work itself; the brevity of training; the increasing evidence that poverty, unemployment and other structural influences are primary variables in much social distress; and rising expectations on the part of the public.

The demanding nature of social work
If we consider the fields of practice of social work, we see how exceedingly demanding they are in that many of them carry profound statutory responsibility. I have written elsewhere (Sutton, 1981):

The legal responsibilities carried by social workers are daunting: they include the investigation of, and intervention in, cases of suspected child abuse, such as violence or incest; the placement of children, often distressed or unmanageable, in such foster homes as can be found, and attempting to support the foster parents; inquiring into the suitability of people interested in adopting children; investigating the appropriateness of supporting an application for the compulsory admission of a patient to a psychiatric hospital; and the carrying out of supervision orders placed by the courts upon, for example, young offenders. In addition, they are required to offer help and support to the mentally handicapped and their families, to the aged, to those discharged from psychiatric hospital and needing help in the community, as well as to members of ethnic minority groups. Readers will be aware of the way in which the media castigate those who err in the judging or management of such impossible responsibilities.

The brevity of training

The Diploma in Social Work is comparable academically to the first two years of a degree. Most students, about half of whom are graduates in another field and half are non-graduates, undertake a common first year of education and training, before choosing to specialize in their second year in work with families and children, probation, group care, residential care or the care of adults in the community. The contribution of psychology, which fell to about 60 hours now seems to have fallen again, as ever new requirements crowd the syllabus. It is daunting to note that, despite their statutory responsibilities, social workers receive less than half the amount of academic training of fully qualified clinical and educational psychologists.

Structural variables and social distress

It is apparent from studies in many different fields of research that structural variables – those associated with disadvantage, poverty and unemployment – contribute overwhelmingly to people's difficulties. Social workers and community workers have only minimal influence in such circumstances. They can ensure that people receive their full entitlement to welfare rights, and seek any additional resources from charitable and other organizations to which their clients may be entitled. They can publicize the fact of the contribution of poverty to social ills, they can organize or join protests against cuts in services but, beyond this, they have little power.

Rising public expectations

The subtlety of some of the influences which affect human behaviour and interaction are only just beginning to be appreciated as researchers attempt to tease out the intricate relationships between innumerable variables. Few psychologists feel confident about making more than very limited predictions about human interaction on the basis of present understanding.

Nonetheless, because the public has become so used to accurate predictions from other disciplines, and because large sums of money are involved in the provision of public services, it is expected that those who call themselves professionals shall make sound judgements and accurate predictions. As we know, many judgements have been flawed and many predictions inaccurate. My point is that *no one* can achieve total reliability, however long the training and however sophisticated the resources. What is shocking is that we continue to require such modestly trained workers to shoulder such responsibilities, and that they are pilloried when their inevitable shortcomings are revealed.

Dilemmas of Social Work

There are many tensions within the practice of social work, of which we have space to consider just four: care versus control; issues of confidentiality; managing conflicts of interest; and the shortage of resources.

Care versus control

Unlike psychologists, whose role in providing support for members of the public is unmixed with statutory responsibilities, social workers are required, in many of the settings in which they work, to play a potentially powerful controlling role alongside that of caring and support. They have the power to apply to court to remove children from parents about whom there is concern, to apply for care orders concerning those children, as well as the power to take back to court those placed on supervision orders who do not comply with the terms of those orders. Probation officers too, have considerable power: for example, to take back to court those offenders who are in breach of the terms of their probation order.

It is not surprising that there is often acute tension between the conflicting roles of caring and controlling. Social workers and probation officers, motivated primarily by concern for people in distress, are often understandably reluctant to penalize further those people who are already among the most disadvantaged members of society. Yet, they are employed to protect those who are even more vulnerable: the very young, the very old and those unable to protect themselves.

Issues of confidentiality

Bromley (1981) has delineated four forms of confidentiality:
1. Absolute confidentiality: in which the listener pledges *never* to reveal what has been divulged.
2. Limited confidentiality: in which the listener clarifies at the outset that he or she is a member of a team, for example, a multi-disciplinary team, with whom information is always shared.
3. Contractual confidentiality: in which there is explicit discussion and agreement about which parts of a disclosure may be revealed, and to whom.
4. Discretionary confidentiality: in which the listener conveys that he or she will use professional judgement about which aspects of a discussion will be divulged – such disclosures being limited to those which are judged as absolutely necessary.

People can easily make the assumption that because we come from professional organizations, we are bound by the first form of confidentiality in Bromley's list. This draws attention to the importance, the necessity in my view, of raising the issue of confidentiality routinely in our professional practice. This should take place as early as possible in our contact with people, so that the limits of confidentiality are explicit from the start and clients know that we carry responsibilities which can sometimes force us to take action on the basis on information received.

This clarity seems to be all the more important in situations where children are involved and where, for example, instances of sexual abuse are being disclosed. To encourage a child to disclose information which may be incriminating of, say, her father, without any prior discussion of the implications of that disclosure, is unethical. Guidelines for the handling of such situations are essential.

Conflicts of interest

These frequently arise in practice. When need is so great in times of diminishing resources, it is all too easy for the person who 'shouts loudest' to claim our attention – at the expense of the person who may have the greater claim on our efforts. Conflicts of interest may arise, for example, between the needs of caregivers and those being cared for, or between the needs of lone parents and those of their children. The following steps can be taken in situations of uncertainty:

❑ Determine who is one's client. As reports have repeatedly stressed, it is imperative that social workers establish their first line of responsibility. Once that is clear, it then becomes easier to know whose interests should be placed first.

❑ Establish whether there are legal factors relevant to the situation. In a conflict of interests, social workers must have detailed knowledge of the relevant law as this often clarifies confusion.

❑ Negotiate the desired outcomes. This approach has already been discussed as part of the ASPIRE process. Whatever the situation, it seems to be helpful if attention can be directed towards clarifying *desired outcomes*, rather than focusing upon present conflicts. Once realistic outcomes are clear, then a range of strategies for attaining them can be implemented. The worker will know of practical resources and personal services which can be drawn upon. The reformulation of a conflict of interests in terms of a 'problem to be solved' rather than a battle to be lost or won can lead to many creative solutions.

Shortages of resources

An acute tension exists between our statutory responsibilities for the welfare of vulnerable members of the community and the lack of resources with which to address these responsibilities. Social workers face particular difficulties concerning:

❑ *Staff shortages.* Many teams of workers are seriously understaffed. Data reported concerning regional variations in shortages (Hatchett, 1991) showed an average ten per cent vacancy rate in the previous two years among full-time field social workers and a five per cent vacancy rate among team leaders. In the South East in 1990, the vacancy rate was over 16 per cent. These figures represent hundreds of empty posts.

❑ *Shortages of specialist workers.* There has been a huge increase in the statutory responsibilities carried by social workers under the Children Act 1989 and the National Health Service and Community Care Act 1990. There is, for example, a great shortage of black counsellors and black psychologists to help people who are leaving large institutions and whose rehabilitation within the community depends upon well-developed and appropriate services.

❑ *Shortages of key resources within the community.* Foster care, for example, has reached crisis point (Lowe, 1991). She writes that 'despite sophisticated recruitment campaigns, the development of better support to carers in some authorities, and the increased participation of black and ethnic minority carers, there are no more foster families in 1991 than there were in the mid-fifties'.

Equal Opportunity

According to the Disabled Persons (Employment) Acts 1944 and 1958, the Sex Discrimination Act 1975 and the Race Relations Act 1976, each local authority has a statutory duty to:

make appropriate arrangements to ensure that its various functions are carried out with due regard to the need to eliminate unlawful discrimination and to promote equality of opportunity.

This legislation is reflected in the statement of values put forward by the Central Council for the Education and Training of Social Workers. This requires that social workers shall practise in ways which respect the value and dignity of individuals and, further, that they must be able to:

recognize the need for and seek to promote policies and practices which are non-discriminatory and anti-oppressive.

The move to competencies has proved useful here. For example, on our own Diploma in Social Work at De Montfort University, students are required, during their first year field placement, to demonstrate five competencies within the unit addressing anti-discriminatory practice:

1. Identify racism and sexism as issues within British society which affect social work practice.
2. Recognize the part the student plays in challenging racism or sexism.
3. Recognize outcomes of racism or sexism in organizations.
4. Recognize the way organizations seek to alleviate racism and sexism and other oppressive practices.
5. Develop anti-racist as well as other anti-discriminatory practice.

Accountability

The challenge posed to professional groups by such books as *The Disabling Professions* (Illich, 1977) together with public concern over the way some so-called professionals have abused their power in recent years, have contributed to demands for 'accountability' from practitioners; that is, they must be answerable for their conduct. This requirement has been put into effect in a number of ways over the past few years, some explicit and others less so. I shall consider four areas: access to personal files; working towards negotiated goals or objectives; working in such a way that work can be evaluated; and working within the boundaries of one's competence.

Access to files
The Access to Personal Files Act 1987 introduced a stringent new requirement of social workers: to make available to clients their personal files, if so requested. (Social workers are not at liberty to reveal all documents, for example, letters and reports written by other professionals.) This responsibility placed upon workers new demands for accuracy, and exacts from them, as the Act of course intended, great care in compiling entries. The ideal is that there should be agreement between workers and clients about what is recorded. This agreement is entirely in line with the openness and targeted nature of practice which I have advocated in this book. Such accountability has been practised for many years by the probation service, who routinely make their reports available to offenders before a court hearing.

Working towards negotiated objectives
This has been a major theme of this book. The ASPIRE process offers a framework for practising in this way which will lend itself to the all but the most specialized of work. According to the Ethical Guidelines of the Behavioural Social Work Group (Hudson and MacDonald, 1986), 'a social worker should endeavour to use procedures which are in the best interests of the client or clients . . . Choice of intervention should always be justified by the available evidence [and] the social worker should make exhaustive attempts to discuss and agree the goals and methods of intervention with the client, family and group'.

I do not underestimate how difficult it is to enable social workers to think of their work in this way. Ovretveit (1986) in an action research project, *Improving Social Work Records and Practice*, reports:

Many social workers had great difficulty writing down what they were aiming to achieve and why, in stating what actions they would take to achieve their aims, and in distinguishing general long- and short-term aims from specific actions and tasks . . . The difficulties experienced by workers in formulating their own aims and actions may partially explain the difficulties they had in helping clients to formulate aims and actions. This is an important area for further attention because defining aims is crucial to making the most effective use of scarce resources, and the skills required are essential to helping clients to direct and regain responsibility for their own lives.

Skills, as we have seen, are acquired through practice. These skills are, however, sophisticated and cannot, in my view, be achieved routinely by social workers on two year courses of initial training. The groundwork for the skills can certainly be laid; the more advanced skills, involving achieving 'shared perceptions and agreement on what is to be done', and this in situations of tortuous complexity, are matters for training at post-qualified level. Courses of education and training in social work have a major responsibility here.

Evaluating the effectiveness of social work
Social workers, probation officers and community workers are under in-creasing pressure to demonstrate the effectiveness of their work. As Hudson and MacDonald (1986) succinctly state:

Social work is a very costly resource, and a scarce one. In order to make rational decisions about its allocation, effectiveness – demonstrable effectiveness – is a bottom-line requirement. If social work is not effective – however one wishes to define that – then the money spent on it would be better spent on interventions of demonstrated effectiveness, such as chiropody and the home-help service.

It is an integral part of social work practice (see the ASPIRE process) to plan and implement intervention in a way that allows for rigorous evaluation.

Working within one's competence
According to the ethical guidelines of the Behavioural Social Work Group (Hudson and MacDonald, 1986):

The social worker should continually reappraise his or her competence both from formal training and from his or her experience. If he or she is faced with a situation in which his or her level of skill is in doubt, he or she should consult with a colleague so that either the case is taken on with adequate supervision and training, or it is appropriately referred elsewhere.

However, social workers are frequently required to practise at levels far beyond their training, and in areas where there exists no reliable body of knowledge. They carry responsibilities which other professions have managed to avoid. Psychologists are seen as behaving responsibly when they decline to take on work for which they are inadequately trained; social workers might sensibly follow their example.

It is important to make all possible use of other professional colleagues in our efforts to conduct ourselves responsibly. For example, we should never take decisions in the medical or psychiatric field, unless, of course, we are acting formally as Approved Social Workers; it is appropriate always to refer people to, and to seek help from, doctors or psychiatrists. Good relationships built up with such colleagues form an important and potentially invaluable network of help for our clients and ourselves.

Empowerment

This is a very popular term at the present time. It has connotations of 'giving away one's own power' to those who have little or who lack it altogether. Let us consider briefly how far it may be attained at the level of the community, the group and the individual.

Community workers and social workers employed in the field of community development have the most explicit commitment to empowering others. Job descriptions often emphasize supporting local people in developing their political awareness and facilitating them in claiming the rights and services to which they are entitled. Some extremely effective work has been carried out in the form of support for campaigns concerning welfare rights, such as those of the Child Poverty Action Group, as well as in addressing the needs and rights of specific groups, such as those of people with learning disabilities. Many campaigns continue as part of the overarching campaign for equal opportunities – such as that for gay and lesbian people to be considered as potential foster parents just like everyone else. Those workers who are employed primarily as group workers can refer to the manual *Self-Directed Group Work* by Mullender and Ward (1991) which sets out how practitioners can actively avoid taking leadership roles and enable others to gain skills by so doing.

Field social workers have perhaps greater difficulty in practising in a way which empowers people because so much of their work is, or is seen as, controlling or policing. I have tried to make the case, however, that within a working alliance, the act of negotiating and implementing objectives and gathering evidence about whether they have been achieved, is itself empowering in that it involves clients in deciding the goals of the work. To be sure, there may be some stipulations, for example of the court, which must be met, but at least the act of negotiating goals makes the whole endeavour open and explicit. Hudson and MacDonald (1986) examine the work of the Alameda Project, in which worker–client agreements formed the basis of decision-making in instances of child abuse and neglect. They write of the agreements which were devised:

These spelled out what was expected of the parents, and the workers agreed to advise the court to return the children to their care if the parents fulfilled their part. The contracts specified outcome goals (return of the child), sub-goals that would have to be achieved in order to attain this outcome, time limits and the responsibilities of workers and clients . . . We have heard the Alameda Project described as 'coercive' – to that we would simply reply that the position of these parents should be contrasted with that of others who, generally speaking, get no clear answer to the question, 'What do I have to do to get my child back?'

Practice of this kind, even if it seems controlling is, on closer analysis, practice which empowers.

Personal Conduct

The British Psychological Society (1993) sets out a clearly worded statement concerning personal conduct which is helpful in its specificity. It states, for example, that psychologists:

shall not exploit any relationship or influence or trust which exists [with] . . . those in receipt of their services to further the gratification of their personal desires;

and that they shall

not allow their professional responsibilities or standards of practice to be diminished by considerations of religion, sex, race, age, nationality, party politics, social standing, class, self-interest or other extraneous factors.

These principles are enforced. Psychologists can be, and are 'struck off' the Register of Chartered Psychologists for significant breaches of the principles. So far, the social work profession has not seen fit to devise a means of ensuring that its members observe a similar code of personal conduct. The sooner it does so, the more responsible it will appear to a public calling, rightly, for higher standards of professional accountability.

References

AHMED, S., CHEETHAM, J. and SMALL, J. (1986) *Social Work with Black Children and their Families*. London: Batsford.

AINSWORTH, M.D.S. (1967) *Infancy in Uganda*. Baltimore: Johns Hopkins Press.

AINSWORTH, M.D.S. (1979) Infant–mother attachment. *American Psychologist, 34*, 932–937.

AINSWORTH, M.D.S., BLEHAR, M., WATERS, E. and WALL, S. (1978) *Patterns of Attachment*. Hillsdale, NJ: Erlbaum.

AINSWORTH, F. and FULCHER, L.C. (Eds) (1981) *Group Care for Children: Concepts and Issues*. London: Tavistock Publications.

ALASZEWSKI, A. and MANTHORPE, J. (1991) Literature review: measuring and managing risk in social welfare. *British Journal of Social Work, 21*, 277–290.

AMERICAN PSYCHIATRIC ASSOCIATION (1987) *Diagnostic and Statistical Manual of Mental Disorders*, 3rd edn. (rev.) Washington, DC: APA.

ANDERSON, E.M. and CLARKE, L. (1982) *Disability in Adolescence*. London: Methuen.

ARCHER, J. (1991) The influence of testosterone on human aggression. *British Journal of Psychology, 82*, 1–28.

ARGYLE, M. (1972) *Social Relationships*. Milton Keynes: Open University Press.

ARGYLE, M. (1983) *The Psychology of Interpersonal Behaviour*, 4th edn. Harmondsworth: Penguin.

ARMSTRONG, R., DAVIES, C. DOYLE, M. and POWELL, A. (1974) *Case Studies in Community Work, Vol. 1*. Manchester: Manchester Monographs.

ASCH, S.E. (1946) Forming impressions of personality. *Journal of Experimental Social Psychology, 1*, 479–495.

ASCH, S.E. (1958) Effects of group pressure upon modification and distortion of judgements. In E.E. MACCOBY, T.M. NEWCOMB and E. HARTLEY (Eds) *Readings in Social Psychology*, 3rd edn. New York: Holt, Rinehart and Winston.

ATKINSON, R.L., ATKINSON, R.C., SMITH, E.E., BEM, D.J. and HILGARD, E. (1990) *Introduction to Psychology*, 10th edn. New York: Harcourt Brace Jovanovich.

AXLINE, V. (1966) *Dibs: In Search of Self*. London: Victor Gollancz Ltd.

BAKER, A.W. and DUNCAN, S.P. (1985) Child sexual abuse: A study of prevalence in Great Britain. *Child Abuse and Neglect, 9*, 457–467.

BANDURA, A. (1977) Self-efficacy: towards a unifying theory of behaviour change. *Psychological Review, 84*, 191–215.

BARROWCLOUGH, C. and FLEMING, I. (1985) *Goal Planning with Elderly People*. Manchester: Manchester University Press.

BECK, A.T. and EMERY, G. (1985) *Anxiety Disorders and Phobias: A Cognitive Perspective*. New York: Basic Books, Incorporated.

BEE, H. (1992) *The Developing Child*, 6th edn. New York: Harper and Row.

BELLMAN, M. and CASH, J. (1988) *Schedule of Growing Skills (Developmental Screening Procedure)*. Windsor: NFER/Nelson.

BELSKY, J. and ROVINE, M. (1988) Nonmaternal care in the first year of life and the security of infant–parent attachment. *Child Development, 59*, 157–167.

BELSKY, J., ROVINE, M. and TAYLOR, D. (1984) The Pennsylvania Infant and Family Development Project III: the origins of individual differences in infant–mother attachment: Maternal and infant contributions. *Child Development, 55*, 718–728.

BENTOVIM, A., BOSTON, P. and VAN ELBURG, A. (1987) Child sexual abuse – children and families referred to a treatment project and the effects of intervention. *British Medical Journal, 295*, 1453–1457.

BLUGLASS, R. (1979) Incest. *British Journal of Hospital Medicine, 22*, 152–157.

BOWLBY, J. (1979) *The Making and Breaking of Affectional Bonds*. London: Tavistock.

BRECHIN, A. and SWAIN, J. (1988) Professional/client relationships: creating a 'working alliance' with people with learning difficulties. *Disability, Handicap and Society, 3*, 213–226.

BRITISH ASSOCIATION FOR COUNSELLING (1985, revised 1991) *Counselling: Definition of Terms*. Rugby: BAC.

THE BRITISH PSYCHOLOGICAL SOCIETY (1993) *Code of Conduct, Ethical Principles and Guidelines*. Leicester: BPS.

BROMLEY, D.B. (1974) *The Psychology of Human Ageing*. Harmondsworth: Penguin.

BROMLEY, E. (1981) Confidentiality. *Bulletin of The British Psychological Society, 34*, 468–469.

BROWN, K. (1981) *What It's Like to Be Me*. Watford: Exley Publications, Ltd.

BROWN, G. and HARRIS, T. (1978) *The Social Origins of Depression*. London: Tavistock.

BROWNE, K. (1988) The nature of child abuse and neglect: an overview. In K. BROWNE, C. DAVIES, and P. STRATTON (Eds) *Early Prediction and Prevention of Child Abuse*. Chichester: Wiley.

BRUMMER, N. (1988) White social workers, black children: Issues of identity. In J. ALDGATE and J. SIMMONDS (Eds) *Direct Work with Children*. London: Batsford.

CAMPBELL, D.A., RADFORD, J.M. and BURTON, P. (1991) Unemployment rates: an alternative to the Jarman index? *British Medical Journal, 303*, 750–755.

CATALAN, J. (1988) Affective disorders. In N. ROSE (Ed.) *Essential Psychiatry*. Oxford: Blackwell Scientific Publications.

CENTRAL COUNCIL FOR EDUCATION AND TRAINING IN SOCIAL WORK (1991) *Rules and Requirements for the Diploma in Social Work*, 2nd edn. London: CCETSW.

CHASE-LANSDALE, L. and OWEN, M.T. (1987) Maternal employment in a family context: Effects on infant–mother and infant–father attachments. *Child Development, 58*, 1505–1512.

CHILDLINE (1993) *Annual Report 1992–1993*. London: Childline.

CLARKE, R.V.G. (1977) Psychology and crime. *Bulletin of The British Psychological Society, 30*, 280–283.

COHN, A.H. and DARO, D. (1987) Is treatment too late: what ten years of evaluative research tell us. *Child Abuse and Neglect, 11*, 433–442.

COLEMAN, P.G. (1986) Ageing and social problems. In HERBERT, M. (Ed.) *Psychology for Social Workers*, 2nd edn. Leicester: BPS Books. (The British Psychological Society) and Macmillan.

COMMUNITY WORK GROUP OF THE CALOUSTE GULBENKIAN FOUNDATION (1973) *Current Issues in Community Work*. London: Routledge and Kegan Paul.

COOPER, C. (1985) 'Good-enough', border-line and 'Bad-enough' parenting. In M. ADCOCK and R. WHITE (Eds) *Good-enough Parenting: A Framework for Assessment*. London: British Agencies for Adoption and Fostering.

COOPER, C.L., COOPER, R.D. and EAKER, L. (1988) *Living with Stress*. Harmondsworth: Penguin.

CORNEY, R.H. (1984) The effectiveness of attached social workers in the management of depressed female patients in general practice. *Psychological Medicine*, Supplement 6.

COROB, A. (1987) *Working with Depressed Women*. Aldershot: Gower.

COX, J. (1988) *Transcultural Psychiatry*. Beckenham: Croom Helm.

COX, J. HOLDEN, J.M., SAGOVSKY, R. (1987) Detection of postnatal depression: Development of the ten-item Edinburgh Postnatal Scale. *British Journal of Psychiatry, 150*, 782–786.

CREIGHTON, S.J. (1992) *Child Abuse Trends in England and Wales 1988–1990*. London: NSPCC.

CROCKENBERG, S.B. (1981) Infant irritability, mother responsiveness, and social support influences on the security of infant–mother attachment. *Child Development, 52*, 857–865.

D'ARDENNES and MAHTANI, A. (1989) *Transcultural Counselling in Action.* London: Sage.

DARE, C. (1985) *Family Therapy.* In M. RUTTER and L. HERSOV (Eds) *Child and Adolescent Psychiatry,* 2nd edn. Oxford: Blackwell Scientific Publications.

DARLINGTON, R.B. (1986) Long-term effects of preschool programs. In U. NEISSER (Ed.) *The School Achievement of Minority Children.* Hillsdale, N.J. Erlbaum.

DAVIS, H. (1993) *Counselling Parents of Children with Chronic Illness or Disability.* Leicester: BPS Books (The British Psychological Society).

DAVIS, H. and CHOUDHURY, P.A. (1988) Helping Bangladeshi families. *Mental Handicap, 16,* 48–52.

DAVIES, G. (1991) Research on children's testimony: Implications for interviewing practice. In C.R. HOLLIN and K. HOWELLS (Eds) *Clinical Approaches to Sex Offenders and Their Victims.* Chichester: Wiley.

DAVIES, W. (1990) Personal communication.

DEPARTMENT OF HEALTH (1988) *Protecting Children.* London: HMSO.

DEPARTMENT OF HEALTH (1991) *Looking After Children. Guidelines for Users of the Assessment and Action Records.* London: HMSO.

DEPARTMENT OF HEALTH (1991) *Patterns and Outcomes in Child Placement. Messages from Current Research and their Implications.* London: HMSO.

DEPARTMENT OF HEALTH AND SOCIAL SECURITY (1985) *Social Work Decisions in Child Care.* London: HMSO.

DEPARTMENT OF HEALTH AND SOCIAL SECURITY (1987) *Reports to Courts. Practice Guidance for Social Workers.* London: HMSO.

DEPARTMENT OF HEALTH/SOCIAL SERVICES INSPECTORATE (1991) *Care Management and Assessment: Practitioners' Guide.* London: HMSO.

DICKSON, A. (1991) *A Woman in Your Own Right.* London: Quartet Books.

DOBSON, K.S. (1989) A meta-analysis of the efficacy of cognitive therapy in depression. *Journal of Consulting and Clinical Psychology, 57,* 414–419.

EARLY CHILD DEVELOPMENT UNIT (1991) *Empowerment, 2,* 1–2.

EDELWICH, J. (1980) *Burn-out.* New York: Human Services Press.

EGAN, G. (1986) *The Skilled Helper.* Monterey: Brooks Cole.

EMMET, N. (1987) A feedback loop suggested by social learning theory. In C. SUTTON (Ed.) *A Handbook of Research for the Helping Professions.* London: Routledge and Kegan Paul.

ERIKSON, E.H. (1963) *Childhood and Society,* 2nd edn. New York: Norton.

FAHLBERG, V. (1988) Attachment and separation. In *Fitting the Pieces Together.* London: British Association for Adoption and Fostering.

FALLOON, I., BOYD, J.L. and McGILL, C.W. (1984) *Family Care of Schizophrenia.* London: Guilford Press.

FALLOON, I., MUESER, K., GINGERICH, S., RAPPAPORT, S., McGILL, C. and HOLE, V. (1988) *Behavioural Family Therapy.* Buckingham: Buckingham Mental Health Service.

FARMER, E. and PARKER, R. (1991) *Trials and Tribulations: Returning C hildren From Care to their Families.* London: HMSO.

FARRINGTON, D.P. (1990) Implications of criminal career research for the prevention of criminal offending. *Journal of Adolescence, 13,* 93–113.

FERNANDO, S. (1988) *Race and Culture in Psychiatry.* London: Tavistock/Routledge.

FERRI, E. (1984) *Step Children.* Windsor: NFER/Nelson.

FINCH, R. and JAQUES, P. (1985) Use of the genogram with adoptive families. *Adoption and Fostering, 9,* 36–37.

FINKELHOR, D. (1984) *Child Sexual Abuse. New Theory and Research.* New York: Free Press.

FISHER, M., MARSH, P. and PHILLIPS, D. with SAINSBURY, E. (1986) *In and Out of Care: The Experiences of Children, Parents and Social Workers.* London: Batsford.

FISHER, R., URY, W. and PATTON, B. (1983) *Getting to Yes.* London: Hutchinson.

FORBES, R.J. and JACKSON, P.R. (1980) Non-verbal behaviour and the outcome of selection interviews. *Journal of Occupational and Organisational Psychology, 53*, 65–72.

FRANKENBURG, W.K. (1992) The Denver II: A major revision and restandardization of the Denver Developmental Screening Test. *Paediatrics, 89*, 91–97.

GELDER, M., GATH, D. and MAYOU, R. (1989) *Oxford Textbook of Psychiatry.* Oxford: Oxford University Press.

GELLES, R.J. (1979) *Family Violence.* Beverley Hills: Sage.

GELSO, G.J. and CARTER, J.A. (1985) The relationship in counselling and psychotherapy. *The Counselling Psychologist, 13*, 155–244.

GEVARTER, W.B. (1975) Humans: their brain and their freedom. *Journal of Humanistic Psychology, 15*, 79–90.

GILBERT, M. (1976) Behavioural approach to the treatment of child abuse. *Nursing Times*, 29 January, 1976.

GILBERT, P. (1989) *Human Nature and Suffering.* London: Lawrence Erlbaum Associates.

GOLDBERG, E.M., WARBURTON, R., McGUINESS, B. and ROWLANDS, J. (1977) Towards accountability in social work: one year's intake into an area office. *British Journal of Social Work, 7*, 257–283.

GOODWIN, D.W. (1989) Biological factors in alcohol use and abuse: implications for recognizing and preventing alcohol problems in adolescence. *International Review of Psychiatry, 1*, 41–49.

GORDON, A. (1975) The Jewish view of death: guidelines for mourning. In E. KÜBLER-ROSS (Ed.) *Death: the Final Stage of Growth.* Englewood Cliffs, New Jersey: Prentice Hall.

GRANT, L. (1992) Counselling: a solution or the problem? *Independent on Sunday*, 19 April.

GRAY, J.A. (1987) *The Psychology of Fear and Stress*, 2nd edn. Cambridge: Cambridge University Press.

GREENLAND, C. (1987) *Preventing Child Abuse and Neglect Deaths. An International Study of Deaths due to Child Abuse and Neglect.* London: Tavistock Publications.

GURMAN, A.S. and KNISKERN, D.P. (1981) *Handbook of Family Therapy.* New York: Brunner/Mazel.

HADLEY, A. (1993) *1992–1993: A Year of Expansion. Brook Advisory Centres Annual Report.* London: Brook.

HALSEY, A.H., HEATH, A.F. and RIDGE, J.M. (1980) *Origins and Destinations. Family, Class and Education in Modern Britain.* Oxford: The Clarendon Press.

HARLOW, H.F. and SUOMI, S. (1979) Nature of love – simplified. *American Psychologist, 25*, 161–168.

HATCHETT, W. (1991) All in a day's work. *Community Care, 877*, 20–21.

HEATHER, N. and ROBERTSON, I. (1981) *Controlled Drinking.* London: Methuen.

HENLEY, A. (1983) *Caring for Hindus and their Families.* London: Department of Health and Social Security/King's Fund.

HERBERT, M. (1981) *Behavioural Treatment of Children with Problems.* London: Academic Press.

HERBERT, M. (1988) *Working with Children and their Families.* Leicester: BPS Books (The British Psychological Society) and Routledge.

HERBERT, M. (1989) *Discipline: A Positive Guide for Parents.* Oxford: Blackwell.

HERBERT, M. (1990) *Planning a Research Project.* London: Cassell.

HERBERT, M. (1991) *Child Care and the Family.* Windsor: NFER/Nelson.

HERBERT, M. (1993) *Working with Children and the Children Act.* Leicester: BPS Books (The British Psychological Society).

HETHERINGTON, R. (1991) Personal communication.

HICKS, H.G. and GULLETT, C.R. (1981) *Management*, 4th edn. McGraw Hill: International Book Company.

HOLDEN, U.P. and WOODS, R.T. (1988) *Reality Orientation: Psychological Approaches to the Confused Elderly*. Edinburgh: Churchill Livingstone.

HOLLIN, C. (1993) *Effective rehabilitation programmes for young offenders: New findings and practical suggestions*. Paper presented at the III European Congress of Psychology, Tampere, Finland.

HOLMES, T.H. and RAHE, R.H. (1967) The social readjustment rating scale. *Journal of Psychosomatic Research, 11*, 213–218.

HOME OFFICE (1989) *Criminal Statistics 1989*. London: HMSO.

HOME OFFICE, DEPARTMENT OF HEALTH, DEPARTMENT OF EDUCATION AND SCIENCE, WELSH OFFICE (1991) *Working Together Under the Children Act 1989*. London: HMSO.

HOPSON, B. (1986) Counselling and helping. In M. HERBERT (Ed.) *Psychology for Social Workers*, 2nd edn. Leicester: BPS Books (The British Psychological Society).

HOWARD, B. (1991) Personal communication.

HOWE, D. (1989) *The Consumers' View of Family Therapy*. Aldershot: Gower.

HOWE, M. (1988) 'Hothouse' children. *The Psychologist*, 356–358.

HUDSON, B. and MACDONALD, G. (1986) *Behavioural Social Work*. Oxford: Blackwell.

HUNTER, M. (1994) *Counselling in Obstetrics and Gynaecology*. Leicester: BPS Books (The British Psychological Society).

ILLICH, I. (1977) *Disabling Professions*. London: Boyars.

INEICHEN, B., HARRISON, G. and MORGAN, H.G. (1984) Psychiatric admissions in Bristol. Geographical and ethnic factors. *British Journal of Psychiatry, 145*, 600–604.

IWANIEC, D., HERBERT, M. and McNEISH, A.S. (1985a) Social work with failure-to-thrive children and their families. Part 1: Psychosocial factors. *British Journal of Social Work, 15*, 243–259.

IWANIEC, D., HERBERT, M. and McNEISH, A.S. (1985b) Social work with failure-to-thrive children and their families. Part 2: Behavioural Social Work Intervention. *British Journal of Social Work, 15*, 375–389.

JEHU, D. (1988) *Beyond Sexual Abuse: Therapy with Women who were Childhood Victims*. Chichester: Wiley.

JONES, D.P. and McGRAW, J.M. (1987) Reliable and fictitious accounts of sexual abuse to children. *Journal of Interpersonal Violence, 2*, 27–45.

KAUFMAN, J. and ZIGLER, E. (1987) Do abused children become abusive parents? *American Journal of Orthopsychiatry, 57*, 186–192.

KETTERER, R.F., BADER, B.C. and LEVY, M. (1980) Strategies and skills for promoting mental health. In R.H. PRICE, R.F. KETTERER, B.C. BADER and J. MONAHAN (Eds) *Prevention in Mental Health*. London: Sage.

KING'S FUND CENTRE (1980) *An Ordinary Life*. London: King's Fund Centre.

KOESTLER, A. (1978) *Janus: A Summing Up*. London: Hutchinson.

LIPSEY, M.W. (1992) Juvenile delinquency treatment: A meta-analytic inquiry into the variability of effects. In T.D. COOK, H. COOPER, D.S. CORDRAY, H. HARTMANN, L.V. HEDGES, R.J. LIGHT, T.A. LOUIS and F. MOSTELLER (Eds) *Meta-analysis for Explanation: A Casebook*. New York: Russell Sage Foundation.

LITTLEWOOD, R. and LIPSEDGE, M. (1989) *Aliens and Alienists*, 2nd edn. London: Unwin Hyman.

LIVINGSTON BRUCE, M., TAKEUCHI, D. and LEAF, P.J. (1991) Poverty and psychiatric status. *Archives of General Psychiatry, 48*, 470–474.

LOCKE, A.E., SHAW, K., SAARI, L. and LATHAM, G. (1981) Goal-setting and task performance. *Psychological Bulletin, 90*, 125–152.

LOWE, M. (1991) Little to lose, much to gain. *Community Care, 851*, 18–19.

McCLYMONT, M. (1991) *Health Visiting and Elderly People. A Health Promotion Challenge.* 2nd edn. Edinburgh: Churchill Livingstone.

McGOVERN, D. and COPE, R. (1987) First psychiatric admission rates of first and second generation Afro-Caribbeans. *Social Psychiatry*, 122, 139–149.

MACCOBY, E.E. and MARTIN, J.A. (1983) Socialization in the context of the family: parent–child interaction. In P. MUSSEN (Ed.) *Handbook of Child Psychology, Vol. 4 Socialization: Personality and Social Development.* New York: Wiley.

MALIN, N. (1983) *Group Homes for Mentally Handicapped People.* London: HMSO.

MARES, P., HENLEY, A. and BAXTER, C. (1985) *Health Care in Multiracial Britain.* London: Health Education Council and National Extension College.

MARSHALL, W.L. and BARBAREE, H.E. (1990) An integrated theory of the etiology of sexual offending. In W.L. MARSHALL, D.R. LAWS and H.E. BARBAREE Eds) *Handbook of Sexual Assault. Issues, Theories and Treatment of the Offender.* London: Plenum.

MASLOW, A. (1970) *Motivation and Personality.* New York: Harper and Row.

MAXIME, J.E. (1986) Some psychological models of black self concept. In S. AHMED, J. CHEETHAM and J. SMALL (Eds) *Social Work with Black Children and their Families.* London: Batsford.

MAYER, J. and TIMMS, N. (1970) *The Client Speaks.* London: Routledge and Kegan Paul.

MILLHAM, S., BULLOCK, R., HOSIE, K. and LITTLE, M. (1986) *Lost in Care: The Problems of Maintaining Links between Children in Care and their Families.* Aldershot: Gower.

MISCHEL, W. (1973) Towards a cognitive social learning reconceptualization of personality. *Psychological Review*, 80, 272–283.

MISCHEL, W. (1986) *Introduction to Personality.* New York: Holt, Rinehart and Winston.

MOSHER, L., MENN, A. and MATTHEWS, S. (1975) Soteria: evaluation of a home-based treatment for schizophrenia. *American Journal of Orthopsychiatry*, 75, 455–467.

MULLENDER, A. and WARD, D. (1991) *Self-Directed Groupwork.* London: Whiting and Birch.

NATIONAL COUNCIL FOR THE CARE AND RESETTLEMENT OF OFFENDERS (1988) *Race and Justice for Young Offenders.* NACRO Briefing: Juvenile Crime Section.

NATIONAL INSTITUTE OF SOCIAL WORK (1982) *Social Workers: Their Role and Tasks.* London: Bedford Square Press.

NATIONAL MENTAL HEALTH ASSOCIATION (1987) Why now? Scope of the problem – Current activity – Need for definition. *Journal of Primary Prevention*, 7, 189–194.

NELSON, S. (1982) *Incest, Fact and Myth.* Stramullion.

NELSON-JONES, R. (1982) *The Theory and Practice of Counselling Psychology.* London: Holt Rinehart and Winston.

NEZU, A.M. (1986) Efficacy of a social problem-solving approach for unipolar depression. *Journal of Consulting and Clinical Psychology*, 54, 196–202.

NEZU, A.M. and PERRI, M. (1989) Social problem-solving therapy for uni-polar depression: an initial dismantling investigation. *Journal of Consulting and Clinical Psychology*, 57, 408–413.

NICOL, R. (1988) The treatment of child abuse in the home environment. In K. BROWNE, C. DAVIES and P. STRATTON (Eds) *Early Prediction and Prevention of Child Abuse.* Chichester: Wiley.

OFFICE OF POPULATION CENSUSES AND SURVEYS (1993) *1991 Census Report for Great Britain.* London: HMSO.

OKINE, E. (1992) The misassessment of black families in child abuse work. In J. MOORE (Ed.) *The ABC of Child Protection*. Aldershot: Ashgate Publishing Limited.

OLWEUS, D. (1979) Stability of aggressive reaction patterns in males: a review. *Psychological Bulletin*, *86*, 29–34.

OPEN UNIVERSITY (1970) Understanding society. Social Science Foundation Course. *Why people live in Societies*. Milton Keynes: Open University Press.

OPEN UNIVERSITY (1980) Systems organization: The management of complexity. T243, Block 1. *Introduction to Systems Thinking and Organization*. Milton Keynes: Open University Press.

OPPENHEIMER, R. (1983) Social work assessment. *Behavioural Social Work Review*, *4*, 9–12.

OVRETVEIT, J. (1986) *Improving Social Work Records and Practice*. Birmingham: British Association of Social Workers.

PAGE, R. and CLARK, G.A. (1977) *Who Cares?* London: National Children's Bureau.

PARKES, C.M. (1972) *Bereavement: studies of grief in adult life*. London: Tavistock.

PARKES, C.M. (1980) Bereavement counselling: does it work? *British Medical Journal*, *281*, 3–6.

PARKES, C.M. (1985) Bereavement. *British Journal of Psychiatry*, *146*, 11–17.

PARRY, G. (1990) *Coping with Crises*. Leicester: BPS Books (The British Psychological Society) and Routledge.

PATTENSON, L. and BURNS, J. (1990) *Women, Assertiveness and Health*. London: Health Education Authority.

PAYKEL, E.S. (1991) Depression in women. *British Journal of Psychiatry*, *158* (Supplement 10), 22–29.

PERKINS, R. and ROWLAND, L.A. (1991) Sex differences in service usage in long-term psychiatric care. Are women adequately served? *British Journal of Psychiatry*, *158* (Supplement 10), 75–79.

PHILP, M. and DUCKWORTH, D. (1982) *Children with Disabilities and Their Families: A Handbook of Research*. Windsor: NFER/Nelson.

PHINNEY, J.S. (1990) Ethnic identity in adolescents and adults: review of research. *Psychological Bulletin*, *108*, 499–514.

PIAGET, J. (1952) *The Origins of Intelligence in Children*. New York: International Universities Press.

PSYCHOLOGICAL CORPORATION (1992) *Beck Depression Inventory*. London: Harcourt Brace Jovanovich.

RADA, R.T. (1978) *Clinical Aspects of the Rapist*. New York: Grune and Stratton.

RAUCH, J.B. (1988) Social work and the genetics revolution: genetics services. *Social Work*, September/October, 389–394.

REID, W. and EPSTEIN, L. (1972) *Task-Centred Casework*. New York: Columbia University Press.

RICHMAN, N. (1985) Disorders in pre-school children. In M. RUTTER and L. HERSOV (Eds) *Child and Adolescent Psychiatry*. London: Blackwell Scientific Publications.

ROBERTS, J. (1988) Why are some families more vulnerable to child abuse? In K. BROWNE, C. DAVIES and P. STRATTON (Eds) *Early Prediction and Prevention of Child Abuse*. Chichester: Wiley.

ROGERS, A. and FAULKNER, A. (1987) *A Place of Safety*. London: MIND.

ROGERS, C. (1951) *Client-Centred Therapy*. Boston: Houghton Mifflin.

ROGERS, C. (1958) The characteristics of a helping relationship. *Personnel and Guidance Journal*, *37*, 6–16.

ROSENHAN, D.L. and SELIGMAN, M.E. (1984) *Abnormal Psychology*. London: W.W. Norton and Co.

RUTTER, M. (1975) *Helping Troubled Children*. Harmondsworth: Penguin.

RUTTER, M. (1978) Family, area and school influences in the genesis of conduct disorders. In L.A. HERSOV, M. BERGER and D. SHAFFER (Eds) *Aggression and Anti-Social Behaviour in Childhood and Adolescence*. Oxford: Pergamon Press.

RUTTER, M. (1986) The developmental psychopathology of depression: issues and perspectives. In M. RUTTER, C. IZARD and P. READ (Eds) *Depression in Young People: Developmental and Clinical Perspectives*. New York: Guilford Press.

RUTTER, M. and RUTTER, M. (1992) *Developing Minds*. Harmondsworth: Penguin.

SANCHEZ, V.C., LEWINSOHN, P. and LARSON, D.W. (1980) Assertion training: effectiveness in the treatment of depression. *Journal of Clinical Psychology, 36*, 526–529.

SARNACKI-PORTER, F., CANFIELD BLICK. L. and SGROI, S.M. (1982) Treatment of the sexually abused child. In S.M. SGROI (Ed) *Handbook of Clinical Intervention in Child Sexual Abuse*. Lexington: D.C. Heath and Company.

SCHAFFER, H.R. (1990) *Making Decisions About Children: Psychological Questions and Answers*. Oxford: Blackwell.

SCHAIE, K.W. and WILLIS, S.L. (1986) Can decline in intellectual functioning in the elderly be reversed? *Developmental Psychology, 22*, 223–232.

SCHWEITZER, P. (1991) A place to stay: growing old away from home. In A.J. SQUIRES (Ed.) *Multicultural Health Care and Rehabilitation of Older People*. London: Edward Arnold/ Age Concern.

SCOTT, A.I. and FREEMAN, C. (1992) Edinburgh primary care depression study: treatment outcome, patient satisfaction and cost after 16 weeks. *British Medical Journal, 304*, 883–887.

SELIGMAN, M. (1975) *Helplessness*. San Francisco: Freeman.

SGROI, S.M. (1982) *Handbook of Clinical Intervention in Child Sexual Abuse*. Lexington: D.C. Heath and Company.

SHAPIRO, D.A. (1986) Psychopathology. In M. HERBERT (Ed.) *Psychology for Social Workers*. 2nd edn. Leicester: BPS Books (The British Psychological Society) and Macmillan.

SHAVER, K. (1977) *Principles of Social Psychology*. Cambridge, Massachusetts: Winthrop.

SHEARER, M.S. and SHEARER, D.E. (1972) The Portage Project: A model for early childhood education. *Exceptional Children, 39*, 210–217.

SHEPHERD, A. (1992) Personal communication.

SHERIDAN, M. (1973) *From Birth to Five Years: Children's Developmental Progress*. Windsor: NFER-Nelson.

SHERIF, M. (1958) Superordinate goals in the reduction of intergroup conflict. *American Journal of Sociology, 43*, 345–365.

SINCLAIR, R. (1984) Decision-making in Statutory Reviews on children in care. Aldershot: Gower.

SLUCKIN, W., HERBERT, M. and SLUCKIN, A. (1983) *Maternal Bonding*. Oxford: Blackwell.

SMITH, M. (1984) *Organise!* Leicester: National Association of Youth Clubs.

SMITH, M. (1991) Providing a framework. *Community Care* (Supplement on Investigating Child Abuse), *869*, V–VI.

SPENCER, J.R. and FLIN, R.H. (1990) *The Evidence of Children, the Law and Psychology*. London: Blackstone.

SPIVACK, G., PLATT, J.J. and SHURE, M. (1976) *The Problem-Solving Approach to Adjustment*. San Francisco: Jossey-Bass.

STEVENSON, J., RICHMAN, N. and GRAHAM, P. (1985) Behaviour problems and language abilities at three years and behavioural deviance at eight years. *Journal of Child Psychology and Psychiatry, 26*, 215–230.

STOCK WHITAKER, D., COOK, J., DUNNE, C. and ROCLIFFE, S. (1984) *The Experience of Residential Care from the Perspectives of Children, Parents and Caregivers*. York: University of York.

STONER, J. (1978) *Management*. Englewood Cliffs, New Jersey: Prentice Hall.

SUBOTSKY, F. (1991) Issues for women in the development of mental health services. *British Journal of Psychiatry*, *158* (Supplement 10), 17–21.

SUTTON, C. (1979) *Psychology for Social Workers and Counsellors*. London: Routledge and Kegan Paul.

SUTTON, C. (1981) Social workers as applied psychologists: A plea for sensitive support. *Bulletin of the British Psychological Society*, *34*, 465–467.

SUTTON, C. (1987) *A Handbook of Research for the Helping Professions*. London: Routledge and Kegan Paul.

SUTTON, C. (1992) Training parents to manage difficult children: a comparison of methods. *Behavioural Psychotherapy*, *20*, 115–139.

SUTTON, C. (1992) Safety and threat: neglected concepts in psychology? *The Psychologist*, *4*, 459–461.

SUTTON, C. and HERBERT, M. (1992) *Mental Health: A Client Support Resource Pack*. Windsor: NFER/Nelson.

TAJFEL, H. and TURNER, J. (1979) An integrative theory of intergroup conflict. In W. AUSTIN and S. WORCHEL (Eds) *The Social Psychology of Intergroup Relations*. California: Wadsworth.

TELLEGEN, A., LYKKEN, D.T., BOUCHARD, T.J. (Jr.) WILCOX, K.J., SEGAL, N. and RICH, S. (1988) Personality similarity in twins reared apart and together. *Journal of Personality and Social Psychology*, *54*, 1031–1039.

THOMAS, A. and CHESS, S. (1977) *Temperament and Development*. New York: Brunner/Mazel.

THOMAS, K.B. (1987) General practice consultations: is there any point in being positive? *British Medical Journal*, *294*, 1200–1202.

THORNTON, D., CURRAN, L., GRAYSON, D. and HOLLOWAY, V. (1984) *Tougher Regimes in Detention Centres*. London: HMSO.

TOBIN-RICHARDS, M.H., BOXER, A.M. and PETERSEN, A.C. (1983) The psychological significance of pubertal change: Sex differences in perception of self during early adolescence. In J. BROOKS-GUNN and A.C. PETERSON (Eds) *Girls at Puberty: Biological and Psychological Perspectives*. New York: Plenum.

TOMLINSON, S. (1984) *Home and School in Multi-Cultural Britain*. London: Batsford Academic and Educational Ltd.

TOWNSEND, P. and DAVIDSON, N. (Eds) (1982) *Inequalities in Health*. (The Black Report). Harmondsworth: Penguin.

TOWNSEND, P., PHILLIMORE, P. and BEATTIE, A. (1988) *Health and Deprivation: Inequality and the North*. London: Croom Helm.

TROWER, P., CASEY, A. and DRYDEN, W. (1988) *Cognitive Behavioural Counselling in Action*. London: Sage.

TUCKMAN, B.W. (1965) Developmental sequences in small groups. *Psychological Bulletin*, *63*, 384–399.

WALLERSTEIN, J.S. and KELLY, J.B. (1980) *Surviving the Breakup*. London: Routledge and Kegan Paul.

WARR, P., BANKS, M. and ULLAH, P. (1985) The experience of unemployment among black and white urban teenagers. *British Journal of Psychology*, *76*, 75–87.

WATSON, J. (1930) *Behaviorism*. New York: Norton.

WEBSTER-STRATTON, C. and HERBERT, M. (1994) *Troubled Families: Problem Children*. Chichester: Wiley.

WEST, D.J. and FARRINGTON, D.P. (1973) *Who Becomes Delinquent?* London: Heinemann.

WESTLAND, P. (1986) Power and the underprivileged. *Social Services Insight*, February 15–22, 18–20.

WESTWOOD, S., COULOUTE, J., DESAI, S., MATTHEW, P. and PIPER, A. (1989) *Sadness in my Heart*. Leicester: University of Leicester.

WILKES, J. (1993) *Sexuality, Young People and Care: Creating a Positive Context for Training, Policy and Development*. London: CCETSW.

WORCHEL, S. (1979) Cooperation and the reduction of intergroup conflict: some determining factors. In W.G. AUSTIN and W. WORCHEL (Eds) *The Social Psychology of Intergroup Relations*. California: Wadsworth.

Appendix A: **Charting several behaviours**

Name: _____   Date: _____

Behaviour	Monday	Tuesday	Wednesday	Thursday	Friday	Saturday	Sunday	Total
Behaviours to encourage and praise.								
1. Does what he or she is asked; begins to follow a request within one minute, e.g. to put clothes away.								
2.								
Behaviours to discourage.								
1. Does not do what he or she is asked; does not begin to follow a request within one minute, e.g. to come for tea.								
2.								

Appendix BI: **An example of an agreement between a worker and a client (cf ASPIRE: work with families p.93)**

A. The agreement

This agreement is drawn up between:

Name: Tracey Harris   Address: The Cedars Hostel   and

Name: Jenny Cooper   worker from (Agency): Middleshire Soc Services

Address: 17 Long Lane, Middleton   Telephone no: 74682

B. What we are trying to do together

Our overall aim is to increase Tracey's feeling of control over her life.

Our particular goals or objectives are:

1. To enable Tracey to feel better in health.

2. To ensure she has claimed all her welfare rights entitlements.

3. To help Tracey manage Kevin's misbehaviour.

4. To give Tracey info. about parent + child drop-in centres.

C. In order to work towards these goals, we have made some agreements:

Agreed by ....Tracey.... (client)   Agreed by ....Jenny.... (worker)

1. To go to the GP serving the hostel for a check-up.

1. To phone Tracey's Health Visitor + liaise with her.

2. To go to the welfare rights office to check her entitlements.

2. To get a list of parent + child drop-in centres + creche facilities.

3. To respond to Kevin's misbehaviour in a consistent manner as suggested by Jenny.

3. To visit Tracey for 3 x 30 minutes to suggest practical ways of managing Kevin.

D. Other points to be noted

1. The above agreement is to be reviewed and updated every ....1.... weeks

2. The agreement can be changed if both parties agree to this

3. Failure on ....'s part to keep the agreement may result in

Our next meeting is on 24 October.

Signed Tracey Harris   Signed Jenny Cooper   Date 17 October

Appendix BII: A framework for an agreement between a worker and a client

A. The agreement

This agreement is drawn up between:

Name: .... Address: .... and

Name: .... worker from (Agency): ....

Address: .... Telephone no: ....

B. What we are trying to do together

Our overall aim is ....

Our particular goals or objectives are:

1. To ....

2. To ....

3. To ....

C. In order to work towards these goals, we have made some agreements:

Agreed by .... (client)   Agreed by .... (worker)

1. To ....   1. To ....

   ....

2. To ....   2. To ....

   ....

3. To ....   3. To ....

   ....

D. Other points to be noted

1. The above agreement is to be reviewed and updated every .... weeks

2. The agreement can be changed if both parties agree to this

3. Failure on ....'s part to keep the agreement may result in

   ....

Signed .... Signed .... Date ....

Appendix C: **A framework for an agreement in one-to-one or family work**

This form to be completed by the worker in discussion with the client and the family. It is all-purpose and can be adapted to a wide range of situations.

A. The agreement

This agreement is drawn up between:

1. .... 3. ....

2. .... 4. ....

and .... worker from: ....

Agency: ....

Address: ....

.... Telephone no: ....

B. What we are trying to do together

We have talked about what we can work towards together, and agree that our goals are to:

1. ....

2. ....

3. ....

4. ....

C. To work towards these goals

The worker agrees to:

1. ....

2. ....

3. ....

The following members of the family agree to:

First person (name) ....

1. ....

2. ....

3. ....

Second person (name) ....

1. ....

2. ....

3. ....

Third person (name) ....

1. ....

2. ....

3. ....

Fourth person (name) ....

1. ....

2. ....

3. ....

D. Other points to be noted

The above agreement is to be reviewed every .... weeks.

The above agreement can be changed if everyone agrees.

Signed: .... Signed: ....

Signed: .... Signed: ....

Date: ....

Appendix D: **Monitoring progress towards goals**

This form to be completed at regular intervals, e.g. once weekly by the client as a means of recording progress towards goals.

Client's name: _____

Worker's name: _____ Date: _____

Record whether you personally feel that you are making progress towards your goal, or are getting further away from it, on average, each week.

Goal

to: _____

_____

_____

_____

+ 10									
+ 9									
+ 8									
+ 7									
+ 6									
+ 5									
+ 4									
+ 3									
+ 2									
+ 1									
weeks	**1**	**2**	**3**	**4**	**5**	**6**	**7**	**8**	
− 1									
− 2									
− 3									
− 4									
− 5									
− 6									
− 7									
− 8									
− 9									
− 10									

Improvement (vertical axis label for + values)

Deterioration (vertical axis label for − values)

Period of intervention   *Follow-up*

Appendix E: **An example of a questionnaire**
(with acknowledgements to Lindy Jeffery, community worker, Leicester)

HEALTH PROVISION FOR WOMEN IN LEICESTER

We are carrying out a survey to find out what women know about health provision for them in Leicester.

We hope the results will be used to increase publicity for Well Woman Clinics.

1) Please tick which age group you are in.

20–24	25–29	30–34	35–39	40–44	45–49	50–54	55–59	60–61	Over 65

( ) 1
a - j

2) Are you in paid employment? Full-time ☐   Part-time ☐   No ☐

( ) 2
( ) 3

3) Which area of the city do you live in? _____

( ) 4

4) I would describe my ethnic origin as:

Asian ☐   African-Caribbean ☐

White ☐   Other (please state) _____

( ) 5
( ) 6
( ) 7
( ) 8

5) Have you had a cervical smear test during the last five years?   Yes ☐   No ☐

( ) 9
( )10

If you answered NO to question (5) please go on to question (7)

6) If you answered YES to the last question, did you have your smear test carried out at:

Your local GP Surgery ☐

Family Planning Clinic ☐

Well Woman Clinic ☐

Other (please state) _____

( )11
( )12
( )13
( )14

7) Have you heard of Well Woman Clinics?   Yes ☐   No ☐

( )15
( )16

If you answered NO to question (7) please go on to question (14)

8) If you answered YES to the last question, do you know where your nearest Well Woman Clinic is situated?

No   Yes   (please state) _____

( )17
( )18
( )19
( )20

9) Do you know how to make an appointment at your local Well Woman Clinic?

No ☐   Yes (please indicate how you would do this)

_____

( ) 21
( ) 22
( ) 23
( ) 24

10) Have you ever attended a Well Woman Clinic? No ☐ Yes ☐

If you answered NO to question (10) please go on to question (12)

( ) 25
( ) 26

11) If you answered YES to the last question,

a) Which clinic did you attend? _____

( ) 27

b) How long ago did you attend? _____

( ) 28

Please now move on to QUESTION 13

12) If you answered NO to question (10), which tests do you think are carried out at a Well Woman Clinic?

_____

_____

_____

( ) 29

( ) 30

( ) 31

( ) 32

13) Have you seen any advertisements for Well Woman Clinics?

No ☐   Yes ☐

( ) 33
( ) 34

14) How important would be the following reasons for you in attending a Well Woman Clinic? (Please tick ONE box for each statement)

	Very Important	Quite Important	Not Important
a) Having a woman doctor			
b) Having a thorough check-up			
c) Being able to discuss health problems			
d) Having a cervical smear test			
e) Learning how to do a self breast examination			

A B C
35
36
37
38
39

THANK YOU FOR YOUR CO-OPERATION IN COMPLETING THIS FORM

INDEX

Access to Personal Files Act 1987 213
accountability 213–15
administrative skills 201–3
adolescence 49–52
affective disorders 147–8
Age Exchange 55
'ageism' 55
aggressive behaviour 18
    in children 26–7, 46–7, 75
agreements (contracts), negotiating and
    writing 76–7, 228
    in child/abuse neglect cases 215–16
    for supervision 204, 205
    in work with families 79, 170, 174–5,
    176, 229–30
aims, formulating 214
    see also goal–setting approaches; object-
    ives
Alameda Project 215–16
alcohol consumption 141
    genetic factors in 50
anger, expression of 125
anti-discrimination legislation/practice 7,
    212–13, 164–5
anti-racist practice 6, 51, 213
anti-sexist practice 7
anti-social behaviour 46–7
anxiety 28, 30, 121
    children's 114
    defence mechanisms against 21, 22–3
    physiological response to 136
anxiety-based disorders *see* neuroses
appreciation, expression of 71
ASPIRE approach 7–12, 76, 79, 88, 213
    in group work 162
    in intervention in emotional abuse
    110–13
    as problem–solving method 130–32
    in residential care context 171–7
    in work with families 93–6
asserting (in negotiation) 195–6
assertiveness training 155
assessment 7–9, 93
    in child abuse 98–101
    of children's development 33–8
    informing 64
    of maternal depression 100
Assessment and Action Records 199

attachment 16, 41–3, 82–3
    and daycare 43–5

Beck Depression Inventory 100
behaviour chart 193, 227
behavioural approaches to learning 26–7
behavioural response to anxiety 121
behaviourism 23
    see also social learning theory
bereavement, response to 120–21, 122–5
biological drives 17
biological perspective 16–19
bonding 41, 44–5
'broken identity' 120
bullying 47, 48
burn-out 203–4

Campaigning activities 159, 160, 215
care vs. control dilemma 210
carers
    of disabled people 80
    of distressed children 115
case conferences 100–101
centile charts 33, 35–8, 103
challenging (in negotiation) 195–6
charts *see* records
child abuse 97–118
    abusers' perceptions of 59, 105
    assessment in 98–101
    caring for survivors 114–16
    categories of 97
        emotional abuse 97, 110–13
        neglect 97, 102–3, 113
        physical injury 97, 98, 103–5
        sexual abuse 97, 98, 105–9, 113, 117,
        125, 141
    children as witnesses 116–18
    ethical considerations in investigating 211
    incidence of 97–8
    intervention in 101–2, 102–3, 107–9,
    110–14
    ritualistic abuse 117
    worker–client agreements (Alameda
    Project) 215–16
Childline 47, 48, 107
children 78–96
    aggressive behaviour in 26–7, 46–7, 75
    communicating with 65–8

development 38–49
  assessment of 33–8
  cognitive 28–30, 49
families as supportive environment 82–4
mental health of 141, 144, 145
National Children's Bureau cohort study 191
needs of 32, 33, 34
patterns of temperament of 18, 40–41
in residential care 114–15, 169–77
  Assessment and Action Records 199
  decision-making in reviews 199
  parents' response 79
separation from parents 80, 114
Children Act 1989 116
  formative influence in 185
  and 'partnership with parents' concept 10, 44, 68, 78, 79, 169–70, 171
  and social workers' responsibilities 212
  and wishes/feelings of children 65, 115
children in distress 114–16
classical conditioning 23
client-centred approach 30, 92, 128
cognitive–behavioural counselling 154–5
cognitive development 28–30, 49
cognitive perspective 28–30
cognitive processes, learning by 26
cognitive response to anxiety 121
communication 64–71
  non-verbal 60–61
  verbal 61–3
  with/within families 68, 84, 85–8
community 156, 157–8
  needs of 158
  community action 159, 160
  community care 182–4
  community development 159
  community group participation 158, 159
  community mothers 101
  community profile 157–8
  community work 2, 65–6, 156–82
  contribution to psychology 6–7
  forms of 158–61
  goal–setting approaches in 27
  see also group work
competence, working within 214–15
conditioning 23
confidentiality 210–11
conflicts
  in family, effects on children 80
  of interests 211

intergroup 167–8
  within-group 163, 165
contingency (tertiary) agreements 76
contracts see agreements
controlled experiment 190
'coping skills' 126
cost–benefit analysis (social encounters) see social exchange theory
counselling 22, 23
  of abusing parents 113
  cognitive–behavioural 154–5
  marital, example of failure 92
  of people in crisis 127–32
court reports 200–201, 213
crime, contributory causes of 19, 20
crisis intervention 119–32
  in child sexual abuse 108–9
cuddling, babies' response to 41
cultural barriers, communicating across 69–70

Daycare, effect on child's attachment 43–4
decision-making 73–4, 199
defence mechanisms 21, 22–3
denial 21, 22
depression 28, 30, 147–8
  assessment of 100
  counselling in 129–30, 155
  treatments 149, 150, 153–4
  in women 129–30, 138, 141–2
descriptive research 188
developmental tasks 38, 39
Diploma in Social Work 6–7, 209, 212–13
disabled people
  interaction with 63
  needs of carers 80
  younger 51
Disabled Persons (Employment) Acts 1944 and 1958 212
disadvantaged children, programmes of early intervention 45
discipline 84
discrimination 6–7, 58
  against elderly people 55
  in schools 47, 49
  see also anti-discrimination legislation/practice
divorce, effects on children 80–81
doctors, consultation styles 189
dominance 63
dominance hierarchies 164

drives 16, 17
drugs
  anti-depressants (tricyclics) 150
  genetic factors in abuse of 50
  tranquillizers (phenothiazines) 149

Ecological approach 13
Edinburgh Post-Natal Depression Inventory
  100
education
  skills 198–9
  social worker's role 18–19, 83
elderly people 54–5
  communicating with 70–71
  depression in 129
  group homes for 180–81
  mental health needs of older women 141
electroconvulsive therapy 143
emotional abuse (children) 97, 110–13
emotions
  response to anxiety 121
  see also psychodynamic/emotional per-
    spective
empathy 59, 71, 127–8
employment 52
empowerment 6, 215–16
  of parents 79
  of people in crisis 126
equal opportunity 212–13, 215
ethics 208–16
ethnic minority groups
  children of 47, 49, 51, 117
    in care 169, 172–7
    sense of identity 52
  elderly people 54, 55
  and mental health 7, 142–4
  need for specialist workers 212
  work with families 79, 100
  see also language barriers
evaluation of effectiveness 8, 9, 10, 214
  by data gathering 150–1, 193
experimental studies 188, 189–90
expression of feelings 86–7, 88, 123, 125

'Failure to thrive' 102–3, 110
families
  communication with/within 68, 84,
    85–8
  and sense of identity 51
  as supportive environment 82–4
  as system 15, 88

work with 78, 79–82
  agreements in 79, 170, 174–5, 176,
    229–30
  ASPIRE 93–6
  see also parents
Family Adversity Index 81–2
family therapy 88–93, 102
feedback, learning via 24–5, 46, 87
feeding difficulties 103
feelings
  coping with 124–5
  expression of 86–7, 88, 123, 125
filtered listening 72
first impressions 58, 59
foster care 212
foster grandparents 101
Freud, Anna 21, 22
Freud, Sigmund 19

Gay and lesbian people 50
  loss of partner 124–5
  self-esteem 52
gender issues 7
gender roles 26, 46, 83
genetic factors 16, 18–19
  in schizophrenia 149
  in substance misuse 50
genograms 89, 90, 115
goal-setting approaches 9–10, 27
  for elderly people 181
  monitoring progress in 193, 194, 231
  within organization 202
group care 169–82
group homes
  for elderly people 181
  for people with learning disability 180–81
group work 161–8
  between-group processes 166–8
  empowerment in 215
  in mental health work 154
  within-group processes 163–5

Health, genetic factors in 18
health care 53–4
holistic approach 14
hospitals visits (children) 83
human development 33–35
  innate factors in 16–19
  psychosexual stages of 21, 22
  see also under children
human needs

hierarchy of 30, 31
  see also under children
humanistic perspective 30–32, 92
hysterectomy 141

Identity, sense of 51–2, 120
imitation, learning by 5, 26
implementation of plan 8, 9, 10
incest 106
infancy, development during 38–45
innate factors in development 16–19
insulting behaviour (in negotiation) 195
interpersonal skills 56–77
interpreter, using 69–70, 86
intervention
  for abused children 101–2, 102–3, 107–9
  for children with learning disabilities 45
  in depressive illness 153–4
  for difficult pre-school children 47
  for disadvantaged children 45
  evaluation of *see* evaluation of effective-
    ness
  for personality disorders 150–51
  for schizophrenia 150
  for young offenders 177–8
  see also crisis intervention
interviewing 64–5
  in child abuse investigation 100, 107
  non-verbal communication in 61
  recording 200

Jargon 63
Jewish community, mourning rituals 123–4

Labels *see* stereotyping
language, acquisition of 5, 83
language barriers, communicating across
  69–70
'learned helplessness' 126
learning *see* conditioning; social learning
  theory
learning disabilities *see* people with learning
  disabilities
legal knowledge 211
lesbian women
  children of 81
  see also under gay and lesbian people
Life Events Scale 120, 136–7
life story books 115
listening 22, 71–2, 86, 124
looking after oneself 203–6

Mansangathan Project 143
marriage counselling, example of failure 92
Maslow, Abraham 30–32
mastectomy 120, 141
menopause 54
mental disorders, classification of 144,
  145–51
mental health 54, 133–55
  of ethnic minority groups 142–3
  genetic factors in 18
  problem-solving techniques in 130
  promotion of 152–3
  women and 140–42
Mental Health Act 1983 143
mental health services 142–3, 151–2
meta-analysis 179
modelling, learning by 26
mourning rituals 123–4
'move to consensus' 100–101

National Health Service and Community
  Care Act 1990 182
  social workers' responsibilities under 212
neglect (child) 97, 102–3, 113
negotiating
  of agreements 76–7
  of objectives 9–10, 215
  skills 193, 195–6
neuroses 145–7
'normality' 133

Objectives
  for children in care 170
  negotiating 9–10, 215
  of organization and individuals 202
  working towards 213–14
  see also goal-setting approaches
observational studies 191
Oedipus complex 21
one-parent families 81
operant conditioning 23
organic syndromes 146, 151

Parents 53
  partnership with 10, 44, 68, 78, 79,
    169–70, 171
  as role models 51
  skills 53, 84–5
  styles 85, 86
    in families of sexual offenders 108
  training of 47, 102, 179

peer group influences 26, 50
penalty *see* punishment
people with learning disabilities
    communicating with 70
    group homes for 180–81
    'normalization' of 196
    programmes of early intervention for 45
perception 56–9, 62
personal conduct 216
personal growth, theory of 30, 32
personal relationships 53
    with clients 56, 71–2
    within family 82–3
    see also interpersonal skills
personality
    disorders of 146, 150–51
    Freud's theory of 19, 21–2
perspectives on human beings 14
    behavioural and social learning 23–8
    biological 16–19
    cognitive 28–30
    humanistic 30–32
    psychodynamic/emotional 19–23
physiological response to anxiety 121, 136
Piaget, Jean 28, 29, 40
planning of action 8, 9–10
play therapy 68
Portage Project 45
post-natal depression 100, 142
post-traumatic stress 119, 122
    in abused children 109
poverty
    and health 54
    and psychiatric disorder 129
    social workers and 209
power 6, 63–4
prejudice 7, 58
pre-school children, development 45–7
primacy effect 58
primary school children, development 47–9
probation officers 2
problem-solving techniques 130–32
psychodynamic/emotional perspective
    19–23
psychology
    contribution to social and community
        work 2–6
    contribution to social work training 209
    profession of 1
    research work in 185, 186–93
psychoses 146, 147–50

psychosexual development 21, 22
public expectations 3–4, 209–10
punishment (children) 24, 27, 75

Questionnaires 191, 192, 232–3

Race Relations Act 1976 212
racial differences 19, 40
racism 6, 142–3, 213
    see also anti-racist practice
rationalization 21
reaction formation 21
reality orientation therapy 151, 181
reordered families 81
records
    access to 213
    of behaviours 112, 113, 227
    keeping 112, 113, 186, 199–200, 213–14
    reading 59
redundancy, response to 120
reinforcement, learning via 24–5
reliability of test 191
report-writing 200–201
repression 21
requests 87
research 185–93
residential care 169–82
    children in 169–77
    elderly people in 181
    people with learning disabilities in
        180–81
    young offenders in 177–9
resource shortages 211–12
respect/regard for clients 30, 32, 127–8
review of intervention 8, 9, 10
rewards (children) 5, 24–5
risk factors
    child abuse 99–100
    depression 138, 139, 142
    mental–emotional disorders 134
    young offenders 179
ritualistic abuse 117
Rogers, Carl 30
role models 5, 51, 83

Safety *see* security
sampling, problems in 191
schizophrenia 148–50
    reported incidence in ethnic minorities
        143
school environment 47, 49, 51

secondary school children, development 49–52
security (safety) needs 32
    children's 83, 114–15
    and intergroup conflict 168
self-advocacy 196–7
self-efficacy 126
self-esteem 47, 51–2
    of elderly people 55
service (secondary) agreements 76
Sex Discrimination Act 1975 212
sexism 213
    see also anti-sexist practice
sexual abuse (children) 97, 98, 105–9, 113, 117, 125, 141
sexuality (adolescents) 50
'shift to risk' 101
similarity, perception of 58
skill acquisition 214
social behaviour, styles of 63–4
social drives 17
social exchange theory 73–6, 161
social interaction 60–64
social learning theory 5–6, 23–8
    and child abuse intervention 103
    and family therapy 90–93
    and treatment of neuroses 147
social work
    complexity of 208–10
    contribution to psychology 6–7
    dilemmas in 210–12
    diploma in 6–7, 209, 212–13
    education and training in 185, 209, 214
    evaluating effectiveness of 214
    profession of 1–2
socialization 46, 47
staff shortages 212
Statement Validity Analysis 118
statistical analysis 188
step-parents 81
stereotyping (labelling) 5, 58, 59, 72
stress 130, 135–8
    coping strategies for 138–40
    in families 81–2

in helping professions 203–4
supervision 204, 205
systems 13–14

Talking to children 83
teaching skills 198–9
team, working as member of 204, 206
theory
    nature of 3–4
    and politics 4–5
time management 202
trust
    children's 115
    clients' 72
    enhancement of (in negotiation) 195
twin studies 16

Unconscious processes 22
unemployment 52, 82, 120
    as indicator of deprivation 151

Validity of test 191
values
    in community work 156
    in social work 6–7, 208–16
violence
    alertness for potential 206–7
    in family 103, 105

Witnesses, children as 116–18
women
    abused 30, 75
    and assertiveness training 155
    depression in 129–30, 138, 141–2
    and mental health 140–42
    needs of 54, 140–41

Young offenders 177–9
    harsh treatment of minorities 7
young people
    communicating with 65–8
    see also adolescence
youth workers 2, 65–6